Wisdom for Parents

Key Ideas from Parent Educators.
Second Edition.

Edited by
Elizabeth A. Ramsey, Ph.D., CFLE

National Council on Family Relations

Wisdom for Parents.
Key Ideas from Parent Educators.
Second Edition

Edited by Elizabeth A. Ramsey

ISBN: 978-0-916174-80-4

Copyright © 2025 National Council on Family Relations

All rights reserved. No part of this publication may be reproduced, distributed, or transmitted in any form or by any means, including photocopying, recording, or other electronic or mechanical methods, without prior written permission of the publisher, except in the case of brief quotations embodied in critical reviews and certain noncommercial uses permitted by copyright law.

The contents of this book represent the views of the author(s), which may or may not represent the position of the entire organization.

Publishers: de Sitter Publications, 2011, NCFR (National Council on Family Relations (NCFR), 2021, 2025

Cover image: Hoo loves you?
Artist credit: Rosemary Johnson

Proceeds from the sale of this book benefit NCFR's Certified Family Life Educator (CFLE) scholarship fund

† Author is deceased

Printed in the United States of America

Contents

Preface vi

About the Editor vii

Note From the Editor vii

Tribute to Robert E. Keim viii

Chapter I. – Communication
Tact Between Mother and Daughter – Mary Bold — 11
The Marriage Legacy: Showing Respect in Handling Differences – Charles L. Cole — 13
"I'm Sorry" – Robert E. Keim — 16
Listening to Our Children: The Key to Building Connection – Ana Morante — 17
The Hidden Pitfalls of "I" Statements – Julie K. Nelson — 18
Home–School Communication: The Key to Student Success – Cynthia J. Small — 21

Chapter II. – Development Across the Lifespan
The Feeling Child – Sharon M. Ballard — 23
"Can't We Just Play?" – Jean Illsley Clarke — 25
The Secrets of Self-Esteem – Julie K. Nelson — 27
Lessons Around the Family Dinner Table – Peggy North-Jones — 30
The Bell Curve of Parenting – Brenda L. Potter — 32
Every Growing Person Needs Basic Care, Stimulation, Guidance, Love, and Affirmation – Lane Powell — 33
Gender Development in Preschool. A Brief Guide to Answering Young Children's Questions – Elizabeth A. Ramsey — 36
"As the twig is bent, so grows the tree": Making the Early Years Count – Amelia L. Rose — 37

Chapter III. – Guidance, Discipline, and Parenting Approaches
"In a Minute" – Rebecca A. Adams — 41
Parenting Using "While Activities" – Jerica Berge — 43
Rewards to Encourage: Spark an Interest in Reading – Mary Bold — 45
Taking (Digital) Candy From Strangers – Mary Bold — 47
Blame the Folks: A Strategy for Handling Peer Pressure – Mary Bold — 49
Discipline – "To Teach" – Dawn Cassidy — 51
"Which Way?" Giving Toddlers Agency – Dawn Cassidy — 52
A Small World Families Live In: Six Degrees of Separation – Kristie Chandler — 53
"Did You Have Fun?" – Jean Illsley Clarke — 55
Is "Good Enough" Enough? – Jean Illsley Clarke — 58
Making Choices and Using My "One": A Toddler's Bedtime Routine – Rebecca A. Cobb — 61

Screen Time: Whose Problem Is It? – Karen DeBord ... 63
The Struggle is Real for Parents at Bedtime – Lori Elmore-Staton ... 66
Positive Discipline Strategies – Lori Elmore-Staton & Alisha Hardman ... 68
"I Gotta Be Me": Every Child Is Special – Cynthia R. Garrison ... 71
Compassionate Parenting: A Case Study – H. Wallace Goddard ... 74
First Compassion, Then Teaching – H. Wallace Goddard ... 77
Parenting With Style – Sharon M. Ballard & Kevin H. Gross ... 82
Harnessing the Power of Failure – Alisha Hardman & Lori Elmore-Staton ... 86
Intentional Parenting: What Are Your Goals for Your Child and Your Relationship?
  – Cameron Lee ... 88
Teaching the Right Lesson: What Do Our Kids Learn From Our Behavior?
  – Cameron Lee ... 91
Imperfection Is Perfectly Fine – Margaret E. Machara ... 93
Want Smarter Kids? Try a Little Roughhousing – Julie K. Nelson ... 95
Why Kids Lie: How to Teach Children Truthfulness and Respond to Lies Helpfully
  – Jody Johnston Pawel ... 98
Stop the Sibling Self Comparison – Elizabeth A. Ramsey ... 102
The "Mom, I Need You" Touch – Elizabeth A. Ramsey ... 103
Life Lessons From the Pandemic: Children Are as Parents Do – Jim Rogers ... 104
Empowering Children – Dorothea M. Rogers ... 106
Giving Children S.M.A.R.T Choices – Hilary A. Rose ... 108
Improving the T.E.N.O.R. of Interactions. Using Logical Consequences
  – Hilary A. Rose ... 110
Actions Speak Louder Than Words: Being Role Models for Our Children
  – Kimberly Van Putten-Gardner ... 114
Four Messages Every Child Longs to Hear – Cynthia B. Wilson, Jim Jackson, &
  Lynne Jackson ... 115

Chapter IV. – Health and Wellness
Raising Sexually Healthy Children – Sharon Ballard & Kevin Gross ... 119
Breaking the Generational Curse: Integrating Family Science to Promote
  Self-Differentiation and Overcome Trauma-Driven Parenting
  – Felisha M. Burleson ... 122
Weathering the Storm – Kristina Higgins ... 125
What's So Hard About Parenting Children With Mental Illness? – Elizabeth Mazur ... 128
Fostering Parent and Infant Bonds in the Neonatal Intensive Care Unit
  – Hannah Mechler ... 131
Breaking the Cycle: Understanding Adverse Childhood Experiences and Trauma
  – Angelina M. Mojica ... 133
Neonatal Abstinence Syndrome: Experiences of Foster Care Parents
  – Elizabeth A. Ramsey ... 136
Attachment Theory and Its Cross-Cultural Applicability
  – Elizabeth Morgan Russell ... 139

Preventing Youth Substance Use: What Parents Can Do to Reduce Risk and Increase Protective Factors – Cynthia B. Wilson & Kaley G. Turner   142

Chapter V. – Life Skills
The Practice Credit Card – Mary Bold   146
"Can You Afford It?" – Elizabeth B. Carroll   148
Lessons Learned: When Transitioning From Being a Mother of a Teen to a Mother of a Teen Parent – Lisa Taylor Cook and Kristina Higgins   151
Invest in 5 to Save 10 – Karen DeBord   153
Time as Money—Using Hour Concepts to Explain Family Finances – Jacki Fitzpatrick   155

Chapter VI. – Perspectives
You—My Daughter – Marcia Pioppi Galazzi   159
Growing Son to Man – Marcia Pioppi Galazzi   160
A Stich in Time: Knit One, Purl One – Clara Gerhardt   160
Imperfect Perfection of Parenting – Clara Gerhardt   162
Parenthood: The Land of Vulnerability – Clara Gerhardt   162
Seasons of Parenting – Clara Gerhardt   164
Silver and Gold: The Family Photo Album – Clara Gerhardt   165
The Daisy Chain of Parental Gifts – Clara Gerhardt   168
Where I'm From – Mark Sfeir   169
Courage – SaraKay Smullens   170
On Gender and Acceptance – Margaret Stridick   173

Chapter VII. – Relationships
Couple Attachment Moments – Jerica Berge   174
The Necessary Rules for Healthy Fighting – John H. Gagnon   176
Commuter Marriages With Children: Benefits and Cautions – Richard Glotzer   180
Embracing Father's Opportunities to Prepare Daughters for The World of Boys – Scott Stanley Hall   182
Nurturing Traditions: Nurturing Family – Arminta Lee Jacobson   185
My Father's Wisdom From Under the Clock Tower: Teaching Forgiveness – Gregory R. Janson   188
Three Pillars of Strength Among Latin American Families – Brian L. Jory & Rachel Bascope-Vidal   190
Parenting Through Turbulent Times – Ainsworth E. Joseph   194
Nurturing the Couple – Dorothea M. Rogers   197
[No] Surprise: Our Children Still Need and Want Us – Sterling Wall   199

Appendices   204

Subject Index   208

Preface

Wisdom for Parents. Key Ideas From Parent Educators, Second Edition, is a compilation of wisdom gathered from Family Science professionals including parent and Family Life Educators, many of whom are Certified Family Life Educators (CFLEs), college professors, marriage and family counselors, social workers, clergy, and more. The authors have contributed their professional knowledge and experiences as well as personal reflections and perspectives through articles, stories, and poems, all woven together to address parenting approaches and techniques, communication, character-building, health and wellness, life skills, guidance and discipline, relationships, trauma, culture, development across the lifespan, and more. This book shares key parenting ideas by way of short articles.

During the past century, many approaches and theories have evolved, which you will discover more clearly in this book. It is filled with interesting, intriguing, insightful, and moving articles. The lessons learned and wisdom imparted help the reader to navigate through the joys and challenges of parenting. This book is for everyone: Professionals, students, and parents can all benefit from it. It is a valuable resource both in and out of the classroom setting. Many of the articles contain discussion questions and activities for use in group settings or independent thought. The appendices include helpful group discussion guidelines and prompts as well as relevant parenting information and suggestions.

Specials thanks to the late Robert Keim, Ph.D., CFLE Emeritus, and Arminta Jacobson, Ph.D., CFLE Emeritus, editors of the first edition of *Wisdom for Parents: Key Ideas From Parent Educators* who contributed their time and energy to this project. The National Council on Family Relations (NCFR) continues to honor their request that proceeds from the sale of this book support the (CFLE) scholarship program.

About the Editor

Elizabeth A. Ramsey, Ph.D., is a professor at Tennessee Technological University in Human Ecology and is a Certified Family Life Educator (CFLE). She worked in the field as a Family Life Educator for years, as well as a Rule 31 Family Mediator, an early childhood development assessor, and as Director of Children's Ministry, Women's Ministry, and Outreach Ministry at a church in rural Tennessee. She has experience teaching English Language Arts and Social Health Education in the public school system. Dr. Ramsey's research and project interests include addiction prevention and support, the training and education of foster parents, social health education in public school systems, implementation of trauma-informed care in helping professions, the mitigation and prevention of adverse childhood experiences (ACEs), and building resilience in children and families who have experienced ACEs and/or trauma.

Note From the Editor

I first discovered *Wisdom for Parents* in 2015 when I was teaching a course on parenting at Tennessee Technological University. I needed a way to incorporate real-life scenarios into my classroom so that my students could apply what they were learning. I implemented weekly reading assignments from the book and included questions based on each article. My students loved it. Many of them shared with me over the years that they were able to understand concepts better because of the supplemental readings from *Wisdom*. I also found certain articles were wonderful resources when working with parents and families on an individual basis. *Wisdom* shared so many wonderful nuggets for parents that changed their family's lives in positive ways.

All those years I used the first edition that was published in 2011, but I could see that it needed an update. I remember reaching out to NCFR to see if there were any plans for a second edition. To say that I treasured the book so much is truly an understatement because I found myself volunteering to be the editor of the second edition. Therefore, over the past year, I have thrown myself into this project. This included many emails, calls for authors, reading, rereading, editing, more emails, more reading more editing, and many weekly meetings with Dawn Cassidy, who served as production editor of this project. She was such a valuable contributor to the second edition, showing up to every Monday meeting with her sunny disposition and special ability to help organize and make sense of a massive project. Thanks also to the many authors who shared their wisdom and knowledge by updating past entries or contributing new ones.

The resulting volume has maintained the heart and intention of the first editors while providing updated information, references, and perspectives, including articles from new authors. As you read this, I hope you find the suggestions and ideas helpful to your parenting situations or practice. May this book empower you, your family, and the lives that you touch.

Tribute to Dr. Robert E. Keim
September 22, 1929–December 20, 2020

"There is a land of the living and a land of the dead and the bridge is love"
—*Thornton Wilder, The Bridge of San Luis Rey*

Dr. Robert E. Keim, or Bob as he was affectionately known to his friends and colleagues, was one of the leading figures in the field of Family Science. He carried the CFLE (Certified Family Life Educator) designation with pride, and upcoming as well as established professionals looked up to him as a role model—someone who opened doors for Family Life Educators and who blazed the trail. The first recipients of the certification as a Family Life Educator were recorded in 1985. Bob obtained his certification 2 years later; giving him pioneer status in the organization.

NCFR and Professional Engagement

Dr. Keim was deeply interested in all facets of Family Science. His extensive relationship as a lifelong member of the National Council on Family Relations (NCFR) started in 1966 and spanned 55 years. He maintained his CFLE designation for 35 years, a tribute of his loyalty to the profession and the organization. He was one of a handful of men who represented this profession in the early years; to be precise, he was the eighth male member of NCFR on record.

During his long professional career, he led various programs for couples and parents in more than 100 settings and was certified in five evidenced-based parenting and family-life-related programs. He was editor of the *Family Science Review* from 1993 through 1996 and published numerous articles on family-related topics, including professional development. He presented at more than 200 conferences on parenting and matters relating to the family and served on multiple committees.

His contributions have been deservedly honored with the CFLE Special Recognition Award, which was bestowed on him at the 2012 NCFR annual conference. This great honor was a deserved tribute for lifelong involvement and support of the profession. At retirement, Dr. Keim moved to Clinton, TN, where he remained active in his academic profession as professor emeritus.

Book Editorship

Most professionals with an illustrious career such as Dr. Keim's would find it tempting to rest on the laurels of their hard-earned labor. Not Bob. He found yet another challenge, one that would overwhelm many of us: He became the coeditor of a remarkable anthology of parenting wisdom. He coedited the book, *Wisdom for Parents: Key Ideas From Parent Educators* (2011) with Arminta Jacobson.

During 2011, Dr. Keim attended the annual regional conference of the Southeastern Branch of the National Council on Family Relations, and I had the honor and privilege to host him in our family home. What amazed me was that as an octogenarian, he had driven across states to attend the conference in Alabama. We had many conversations, and I was touched by his humility and genuine kindness. Of course, I also wanted to know how the book became a reality. This is what Dr. Keim shared with me:

> Truly, one of the great joys of my life was the task of co-editing the book, *Wisdom for Parents: Key Ideas from Parent Educators,* along with Arminta Jacobson of the University of North Texas. The idea of the book occurred in Phoenix at our previous NCFR Conference. There was mention of a fund-raising project. At our Parent Education focus group, the idea of the book "lit up" just like the proverbial light bulb: "wisdom for parents" and "key ideas." Soon thereafter Arminta and I were off on the task. Our special thanks continue to go out to some 50 contributing authors.
>
> My experience of editing the *Family Science Review*, for a few years, helped. Much is written about the "platform" from which one is writing; that is, who is the group or audience who will promote the book. In our case, the target audiences are CFLEs. It is our sincere wish that the book finds a home in local libraries and faith communities and gains wider readership amongst Family Life Educators. A good number of the articles were from practitioners and like-minded colleagues who value the work CFLEs do. The book does contain some unique ideas and messages for parents.

Formative Years
Dr. Keim was born in Tulsa, Oklahoma, to Roy and Marion Keim. His father was a civil engineer who worked on several dams, and so the family moved from project to project, which included the construction of the TVA Norris and the Fontana Dams. By age 20, Bob had lived in 16 residences. Maybe this contributed to his adaptability—he repeatedly had to create new circles of friends and colleagues. Once he found his professional niche in later life, he stayed put for about three decades, firmly rooted in the place he loved.

Education and Early Career
Bob graduated from the University of Washington, Seattle, in 1952. He served in the U.S. Army, with a tour in South Korea, followed by several years as a Certified Public Accountant. He attended the Pacific School of Religion in Berkeley, graduating with a master's of divinity degree in 1960. He was ordained in the Congregational/United Church of Christ and served several churches in California before pursuing his doctorate in Family Science. As part of his extensive training, he also completed two full-time clinical internships: one at a large state mental hospital and one at a youth authority reception and evaluation center. He graduated with a Ph.D. in marriage and family living in 1971 from Florida State University.

Academic Calling
Bob taught briefly at Florida State and Colorado State Universities before moving with his children to DeKalb, IL, to teach Family Science at Northern Illinois University, where his career spanned 28 years. For 21 years, he taught a course on parenting education. Dr. Keim retired from this university as professor emeritus.

Personal and Family Life

In 1950, Bob married Patricia, and the couple had four children. From 1967 onward, Bob raised the four children as a single parent and did so in an exemplary manner. One cannot but wonder if this solo parenting task directed him toward his interest in the formal study of parenting as a discipline; after all, in his personal life, he had passed the practical exam of parenting as a life skill many times over. Bob experienced the deep pain of the loss of two of his adult children. Later in life, he was blessed with the joys of grand- and great-grand-parenthood.

Remembering and Honoring Dr. Keim

Bob is remembered for his positive, upbeat outlook; his wry sense of humor; his love of games and family; his rock-solid, steadfast loyalty; and his gratitude and kindness towards the people he met or befriended. In the Family Science profession, he truly was one of the first strong voices. His teachings were foundational to the education of hundreds of students. As an educator he shaped our profession; for this and so much more we extend our gratitude and pay tribute to Dr. Robert Keim.

This work was based on the following:

Gerhardt, C. (2012, Winter). Dr. Robert Keim, CFLE Special Recognition Award Recipient. *CFLE Network*.

Personal communication with Dr. Robert Keim, 2011.

Dr. Robert Keim's obituary, published in 2020.

Clara Gerhardt, Ph.D., CFLE
Clinical Psychologist and Distinguished Professor
Department of Human Development and Family Science
Samford University, Birmingham, AL

Chapter I
Communication

Tact Between Mother and Daughter

Mary Bold, Ph.D., CFLE
Financial Planner
Abacus Financial Planning, LLC

Mothers and other female relatives are often the supervisors for clothes shopping for early adolescent girls. The responsibility to supervise wise clothing choices sometimes leads to unwise comments about how young girls look as they try on items. With awareness and a little practice, parents or caregivers can adopt wise language that will spare feelings and avoid arguments.

Keeping in mind the broad contexts of self-esteem and body image, the activity of clothes shopping can have a large influence on children's awareness of body shapes, both their own and others. Shopping represents an investment of time, energy, and money, so the stakes are already high. On the positive side, clothes shopping provides an opportunity to spend quality time together.

According to research, adolescent girls' self-esteem is related to many factors. For instance, parent–child communication has been tied to self-esteem stability for 11- and 12-year-olds, suggesting that lower self-esteem is associated with critical messages from parents (Kernis, 2000). Criticism can come in different forms, such as behaviors or spoken words. Regarding clothes shopping, adults' level of patience can be a powerful message as well.

Likewise, body image has multiple influences. Family influences (such as pressure to diet, negative remarks about a child's body, or supportive communication about body shape) contribute to self-image and perception of body image (McCabe & Ricciardelli, 2003). At the same time, society's influence is also great. Mass media's information directed to younger audiences carries messages about body shape, dieting, and fashion. Social media platforms can also play a role in body dissatisfaction and low self-esteem (Vincente-Benito & del Valle Ramiez-Duran, 2023).

Specifically, social media are often targeted as detrimental to young people's self-esteem, especially for prompting comparisons of attractiveness. Magson et al. (2023) recommended that parents and educators help young people understand that beauty stereotypes are perception-based and that attractiveness is not critical to self-worth. These researchers pointed out that some social media platforms have run campaigns to promote acceptance of diverse body sizes, and thus the media themselves can help counter stereotypes.

Clothing manufacturers and designers do not provide all clothes for all body types. Still, adolescent girls may want to try a variety of fashions. For the adult accompanying the girl into fitting rooms, an impulsive comment might be, "That looks awful" or "You can't fit into that." A more tactful response is in order: "How do you feel in that?" or "I think I preferred the first outfit—it looked so good on you" or "That flatters you."

As a mom who hates to shop, I had to pace myself to satisfy my daughter's interest in clothes shopping. I knew my own irritation with shopping could influence my attitude and my language. When I happened upon the phrase, "It doesn't flatter you," my daughter reacted positively, and I made the phrase my standard comment when the fit was poor or the outfit was inappropriate. My daughter picked up on the phrase and soon was asking, "Does this flatter me?"

This simple phrase not only steered us away from hurt feelings and arguments, it also properly shifted any negativity to the article of clothing and away from my daughter. She was not unflattering; it was the clothing that was the problem.

You may find another phrase that works better with your own daughter, such as "Does this compliment me?" or "Which outfit looks best?" Such phrases prompt honest feedback but in a supportive way. They also can avoid conflict and help your daughter more easily make decisions that are important to her. Similarly, you can deemphasize clothing sizes or point out that sizing differs across brands. You may also be able to share how you have seen sizing standards change over your lifetime.

The more tactfully and thoughtfully we speak with our children, the more we can help build their positive self-esteem. This doesn't happen in one conversation or on one shopping trip. All our exchanges contribute to a supportive relationship.

Discussion Questions & Activities

1. What role does language play in body image? Are there forbidden words in the body image discussion, or is the entire discussion forbidden?

2. Acceptance of diverse body shapes appears to be challenging for some people. Consider two sides of it: how I accept/do not accept my body shape, and how I accept/do not accept other people's body shape.

References

Kernis, M. H., Brown, A. C., & Brody, G. H., (2000). Fragile self-esteem in children and its associations with perceived patterns of parent–child communication. *Journal of Personality, 68*(2), 225–252. https://doi.org/10.1111/1467-6494.00096

McCabe, M. P., & Ricciardelli, L. A. (2003). Sociocultural influences on body image and body changes among adolescent boys and girls. *The Journal of Social Psychology, 143*(1), 5–26. https://doi.org/10.1080/00224540309598428

Magson, N. R., Oar, E. L., Fardouly, J., Rapee, R. M., Freeman, J. Y. A., Richardson, C. E., & Johnso, C. J. (2023). Examining the prospective bidirectional associations between subjective and objective attractiveness and adolescent internalizing symptoms and life satisfaction. *Journal of Youth and Adolescence, 52*(2), 370–392. https://doi.org/10.1007/s10964-022-01700-7

Vincente-Benito, I., & del Valle Ramiez-Duran, M. (2023). Influence of social media use on body image and well-being among adolescents and young adults: A systematic review. *Journal of Psychosocial Nursing and Mental Health Services, 61*(12), 11–18. https://doi.org/10.3928/02793695-20230524-02

The Marriage Legacy: Showing Respect in Handling Differences

Charles L. Cole, Ph.D., CFLE
Professor, Marriage and Family Therapy Center,
The University of Louisiana at Monroe, Calhoun, LA

Ideally, parents realize that what they model for their children about marriage becomes their child's primary role model for how to create and maintain relationships. If you think about the opportunities, we have to teach our children how to resolve conflicts respectfully with our mate, you can see a microcosm of how your child learns to treat others and handle differences when conflicts arise. This is a heavy responsibility, yet it is an awesome opportunity to leave our children a legacy, which they will be able to use their entire life.

In this brief essay on the marriage legacy, I share some key ideas I have learned as a marriage and family therapist and Family Life Educator over the past 4 decades. I use illustrations from couples with whom I have worked and cite research that demonstrates how respect is a fundamental legacy, which I see parents modeling in how they deal with each other as spouses—behavior that the children see in the day-to-day life of growing up in the home.

It is common to hear children say, "I learned that from Mom and Dad," when you ask them how they learned to treat their playmates, siblings, and others by yelling, getting mad, and hitting each other. That is a sad commentary but all too often true. Our children can learn how to disrespect others from watching us (the parents), acting out the drama of conflict before their very eyes. The good news is that, conversely, our children also learn how to respect others by watching their parents interact in a loving manner that conveys respect for each other, even when we disagree and are angry with each other.

In John Gottman's (Gottman et al., 1999; Gottman & Levenson, 1999) research on marriage and parenthood, he reports that what he calls the *four horsemen of the apocalypse* are highly predictive of marital outcomes. The four horsemen are *criticism, defensiveness, contempt,* and *stonewalling*—things that we should seek to avoid in our relationships. Gottman says, and I have found this to be true in my own clinical work with couples and families, that couples who are highly disrespectful toward each other are less likely to stay together and have more problems parenting their children. Gottman can predict with 94% accuracy which couples are likely to get a divorce within 3 years, just based on watching them interact for as little as 15 minutes.

It is the *contempt* that is the most devastating in showing a clear disrespect and disregard for the value of the partner. When contempt is present, it is hard to see the love behind the ridicule, put-downs, and eye-rolling that conveys, "I not only disagree with you, but I think you are a worthless bum." When the contempt is coupled with an emotional distancing and stonewalling response of not even acknowledging your presence by not responding and walking away, it sets in motion a cascade of negative forces that drive the couple further apart, emotionally and physically, to the point where little opportunity for repair and reconnection occur. Children can see the parents giving up on each other and walking away or only giving negative messages when they do bother to engage each other. And our children can learn this pattern well and then all too often have difficulty making and maintaining meaningful friendships and loving relationships.

Even when parents separate and divorce, they often continue to send the negative messages about the spouse or ex- spouse to their children in how they interact with their "ex" because there is a lifetime connection with the children (Cole & Cole, 1999). Occasions such as children graduating from high school or getting married, for example, are often a source of tension for the entire family because the ex-spouses never learned to work out differences respectfully for the sake of the children.

We have seen family gatherings turn into war zones over seating arrangements at weddings. What kind of message does that send to the child on an occasion that should be one of the happiest days of their life? It is common to see the anxiety so high that no one really knows how to handle the situation and the child is literally holding their breath that their parents do not have an "ugly incident" in front of everyone. Imagine the tension in the faces when the pictures are taken to capture the event that will be passed down to future generations as they see the scowls and frowns on the faces of their grandparents.

How can respect be maintained and passed down to future generations when all the children have seen is disrespect and maybe even hate? The task is so overwhelming to many families that they simply coexist, never getting over the issues and they simply try to push it under the rug, hoping no one really notices and that the children are not hurt too badly. According to William Pinsoff (2002), the norm of the 21st century is likely to continue to be that the majority of homes will be broken by divorce before the children are reared. At present, about half of the couples that marry do not stay married, and the norm is less common for marriages to last for a lifetime than it was up to the final quarter of the 20th century.

For many of these families, help is on the way to learn to move past the struggles and to learn to treat each other with respect even when they disagree. It is still not normal for couples to seek help soon enough to avoid the pains of conflict and disagreements for most. The majority of those that do seek help from trained marriage and family therapists report that they do better after treatment than before. And we now have solid scientific evidence that both marriage enrichment and marriage and family therapy have demonstrated positive benefits compared with control groups receiving no treatment (Giblin et al., 1985; Shadish & Baldwin, 2002).

When either partner becomes aware that they are hurting their children when they see their parents attack each other, it is time for the couple to use this warning sign to slow down the process and stop the cycle of attack and counterattack with their spouse. A simple way to put on the brakes might be to say calmly to one's spouse, "Our children are being hurt by us being so angry and disrespectful to each other. And I want to take responsibility for my part in this and promise you now that I don't want our children to be harmed, I don't want our marriage to be harmed, and I don't think you do either. So let's back off for a few minutes and try to calm down."

When couples can purposefully take control of the situation by calming the intensity of the conflict, they can more effectively communicate what each spouse wants. And each spouse can begin to empathize with their partner and be less likely to feel threatened by the contemptuous messages of "I hate you" that might have slipped out of one's mouth in a moment of anger.

Disagreements are normal, and all marriages have them. It is not the disagreement that hurts the relationship; it is the way the disagreement is handled that makes the difference in sending a message of "I value you and love you, and because I love you, I want to let you know what is bothering me." Many times, the intensity of disagreements has little if anything to do with the spouse but rather how we communicate the concern and process the issue by talking about it in either a fair or unfair manner. We want to send a message that we are going to get closer and understand each other better by sharing this concern openly in a respectful manner that doesn't hurt either of us. When we choose that strategy for handling our disagreements, we are modeling respect and love for each other and our children are learning how to handle their disagreements in a manner that helps build relationships, not tear them apart.

Parents reading other articles in this book might find writings that inspire them to seek better relationships with all members of their family, including their partner. Another step that could be taken is to attend workshops or retreats that focus on marriage enrichment, a movement that has been developing for about a half a century. One might find out about these programs at their local church, parish, or synagogue, or local extension agency.

Concluding Comments
Respect for our mate is vital for both developing a meaningful marriage relationship and establishing an effective parenting partnership. What we do with our marital partner, or former spouse, becomes images in the blueprints from which our children will draw upon to construct their meaningful relationships. The legacy we pass on to our children about relationships will last them a lifetime and become the fundamental models that they will learn from us on how to treat others.

References
Cole, C. L., & Cole, A. L. (1999). Boundary ambiguities that bind former spouses together after the children leave the home in post-divorce families. *Family Relations, 48*(3), 271–272.

Giblin, P., Sprenkle, D., & Sheehan, R. (1985). Enrichment outcome research: A meta-analysis of premarital, marital and family interventions. *Journal of Marital and Family Therapy, 11*(3), 257–271.

Gottman, J. Gottman, J. M., & Levenson, R. W. (1999). Rebound from marital conflict and divorce prediction. *Family Process, 38*(3), 287–292.

Gottman, J. M., & Levenson, R. W. (1999). What predicts change in marital interactions over time? A study of alternative models. *Family Process, 38*(2), 143–158.

Pinsoff, W. (2002). The death of "Till death us do part": The transformation of pair bonding in the 20th century. *Family Process, 41*(2), 135–157.

Shadish, W., & Baldwin, S. (2002). Meta-analysis in MFT interventions. In D. Sprenkle (Ed.), *Effectiveness research in marriage and family therapy* (pp. 339–370). The American Association for Marriage and Family Therapy.

"I'm Sorry"

Robert E. Keim, Ph.D., CFLE Emeritus†
Professor Emeritus, Northern Illinois University, Clinton, TN

While teaching Parent Education at the university, I frequently asked students how many of them recalled hearing their parents say to them, "I'm sorry." Quite honestly, at first, I was astonished to find that only one or two (out of 30–40) would raise their hand. For a reality check for myself, I once asked my youngest daughter (then still living at home) how many times she recalled me saying it, and she responded by saying: "Gobs and gobs of times." It might sound like I must have been a terrible parent, having to say "I'm sorry" so many times. However, somewhere in the distant past, I seem to have been fortunate to have been impressed with the merits of saying "I'm sorry" when it seemed to fit—with my kids, and with others.

This notion of saying "I'm sorry" is well supported over time by various authors and scholars and involves responding rationally to our self-talk (cognitive behavior theories; Ellis & Harper, 1975; Stoop, 1996; Morin, 1993); being open and honest (the "transparent self"; Jourard, 1964); and communicating our own feelings to another person with good "I" messages.[1]

"I'm sorry." These two simple words, when said with sincere meaning and feeling, can make a world of difference in a relationship. Saying "I'm sorry" (with warmth in the voice) can help make the hurt, offended, or injured person feel as if the person speaking these words really cares, that the person is being genuine, that he or she is reaching out to the other person—trying to make amends, trying to reestablish more honest and open communication. We occasionally experience this with others in our lives; we usually know how it feels, how it can bring back a warmer feeling between two people who were previously being pushed apart by some conflict or misunderstanding. Ample research indicates the power of forgiveness in relationships (Fincham et al., 2006), and this can best happen when someone says "I'm sorry."

When should we say it? Probably when our self-talk tells us something like "That wasn't nice," "You shouldn't have said that or done that"; or "It would be good to tell them 'I'm sorry.'" We need to act on those messages to ourselves, whether they are to our children or another adult. Saying "I'm sorry" to our children can begin when they are young enough to understand (which is usually younger than we think) on up through their teen and adult years. And it will usually pattern their ability to respond as well to the parent with "I'm sorry" when appropriate.

Occasionally, I've heard people express concern that they might lose respect from another, including their child, if they admitted that they had done something "wrong."

On the contrary, people usually seem to respond positively when we express a sincere apology. As it applies between two adults, it also can apply to parents and children.

Yes, saying "I'm sorry," conveyed with sincere meaning and feeling, may be crucial in building a healthy relationship between parent and child.

References

Ellis, A., & Harper, R.A. (1975). *A new guide to rational living.* Prentice Hall. (Note: a classic on avoiding stupid thinking.)

Fincham, F. D., Hall, J., & Beach, S. R. (2006). Forgiveness in marriage: Current status and future directions. *Family Relations, 55*(4), 415–427.

Jourard, S. M. (1964). *The transparent self.* Van Nostrand.

Morin, A. (1993). Self-talk and self-awareness: on the nature of the relation. *The Journal of Mind and Behavior, 14*(3), 223–234.

Stoop, D. (1996). *Self-Talk: Key to personal growth* (2nd ed.). F. H. Revell.

Note

[1] "I messages," perhaps are to be attributed first to Martin Buber in his 1958 book I and Thou (2nd ed.). They are most thoroughly described by Thomas T. Gordon in his 1970 classic book, *P.E.T. Parent Effectiveness Training: The Proven Program for Raising Responsible Children.*

Listening to Our Children: The Key to Building Connection

Ana Morante, L.M.F.T., CFLE
Family Wellness Partner/Trainer
Resilient Families Gilroy, Director

So many of us may think that we know how to listen to our children. After being a family wellness instructor for several years and teaching others the importance of listening to our children, I received a lesson on listening from my own daughter. When she was very young, her father and I separated for a while. During that time, we were surrounded by the love and support from family and friends. From my point of view, she was well sheltered from our marital crisis, and she had frequent and loving access to her father. Throughout the years, when the topic came out, I always made the comment of how loved she was.

Finally one day, she made me realize that I did not take the time or space to listen to her feelings about her own experience. She mentioned that she did not feel she could share with me that she felt deeply affected by our separation, even if we had plenty of support. She needed to share that with me and believe that her feelings were welcomed and validated, despite my own viewpoint or even my fear of how the separation had impacted her.

Sometimes, our children need to share their feelings with us—not so much for us parents to look for a solution or to feel blamed. Rather, they simply need to have their feelings mirrored and validated so that they can feel soothed and move on with their lives with more resilience.

Parents, I know that most of us do the best we can with what we have. Life needs to be seen and witnessed not only from our perspective as a parent, but also from our children's perspectives. This is the best way to help them feel connected to us and more secure in themselves.

Discussion Questions and Activities

1. What are some of the challenges a parent or primary caregiver faces when they see their child struggle?

2. How can a parent balance the goal of having a child follow rules and behave well with the need to make space for a child that is struggling with difficult/challenging behavior? Can you identify a time when you were triggered by a child's behavior to respond in a negative way? Discuss ideas for parents or caregivers to respond with patience and understanding instead of frustration and anger or disconnection.

The Hidden Pitfalls of "I" Statements

Julie K. Nelson, CFLE, MFHD, SFHEA
Associate Professor in Family Science
Utah Valley University, Orem, UT

"I" statements are a simple formula that promises peaceful, conflict-free homes by getting us what we want. Are they really that effective? Is that really the point? Do we even understand how to use them correctly? When do they work and when do they mess us up? This article introduces the hidden pitfalls of "I" statements.

We've been taught to use an "I" statement (also known as "I- messages") from self-help books or Communications 101. Begin a sentence with "I" and then state your desires. "I want you to be more kind to your sister." And the child just complies like you've waved a magic wand over her head, right? Not so fast. *I started with the word "I," so why didn't I get my wish fulfilled?*

When there is no conflict, or we have a compliant child, an "I" statement is effective in expressing what is needed, such as, "I need you to help me unload the car." The child who is ready and willing will respond easily to this request. However, what about situations of conflict? What about a noncompliant child or partner who sees things differently on weightier matters? How is an "I" statement intended to be used in these situations?

Look at these statements:

Statement 1. "I feel you are not listening to me when we discuss finances."
What is the intent and motivation behind this statement?
Putting blame on the other; assuming we read their minds.

What reaction might it produce?

Response: "What do you mean? I am here right now and listening. You always blame me for everything going wrong with money. What about your reckless spending habits?"

Statement 2. "I want you to do your homework right now."
What is the intent and motivation behind this statement?
Perhaps control and power. Likely, the parent has good intentions, but using a demanding statement with a stubborn child will often produce poor results.

Response: "Well, I don't want to. And you can't make me!"

<u>*Try this one:*</u>
Statement: "I don't want your sass anymore. Stop talking to me that way."
What could be the parent's intent and motivation behind this statement?
What reaction might it produce from a willful child?

Beginning a sentence with "I" doesn't guarantee compliance from the other person. Tensions will escalate. Examine your motives before using an "I" statement during a disagreement. Are you using it to seek to understand or to get what you want? If it's to get what you want without regard for the other person's perspective, don't use it in that way. Rather than a communication tool, it has become a relationship weapon.

The purpose of using an "I" statement during conflict is to express our needs, wants, and feelings about ourselves, not anyone else. They are offered with humility and sincerity to seek understanding when the other person has a difference of opinion. The "You" statement that follows is for the listener to restate what they heard. They restate the feelings, ideas, and wants they understood from what the person said. This approach is known as the "Speaker–Listener Technique" in the book *Fighting for Your Marriage* (Markman et al., 2010).

Speaker: "**I** feel so tired at the end of the day and would appreciate help in the kitchen."

Listener: "**You're** tired when you come home from work and need me to help get dinner ready."

The "I" statement person will confirm whether they were heard and understood correctly. If not, they state it again, and the listener reflects what they heard. The important thing is to have no agenda for "winning" or getting your way. The purpose is just to be understood. Then the other person takes a turn and delivers their "I" statement that reflects how they feel about the issue, stating their own needs.

From Boston University, we learn, "Ultimately, I-messages help create more opportunities for the resolution of conflict by creating more opportunities for constructive dialogue about the true sources of conflict" (Montemurro, n.d.). I encourage readers to download the Montemurro (n.d.) handout for helpful "I" message fill-in exercises.

Ideally, the "I" and "You" statements are to discover underlying issues: **power, caring, recognition, commitment, integrity**, and **acceptance**, as defined by Markman et al. (2010). Once we can identify these needs in our statements, the real power of connection and understanding begins. Often, being understood is all we need, and we'll be okay if the issue isn't resolved immediately or exactly the way we had hoped.

These two steps are crucial for seeking understanding in conflicted, complex situations. There is no way to solve a problem effectively unless we seek to understand, without criticism, agenda, blame, or power involved. Set aside your desire to fix or change the other person. The battle is not with them; rather, the two of you are a team to tackle a problem together.

The "I" statement is followed by a "You" statement and then a "We" statement. The "We" compromise part may naturally happen after this back and forth. The two people may need to spend some time considering the other person's point of view. Later that night, or a few days or a week later, both parties will have had time to consider the validity of the other person's view humbly and respectfully.

Compromise is not always an easy 50/50, "I get half my way if you get half your way." Consider if one partner wanted cherrywood cabinets and the other wanted pine and they'd met somewhere in the middle and got oak ... both would hate their kitchen cabinets! Rather, it is working as a team to find creative solutions and new perspectives to see a problem and working together to get an answer. No magic wand. No fairy dust. No easy answers. Just plain and simple "I" and "You" talking and listening sincerely, without wanting to win.

Discussion Questions and Activities

1. Take the following "Speaker" statement and re-state it as a "Listener" might to reflect the tone, energy, and intent:

"Every time you come to the dinner table with your phone out, I feel I don't matter as much as your virtual friends."

2. Following the 4-step pattern prompts on the referenced handout, identify a parenting situation you would like to address and follow the steps below:
   a. How you feel;
   b. What you have that feeling about;
   c. Why you feel this way;
   d. What you would like to see instead.

3. Translate these heated remarks into an effective "I" statement:

"You never listen to my side about what I want to do for our Christmas vacation."
"I cannot believe you are still wasting your time on that video game. Go to bed at once."
"You're never going to grow up to be a responsible adult if you don't do better at school."

References

Markman, H. J., Stanley, S. M., & Blumberg, S. L. (2010). *Fighting for your marriage: A deluxe revised edition of the classic best seller for enhancing marriage and preventing divorce.* Jossey-Bass.

Montemurro, F. (n.d.). *I-messages—handout.* Office of the Boston University Ombuds. https://www.studocu.com/en-us/document/western-governors-university/introduction-to-communication/i-messages-handout-handout/64167217

Home-School Communication: The Key to Student Success

Cynthia Jackson Small, D. Min, CFLE
Executive Director, Family Dimensions
Carrollton, TX

Communication is one of the keys to building a lasting relationship between schools and families. It is the foundation of a solid partnership. When educators and families communicate effectively, positive relationships develop, problems are more easily solved, and students make greater progress. Although this may seem to be a simple process, it usually does not happen overnight and takes practice and time.

As a mom of three children, I understand that family schedules are often hectic and busy, especially during the school year. We're living in such a fast-paced world where everything must be done in a hurry and instantly. Sometimes our daily schedules and journeys in life are so busy that it's difficult to find time to sit down at the dinner table with the family. Despite our chaotic timelines and schedules, it's important to make priorities for our children from the early years through high school and keep the lines of communication open daily. One of the major items that must be at the top of our busy family schedules is to take time to build relationships with teachers and strengthen home–school partnerships.

Partnering with teachers is just one avenue for becoming involved in the education of youth today. One of the defining features of family engagement is effective communication between parents, schools, and the community. This can be a challenge for both parents and teachers, but can happen using a variety of ongoing communication techniques including in-person and online family conferences, workshops, telephone calls, emails, school websites, home visits, and so on. With the advancement of technology, schools have a greater opportunity to reach families using various family-friendly digital tools that are designed to bridge home–school learning. As families begin to feel more comfortable communicating with schools in a digital world, this will open new avenues for engaging families as VIPs (Very Important Partners) in teaching and learning.

As a former classroom teacher and administrator, I have learned that a family–teacher conference is an effective pathway to building meaningful partnerships between the home and school. This best practice is a wonderful way to get to know families while building positive relationships and trust between the school staff and family members. It is essential for schools to create a welcoming atmosphere and comfort zone for successful conferences. Sharing tips for successful conferences is always helpful in easing families' stress and anxieties. To help parents and family members prepare for successful family–teacher conferences, I developed a list of sample questions to show parents how to begin a positive conversation with their child's teacher. The following questions are designed to promote ongoing, two-way communication with a focus on student learning.

- What can I do to help improve my child's study habits and performance in school? How can I help at home?

- Are there any areas of concern regarding my child's behavior or schoolwork?
- What are the school's homework and grading policies?
- What are age-appropriate strategies that I might use to reinforce skills at home?

One reminder that I often share with teachers and parents is this: Conferences should not be used as an open forum for complaints and negative remarks about the school, the teachers, or other students. The focus is primarily on the child. Additionally, conferences are avenues for teachers and families to communicate shared goals that may be determined collaboratively to support teaching and learning throughout the school year. By communicating positive messages regularly with families, schools will be able to strengthen home–school connections and build successful family partnerships.

As teachers begin to communicate intentionally and exchange good news with families, meaningful family engagement may take place. Further, as schools shift their focus to catching children doing something good at school, it is my belief that families will feel more comfortable serving as partners in their child's education. I remember one occasion when my son's fourth-grade teacher called me at home on a Sunday night. My first thought was, "Oh no!" What has Jason done now?" But to my surprise, she was calling to let me know that she had just scored Jason's math test and he had earned an A. She wanted to let me know how proud she was of Jason. What a refreshing phone call from the school! Yes, I was a proud mom knowing my son was not in trouble but accomplished something great at school! I must admit that I was initially shocked because I had been conditioned to expect bad news whenever a teacher called me at home. But after hearing such a positive message, I saw Jason's teacher as an individual who took time out of her weekend to give me a call and make my day. The teacher really made a difference by sharing good news and allowing me to see how much she cared about my son. This one phone call changed my perception of teachers as I began to view them from a new lens. I am happy to say that from this unexpected phone call, I began to view teachers as true advocates for students and families.

I often share this special story with teachers during professional development trainings. Essentially, my message to educators around the globe is to focus on communicating good news and positive messages with families throughout the school year. The message does not need to be a lengthy one that takes a long time to read or understand. On the contrary, just a phone call or a text message is a simple and effective process that could make a difference in building positive relationships with families.

In closing, I am confident that as school teams and families make a commitment to participate in ongoing, two-way communication, we will discover greater partnerships in school districts and communities around the world. Working and communicating together, we can build home–school partnerships that will impact student success in school and in life.

I've learned that people will forget what you said, people will forget what you did, but people will never forget how you made them feel.—Maya Angelou

Discussion Questions and Activities

1. Share innovative ideas for strengthening communication with families in the digital world to impact student learning and success.

2. Discuss recipes for promoting two-way communication with families designed to increase active family engagement in schools. Identify key "communication"

ingredients for creating a family-friendly school that welcomes all families as partners in teaching and learning.

Additional Reading

Constantino, S. M. (2008). *101 ways to create real family engagement.* Engage Press.

Joyce L. Epstein and Associates. (2019). *School, Family and Community Partnerships: Your Handbook for Action, Fourth Edition.* Corwin. Thousand Oaks, California.

Koralek, D., Nemeth, K., & Ramsey, K. (2019). *Families and educators together: Building great relationships that support young children.* National Association for the Education of Young Children.

Chapter II
Development Across the Lifespan

The Feeling Child

Sharon M. Ballard, Ph.D., CFLE
Professor and Department Chair
Human Development & Family Science
East Carolina University, Greenville, NC

"Big boys don't cry." "Little girls are supposed to be happy." "Don't be sad." Children are often told how they are supposed to feel. Children learn "display rules" very early in life. In other words, they learn where and with whom they can show certain emotions and at what times they are supposed to stuff an emotion deep inside and not let it show. Consequently, children may grow up not knowing how to identify, interpret, and appropriately express their emotions.

More and more attention is being given to the idea of emotional intelligence (EQ)— the ability to recognize our own feelings and those of others, to motivate ourselves, to control impulses, and to regulate emotions well within ourselves and in our relationships. In his book *Emotional Intelligence,* Daniel Goleman (1995/2020) was one of first to discuss the important role that emotions play in our lives. Emotions guide our actions; each emotion serves a function in leading us to particular actions. Children who are more skilled with their emotions often experience fewer social problems, fewer behavior problems, and less withdrawal and depression.

There are three basic steps to facilitate young children's emotional development and help them to develop a positive EQ. First, help children identify their emotions. Preschoolers often have trouble identifying what they are feeling (sometimes adults do too!). Start with introducing terms when the emotions are present, such as anger, fear, hurt, happiness, and sadness and then move to self-conscious emotions, such as jealousy and pride as your child gets older.

Second, children need to learn how to interpret their emotions. Children need to know that emotions are never bad. Avoid using emotion-minimizing language (e.g., "You're okay") that may lead to internalizing emotions (King, 2021). Instead, use emotion-affirming language that validates a child's emotion (e.g., "I know you are sad right now. I would be sad too if my friend had to go home"). We are given the ability to experience endless emotions, and these emotions should be experienced and not pushed aside.

Third, children need to learn to express emotions appropriately. "I understand that you are angry, but it is not okay to hit." Children need to learn outlets for appropriately discharging their emotions. Children may discharge emotions by talking about how they feel, running around the yard (how many of us use exercise as a stress release?), or punching a pillow. For many children, it also might mean crying. Crying tends to make many adults uncomfortable, and they try to get children to stop crying, but crying can be an important expression of emotion. The hurt has already occurred, and the crying is the release of that hurt. If a child (or anybody for that matter) is not allowed to express or discharge the emotion, it will get hidden inside, and eventually it will come out—and not always in a positive manner. For example, we likely all have had experiences when something minor happens and we completely lose control. We either start to sob, or we yell or use some other mechanism for releasing the strong emotions that have built up. It was not necessarily the minor incident that just occurred that caused the blow-up but all the incidents and hurts that have been stuffed inside. Pretty soon, there is no more room, and it must come out. If children's emotions are validated and they are allowed to experience and discharge their emotions on a regular basis, that build up is less likely to occur.

Consequently, we should give children permission to feel an emotion and help them to identify and label the emotion. As they are experiencing the emotion, offer to be with them while they do or offer suggestions on discharging the emotion. Sometimes it is scary to have strong emotions, and it is comforting to a child to have a trusted adult there. For example, when your daughter realizes that she left a favorite toy at Grandma's house, it will be a loss for her. Rather than trivializing her emotion and asking her to stuff it inside by saying something like "Don't be silly, this isn't something to be sad about, forget it and come play," instead, try saying something like "I know that you are sad. I'll call Grandma and have her put it in a safe place until we return, and I will sit with you while you are sad and then when you are ready, we can go play." The child that is given permission to feel sad is going to be much more likely to let the sadness go, start playing, and have a happy day, than the child who is told to forget about it and then carries that sadness with them all day.

Like other areas of development, if children are not given the opportunity to develop skill in identifying, interpreting, and expressing emotions, they will not automatically have those skills as adults and will not develop a strong EQ. Because many of us did not have good opportunities to develop these skills as children, we need to examine our own EQ. We will then be more prepared to help our children be successful in their emotional development.

Discussion Questions and Activities

1. What are healthy ways that you like to discharge emotions? How can these methods be modeled for young children?

2. Children's books can be a wonderful tool for initiating discussions about emotions with children of all ages. Visit the children's section of your local library or ask your librarian for suggestions on appropriate books.

3. Sometimes our emotional vocabulary is limited. Check out https://feelingswheel.com/ for a feelings wheel that can help you and your child label emotions.

For more resources, visit The Best SEL Picture Books About Feelings and Emotions (imaginationsoup.net), which features a great list of picture books about feelings and emotions.

References

Goleman, D. (2020). *Emotional intelligence* (25th anniversary ed.). Bantam Books. (Original work published 1995)

King, E. K. (2021). "You're okay" may not be okay: Using emotion language to promote toddler's social and emotional development. *Young Children, 76*(1), 4–19.

"Can't We Just Play?"

Jean Illsley Clarke, Ph.D., CFLE †
Author and parent educator
Minneapolis, MN

"Can we play now?" Clarissa's children begged. Clarissa was perplexed. Why did her children ask to play? They had been playing all day. In the morning, they had been at Saturday swim classes, and their mom had spent the entire afternoon playing with them. They had played a competitive math game with flashcards. Clarissa had taught them three games from *Taking No for an Answer*: Follow Me, Follow You; Traffic Cop; and Red Light, Green Light (Simmons, 2000). They had also gone on a nature walk to see how many kinds of birds they could spot. All of that had been fun, at least Clarissa hoped it was. Actually, she was getting tired when Mason declared he was bored with birds, and Madison whined, "Can we play now?"

"But we've been playing all afternoon," Clarissa snapped, perplexed, and slightly irritated—well, more than slightly, when she questioned, "What do you want to play now?" The children responded, "Just play, Mom. We want to play."

All the "play" they did with Mom was important. It strengthened connections with Mom and was a good learning time for the children. However, adult-directed activities need to be balanced with child-directed free play, which is the time children consider to be *real* play.

Mason and Madison needed some time for *real* free play. Time to select an activity, engage in it, create their own play scenario (free of adult direction), and bring the activity to closure (Zosh et al., 2018). This need for free play time spans the childhood years.

Infants need some time to themselves. Babies who are entertained full time fail to develop self-comforting skills.

Toddlers must have free time to explore the environment—to touch, drop, taste, wiggle, throw, stack, smell, and listen to a wide variety of safe objects and, yes, people. All are essential brain-building activities.

Two-year-olds need free time to practice their newfound physical capabilities, to struggle, and to master.

Three to 5-year-olds need free play time to explore their own creativity and their relationships with peers—real or imaginary.

School-age children must have free time to develop and test their knowledge of rules. Who makes the rules? Who follows the rules? What happens if you follow them or break them? A lot of learning happens when two thirds of a child-initiated softball game is spent arguing, which cannot happen if an adult coach is running the show.

Adolescents need time to explore their relationships, to think about their values, and to dream about their futures.

Free playtime is not time controlled by screens or game scenarios. It is time controlled by the children themselves, and if they have lost the skill to do that, adults need to act to alter the children's schedules.

How can free time be provided?
- Allow for time to play outdoors.
- Spend less time plugged-in to screens.
- Create a limit for lessons, organized sports, clubs, and volunteer activities.

Are those activities bad? Not necessarily. Just carve out enough time for free play.

Zosh et al. (2018) view play as a continuum from free play to playful instruction, with several types of learning happening across the range. On this spectrum, **free play** corresponds to social learning and self-regulation. **Guided play,** like the nature walks and the adult-guided games such as *Taking No for an Answer*, can lead to discovery, receptive and academic learning, and meaning-making. **Playful instruction**, such as the math flashcards Clarissa used, lead to rote and academic learning.

How much free playtime does your child need? It varies with the child's temperament, but we can safely plan for a minimum of half an hour to 1 hour of free playtime daily.

In research studies on overindulgence, many adults who were overindulged as children complained about being overscheduled and not having enough free time for themselves (Clarke et al., 2014). We can avoid this for our children by providing free play time, which can benefit them in so many ways.

Discussion Questions and Activities
1. ***Reflecting on Childhood Play:*** Ask participants to reflect on their own childhoods. How much of their play was directed by adults versus chosen by them? How do they feel this balance affected their development and creativity?

2. ***Challenges to Free Play:*** In the context of today's fast-paced, screen-oriented world, what challenges do families face in ensuring children get enough free play? How can these challenges be addressed?

3. ***Understanding Free Play:*** What does free play mean to you? How does it differ from structured activities or games with rules set by adults?

4. ***Barrier Breakdown:*** Create small groups to discuss and identify personal and societal barriers to free play (e.g., safety concerns, feeling the need to constantly entertain or educate children). Each group can present their solutions to these barriers (Open AI, 2024).

5. ***Playtime Audit:*** Have participants complete a "playtime audit" for a week, noting how their child spends their playtime. This can include categories such as free play, screen time, and structured activities. Review and discuss the findings in the next session (Open AI, 2024).

6. ***Resource Sharing Circle:*** Encourage participants to share resources, such as safe play areas, free play ideas, or books/articles about the importance of play. This can be done in person or through a shared digital document or platform (Open AI, 2024).

References

Clarke, J., & Dawson, C., & Bredehoft, D. (2014). *How much is too much? Raising likable, responsible, and respectful children—from toddlers to teens—in an age of overindulgence.* De Capo. (For more information about the Overindulgence Research Studies, see www.overindulgence.org.)

OpenAI. (2024). Activities created with *ChatGPT* (3.5) [Large language model]. https://chat.openai.com

Simons, L. (2000). *Taking "no" for an answer and other skills children need.* Parenting Press, Inc.

Zosh, J. M., Hirsh-Pasek, K., Hopkins, E. J., Jensen, H., Liu, C., Neale, D., Solis, S. L., & Whitebread, D. (2018). Accessing the inaccessible: Redefining play as a spectrum. *Frontiers in Psychology, 9,* 1124–1124. https://doi.org/10.3389/fpsyg.2018.011245

Thank you to Lisa Krause, M.A., CFLE, Jean's colleague and friend who reviewed the entries and provided updated references.

The Secrets of Self-Esteem

Julie K. Nelson, CFLE, MFHD, SFHEA
Associate Professor in Family Science
Utah Valley University, Orem, UT

Self-esteem is often mistaken as a product of someone's success. Once a child makes the team, wins the blue ribbon, or gets straight A's, *then* she will feel good about herself, right? Not necessarily. What about when they don't? Life is not usually filled with spectacular moments of basking in the spotlight. Can we feel worthwhile when we are just okay? Self-worth is not just built on extraordinary achievements but on *all* experiences in life.

There is really no secret when parents build their child's self-esteem on evidence-based, day-to-day proven practices. The following outlines three key ingredients: valuing the worth of others, learning from mistakes, and hard work.

Valuing the Worth of Others
All too often, we see the success of others contrasted with our inadequacies. There is usually only one winner in a race, only one lead in the school play, and only one person picked to be the team captain. One surprising part of fostering a child's sense of self-worth is teaching them to value the worth of others. The secret to self-esteem is developing the capacity to feel and express joy in others' accomplishments. It seems paradoxical, but it's a key to self-worth: I'm not just valuable when I am the best but also when I allow others to succeed and to recognize their achievements.

We need to model this as parents. We cannot show pettiness or jealousy when someone seemingly moves out ahead of us in life. Our culture is loaded with the message that if others get the bigger piece of the pie, we go hungry. It's so unfortunate when children hear their mother say, "Well Honey, you didn't win the spot on the team because the other parents are friends with the coach. Their daughter got on the team by favor and not any talent." Whether that is true or not, think of what that acrimonious message models for children. Instead, we need to applaud another person's success, even if we have to fake it at first. By so doing, we model how we have character, and character is part of our sense of worth.

When a child is happy for another person, they learn that it doesn't diminish their own happiness; rather, the joy spills over and multiplies. In a real-life example, a teenager auditioned for a particular role in a play, but her friend got the part instead. The disappointment stung for a while, but this young lady decided to celebrate the accomplishment with her friend. She went over to her house and congratulated her. She asked how she could help. Turning outward helped this young lady to focus less on her pain and to embrace positivity. She helped her friend memorize her lines and learned there was more than one way to express her talents. When it came time to perform, she sat in the audience in amazement. Her friend's accomplishment became her accomplishment. It was a defining moment for their friendship, and they remained friends for life. This young lady turned this negative experience into a huge boost in her self-esteem.

Here are some phrases to get you started. Add a few more and practice them in the right situation:
"I'm so happy for her."
"What a great thing to happen to him. He deserves so much credit. He worked hard for that."
"What can we do to congratulate her?"
"What a great accomplishment. I'm super proud of him."

Question: *What other phrases can you think of?*

These sentiments trickle down to our kids and teach them that there's always enough of the pie to share, even if we make the pie ourselves and take it over to celebrate together.

Learning From Mistakes

Parents can do a lot to reinforce a child's worth when mistakes happen. Unfortunately, some parents do the opposite: They humiliate or rage about their child's incompetence. Perhaps, in part, they are responding the same way their own parents did—kick them when they're down. According to Smith et al. (2022), "Parental criticism reflects perceptions of one's parents as overly disapproving and judgmental of their so-called imperfections" (p. 2). When we send the message that our love is conditional on their performance, it contributes to "toxic perfectionism" and the feeling of "I'll never be good enough!" Additionally,

> Anytime we explode at children for something they do to themselves, we only make the problem worse. We give kids the message that the actual, logical consequence of messing up is making adults mad. The children get swept away in the power of their anger rather than learn a lesson from the consequences of their mistake. (Cline & Fay, 2020, p. 77)

We forget that growth means learning to improve, and imperfection is part of the natural world. We still fail and we've had a lot more experience than children. We want others to be gentle with us when we make a mistake. It's good to remember that children are new to life. They are still learning, and making mistakes is part of the learning process.

A few questions to ponder: Think about the last time you really messed up. How did others react? How did that response make you feel less or more confident and capable? Now think about the last time your child made a big mistake. What words and emotions did you share with them? Did you engender a closer relationship, or did you drive distance between you and your child? How did that communicate your feelings about their worth?

No doubt it is appropriate to express our disappointment when our children do something wrong. But, at the same time, parents need to see these moments as opportunities to teach the value of the individual and self-compassion. We affirm their goodness even if what they did was not so good. "Wow, that wasn't so smart, but you are smart. In fact, I know you are better than this, and I know you'll figure out a way to fix it."

I am not advocating for parents to neglect enforcing a consequence when needed. However, many times, kids just mess up because they were not thinking or they were being careless, not because they were doing it on purpose or being malevolent. Words matter when we say, "What were you thinking? You're such an idiot! How many times must I tell you? Are you deaf?" These are moments when fragile or emerging self-esteem takes a beating. These words are tearing down an already low-spirited child.

Let's not kick the child when he's down. Let's offer a hand up, dusting off, and the confidence to step up and do better.

Hard Work

This one is less obvious and can be the real secret sauce. One of my daughters got a job as a cashier at a fast-food restaurant when she was 14 years old. She could barely see over the counter. She locked her knees when taking orders on the first day and was so nervous she fainted in front of the customer. We laugh about that now, but she proved her persistence by going back after that disastrous first day and working there for the next three summers. She knows that if she could get through that, she could do anything.

A measure of success, according to psychologist and author Angela Duckworth (2018), is having "grit," the passion to persevere in pursuit of something difficult. Children will learn they have value when they do hard things over time and persevere without an immediate reward.

My children learned how to mow our expansive lawn and did so for years. At times, it was challenging to get them to do it. There was occasional griping, but sweat and raw hard work is good for the muscles and building self-worth. The accomplishment is rewarding even when there is no standing ovation after finishing a grimy job. You learn to dig deep and finish what you started.

Discussion Questions
1. What chores or family contributions did you make as a child? Was the system successful or not?

2. How did working around the house contribute to family cohesiveness and feelings of individual worth?

References
Cline, F., & Fay, J. (2020). *Parenting with love & logic: Teaching children responsibility.* NavPress.

Duckworth, A. (2018). *Grit: The power of passion and perseverance.* Scribner.

Smith, M. M., Hewitt, P. L., Sherry, S. B., Flett, G. L., & Ray, C. (2022). Parenting behaviors and trait perfectionism: A meta-analytic test of the social expectations and social learning models. *Journal of Research in Personality, 96,* Article 104180. https://doi.org/10.1016/j.jrp.2021.104180

Lessons Learned Around the Family Dinner Table

Peggy North-Jones, Ph.D., CFLE †
Associate Director, Caregiver Connections, Quincy, IL

At the family dinner table, I grew up knowing that my father, a son of southern parents, did not like his food hot. In fact, he preferred turning everything into a "salad" by covering it with mayonnaise. My mother, a New Englander, liked her food pure and piping hot. The negotiations that went on between them on how to live with these differences characterized the time we spent at the dinner table as a family.

On my first visit to meet my future in-laws, I had just returned from the West Coast where I had fervently joined the ranks of bra-burning feminists. Seated at the dinner table in a midwestern town, I was handed two rolls on a plate. I watched as both of my soon-to-be sisters-in-law and mother-in-law carefully buttered one roll for themselves and then handed the other split and buttered roll to their spouses. I looked at my fiancé with incredulous disbelief and said, "You have got to be kidding." Only later did I realize that this dinner table experience was an introduction into the study of contrasts between my new family and my family of origin.

I knew that on every holiday, my grandmother would arrive in her pretty dress and high heels and place a cut-glass bowl of ambrosia on the dinner table. It was not important what else was for dinner. She brought this dessert that stemmed from her own family tradition.

From these experiences and others, I learned about marriage, conflict, communication, compromise, and life's blessings at the dinner table. There is a wonderful Norman Rockwell painting, *Freedom From Want*. It depicts a smiling family at Thanksgiving dinner, and highlights parents who are proudly presenting the perfectly cooked turkey. For many today, this illustration would have little meaning other than nostalgia. The family dinner up until about the past few decades punctuated family life with a sense of both time and of a shared meaning; it now seems to be disappearing for many. The image that might come to mind for a painting today would be cars in a fast-food drive-through lane or parents serving takeout to their children.

With families today eating an average of only four meals a week together in the home, family dinners have declined by one third since the mid-1970s (Doherty, 2000). The percentage of food consumed by children in restaurants and fast-food outlets nearly tripled between 1977 and 1996 (St.-Onge et al., 2003). According to Hofferth and Sandberg (2001), mealtime, when children and parents come together to share the stories of their day, tends to correlate with overall child well-being. It seems important to reflect on the apparent impact of these changes on family mealtime.

The family dinner represents time shared and a place to pass on rituals, customs, and special-occasion traditions to the next generation. On a daily basis, manners can be taught, gossip shared, adult relationships modeled, and sibling rivalry expressed and resolved. Even when mealtime takes on an unpleasant tone, the experience is still a sharing of who we are as a family. It provides a definition and experiences to remember, as well as predictability: Dinner is at a specific time, and everyone in the house is expected to be there. The routines and rituals around meals and the family table are components of the characteristics that underlie each family's uniqueness.

Nutrition can be taught at the family dinner table. Parents in many cases have stopped being the primary source of information for their children on what and when to eat. I grew up with no pantry, no snacks available, and I asked my parents if I could have something to eat before I could have it. The lack of fast-food places meant that except for a special treat-trip to the corner market, my mother and father controlled food availability. And although I saw some food advertisements in magazines or the newspaper, I did not have a television or computer offering information to me about food. The dinner table, then, provided a time to eat and to learn about what I liked, what was good for me, and what my mother was willing to supply. The kitchen and dining tables provide key learning opportunities that can represent family values.

Manners can be taught at the dinner table. Although the lessons often evoke eye-rolling on the part of children, they go with us as we venture out in the world. These include how to act: "If you don't have anything nice to say, then don't say anything"; how to look: "Sit up straight and put your napkin in your lap"; how to manage food:

"Chew with your mouth closed"; and how to be social and conversational: "You need to stay at the table until everyone is finished." Few of us are very tolerant of sharing mealtime with those who did not have the experience of this training in table manners and etiquette, even if we found the learning tedious at the time.

Family time happens naturally at the dinner table. With today's multitasking, for overextended dual-career or single-parent families, time together is often lacking or at a premium. Now, even restaurant eating may find families together but with one parent on a cell phone and a child engaged in playing a handheld videogame. The experience of dinner table conversation, of shared time where nothing can interrupt the family togetherness, is not a frequent occurrence today. Televisions are on, telephones ring, and family members come and go and often eat different foods at the same meal. The sharing, of so many types, that is fundamental to the experience of the family table seems to have been replaced—if family members even get to the table.

What lesson have I learned from listening to families with whom I have worked over the past 35 years? I've learned that there is so much to be gained by taking the time and putting forth the effort required to get family members to the dinner table. Family bonding, communication, good nutrition, and the sharing of family values all increase when this simple routine is created. According to Brendtro et al. (2001), the sense of belonging that is fundamental to children's healthy development is supported when they are made to feel an important part of a daily event in the life of the family. "Everyone please come to dinner"—what delightful words!

Change is part of life. So are lessons. I wonder ... if the lessons outlined here are not being learned at the dinner table, where will there be learned?

References

Brendtro, L. K., Brokenleg, M., & Van Bockern, S. (2001). *Reclaiming youth at risk: Our hope for the future.* National Education Service.

Doherty, W. J. (2000). *Take back your kids: Confident parenting in turbulent times.* Sorin.

St.-Onge M., Keller, K., & Heymsfield, S. (2003). Changes in childhood food consumption patterns. *American Journal of Clinical Nutrition, 78*(6), 1068–1073.

Hofferth, S., & Sandberg, J. (2001). How American children spend their time. *Journal of Marriage and Family, 63*(2), 295–308.

The Bell Curve of Parenting

Brenda L. Potter, M.S. Ed., CFLE
BLP Consulting,
North Kingstown, RI

A wise friend once told me "We are active parents for just a quarter of our lives." I first digested my friend's wisdom back in my mid-30s, when I was well into my "active parenting quarter" with three children aged birth to 8 years. It seemed inconceivable that the very active parenting stage wouldn't be the norm forever!

With a predicted life expectancy of 80 to 100 years, many of us live the first quarter of our lives before "actively" parenting children. Once our second quarter of 20 to 25 years of parenting begin, our "active parenting" efforts seem to intensify with each year (and child), culminating with the fledging of our children, creating a nice taper to the bell curve image.

As a parent educator, I used this reference as a yardstick to help parents of young children take stock of their own growth and appreciate the intentionality of their parenting focus and purpose within the curve. It is truly an extraordinarily active period of development and understanding.

I recently reflected on the "active parenting quarter" with my wise old friend who is now also in her third quarter of life. We marveled at the physical activity and stamina allowed by our younger bodies! We admired each other's growth and understanding of our active children's journey along the curve and acknowledged the periods of uneven distributions of activity.

As a parent of a child with disabilities, I shared my own bell curve iteration; one with a less distinct midpoint, an uneven distribution of data and a sustained taper for one child that will carry well into my fourth quarter. We agreed the second quarter of our lives was consumed with very "active parenting," and it was the critical developmental foundation for our parental journeys into the third and fourth quarters!

Discussion Question
Besides parents of children with disabilities, what other parents might experience an atypical stage of active parenting? How might you as a Family Life Educator support atypical active parenting?

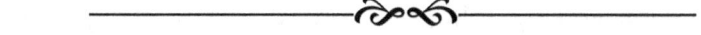

Every Growing Person Needs Basic Care, Stimulation, Guidance, Love, and Affirmation

Lane H. Powell, Ph.D., CFLE †
Consultant
Lubbock, TX

Parenting advice in books and media programs can be confusing. Many of the sources offer a dizzying number of suggestions, advice, and precautions for anxious parents. Although most of us only go to the "school of our family of origin" (our parents) to learn how to parent, we have also seen a variety of styles, reactions, and philosophies of parenting modeled for us—some positive and many negative. There is certainly a need to gain a clearer grounding of the principles of human development that are consistent over all circumstances and stages of life. These essential principles have been confirmed in my own life experience with children, adult relatives, and grandparents.

Human development is the study of growth across the lifespan. Every person who is alive—young or old—is still capable of growth and needs to grow. It will not be in the same way or at the same rate for everyone because growth is different for each person. It is more than just getting bigger. It also involves emotional and mental growth. Just as a growing plant needs soil, light, and moisture, so a growing person has some essential requirements that allow growth to occur.

The four essential needs are *basic needs, stimulation, guidance,* and *love and affirmation.* Each is important for the growing person—the child in the family as well as the parents.

Basic Needs. Years ago, Abraham Maslow (1954) proposed a *hierarchy of needs* in human development. He arranged six categories of need into a pyramid of importance that he believed every human must satisfy to reach their full potential of self-actualization. The base of the pyramid is labeled *physiological needs:* the need for food, clothing, shelter, and protection from harm. If these basic needs are not met or are inadequate, the human may die. *Basic* needs are necessary for *survival.* Sadly, many people in our world will not survive this day because of a lack of basic needs fulfillment. But those who read this book will probably be able to check off this need with a flourish.

Stimulation. The stimulation of the five senses (hearing, sight, touch, taste, smell) is necessary for *growth*—mental as well as physical. New technology has allowed for the advanced study of brain development in newborns. We now know that the infant's brain is not fully formed at birth. It is in a state of plasticity. Neurons in the brain are waiting to be stimulated to form pathways of thought, memory, reasoning, and association (Huttenlocher, 2002). That's why warm and gentle talking to an infant—even though he or she has no idea what you are saying—is so vital. It stimulates the brain to form connections and actually raises the IQ! Research has shown that premature babies who are touched, patted, rocked, and talked to actually gain weight and recover much faster than those who are left in incubators without stimulation. Human development specialists John Bowlby (1953) and Mary Ainsworth (Ainsworth & Bell, 1970) studied children raised in overcrowded orphanages where emotional and physical growth was stunted by neglect. It was the beginning of their work on the importance of parent–child attachment. An actual diagnosis, *failure to thrive,* defines infants who do not gain weight after birth and are listless and quiet. Although things other than neglect can cause this condition, most sufferers have had little sensory stimulation in their environments. Parents of such infants can be given special lessons on how to provide sensory stimulation. They can be shown the importance of holding the baby while feeding, talking to the baby and making eye contact, and playing little games that stimulate growth and attachment.

Do teens still need stimulation? You bet! And they will find ways to get it that are either productive (we hope) or risky. They can still be hugged, their hair brushed, backs rubbed, or feet massaged. Adults of all ages also crave stimulation. Often vigorous adults begin to decline when forced retirement or illness takes away their options for stimulation.

Guidance. Instruction in social skills, protection, and necessary limits and boundaries are essential for *socialization.* Without guidance, a person has little chance of becoming a socially accepted and approved human being. Consider all the things that parents, or other adults, must teach a young child: how to eat, dress oneself, use the toilet, talk (with respect), act (with kindness), share resources, respect other persons' rights, and on and on. Human beings are social animals. They crave interaction and acceptance by other human beings. Maslow (1954) termed this the "need to belong." The parental task of *guidance*, when successfully accomplished, teaches children the socialization that will allow them to live peacefully and productively with others—siblings, parents, friends, spouses, and coworkers.

Parents often talk of "disciplining" their children. In most cases, they are referring to various forms of punishment: spanking, scolding, shouting, reprimanding, taking away privileges, criticizing, threatening, or just ignoring misbehavior. Why not look instead at the root word of discipline, which is "disciple"? A disciple is the student of a teacher. And what are the characteristics of a good teacher? Think for a moment of the best teacher you ever had. What made him or her so good? I have asked this question of many students, and the answers always include the following: She had a good sense of humor; he wanted us to learn and was excited about the subject; he spent extra time with us; she made learning fun and interesting; she was tough and expected a lot, but I knew she cared. The good teacher offers *guidance:* patient, loving, interested, and caring, but setting boundaries and having expectations.

Research on adolescents who avoid high-risk behaviors identified two important characteristics of parents: They provide a warm and loving climate of acceptance in the home, and they do "parental monitoring" (Walsh, 2003). This is not to be confused with parental policing. Parental monitoring describes the parent who is a loving and concerned guide and wants to know where the teen is going and with whom and who also establishes reasonable boundaries and guidelines for behavior. Whether we are 8 or 80, there is still a need for guidance in different forms and different amounts, because following the rules of society opens the door to social acceptance and satisfaction.

Love and Affirmation. Love is best described as unconditional positive regard of other persons (Rogers, 1959/1989). When one is valued and affirmed, no matter how he or she looks or performs, it provides the basis for the development of positive *self-esteem* and *self-actualization*. Human beings are so hungry for love that they will often be seduced by shallow substitutes (praise, manipulation, promises), particularly if they have had little experience with the "real thing." A strong dose of *love and affirmation* that results in positive self-esteem and self-actualization makes it possible for adults to parent the next generation successfully. It allows them to feel comfortable putting aside their own needs to care for very dependent and needy infants and young children, thus providing the basic needs, stimulation, and guidance essentials for the next generation. What is considered a strong dose of love and affirmation? Marriage relationship researcher John Gottman (2000) observed that committed partners must have a 5 to 1 ratio of positive to negative interactions if they are to remain happy in the relationship. Children need an even higher ratio of hugs, positive attention, smiles, and comments of affirmation for who they are and what they do right (vs. the tendency to target what they do wrong).

If a person's need for love and affirmation is unmet in the early years of life, he or she tends to become a self-centered, grasping adult who is never satisfied with the attention given or able to anticipate or empathize with another's needs and pain. Is an adult who missed out on unconditional love and a high ratio of affirmation as a child doomed to be incapable of freely giving these essential qualities to another generation? The good news is that adults have the capacity to grow beyond an emotionally abusive childhood but not without intentionally working on it, with desire (Johnson, 2006). The end result is definitely worth it.

To recap, every growing person has four essential needs:
- Basic—for survival
- Stimulation—for growth
- Guidance—for socialization
- Love and affirmation—for self-esteem and self-actualization

So keep on growing for as long as you live while helping to guide your child!

References

Ainsworth, M. D. S., & Bell, S. M. (1970). Attachment, exploration, and separation: Illustrated by the behavior of one-year-olds in a strange situation. *Child Development, 41*(1), 49–67. https://doi.org/10.2307/1127388

Bowlby, J. (1953). *Child care and the growth of love.* Penguin Books.

Gottman, J. (2000). *Clinical manual for marital therapy: A research-based approach* (rev. 2001). The Gottman Institute.

Huttenlocher, P. (2002). *Neural plasticity.* Harvard University.

Maslow, A. (1954). *Motivation and personality.* Harper and Row.

Johnson, D. W. (2006). *Reaching out: Interpersonal effectiveness and self-actualization* (9th ed.). Pearson.

Rogers, C. R. (1989). *A theory of therapy, personality, and interpersonal relationships as developed in the client-centered framework.* In H. Kirschenbaum & V. Henderson (Eds.), The Carl Rogers reader (pp. 236–257). Houghton Mifflin. (Original work published 1959).

Walsh, N. (2003). Early puberty, ethnicity may contribute to teen smoking: Parental monitoring matters. *Clinical Psychiatry News, 31,* 32.

Gender Development in Preschool
A Brief Guide to Answering Young Children's Questions

Elizabeth A. Ramsey, Ph.D., CFLE
Assistant Professor
Tennessee Technological University, Human Ecology
Cookeville, TN

According to Kohlberg's (1966) theory of gender development, gender identity begins in the early toddler and preschool years. Two-year-olds are becoming conscious of the physical differences between boys and girls, and by age 3, most children will label themselves boy or girl, also known as gender-typing (Kohlberg, 1966; Martorell, 2023; Rafferty, 2024). In Kohlberg's cognitive-developmental theory, gender constancy, or sex-category constancy, has three stages: (a) gender identity, the awareness of one's own gender; (b) gender stability, the awareness that gender does not change; and (c) gender consistency, awareness that a girl remains a girl, even if she prefers to play with trucks and a boy is a boy, even if he has long hair (Kohlberg, 1966).

The last stage typically occurs between 3 and 7 years of age. Recently, cognitive-developmental theorists reject that, as originally stated by Kohlberg, gender constancy must precede gender-typing (Martorell, 2023).

In today's world of gender fluidity where gender can be viewed on a spectrum rather than dichotomy, I'm often asked by parents, "How should I answer or confirm my child's statements or questions about gender at the early age of 2 or 3?" Parents disclose that they are asked by their littles, "Am I a girl?" or "Am I a boy?" The answer is simple: Answer the questions and confirm the statements using a biological approach appropriate for the child's cognitive stage.

The toddler and preschool years are time for simple answers to their questions. Use a biological approach, and don't worry when you are asked by your preschooler if they will always be a girl or if they will always be a boy. It is a common question for them to ask. Keep it simple, Mom and Dad, and don't worry when the question arises; it is a typical part of their development.

Discussion Questions
1. Explore the biological approach to gender development. What are the basic points of this theory?

2. Explore the social learning approach to gender development. Explain how people learn gender roles according to this theory.

3. Explore gender-schema theory. According to this theory, explain the role that culture plays in gender identity.

References

Kohlberg, L. (1966). A cognitive-developmental analysis of children's sex role concepts and attitudes. In E. E. Maccoby (Ed.), *The development of sex differences.* Stanford University Press.

Martorell, G. (2023). *Child* (3rd ed.). McGraw-Hill.

Rafferty, J. (2024). *Gender identity development in children.* Healthy children.org https://www.healthychildren.org/English/ages-stages/gradeschool/Pages/Gender-Identity-and-Gender-Confusion-In-Children.aspx

"As the twig is bent, so grows the tree": Making the Early Years Count

Amelia I. Rose, Ph.D., CFLE
Family Life Pathways, Inc.
West Palm Beach, FL

"As the twig is bent, so grows the tree" is an old adage grounded in folk wisdom. Its origin can be traced back to Alexander Pope in the 1700s, although several others have taken credit for some version of it. Regardless, sayings such as this have withstood the test of time for a good reason: There is some degree of truth to them.

This adage was widely used in the Caribbean by elders in the community, who were thought to be the authority on what constitutes successful childrearing practices. The prevailing conviction was that children's character is formed in the early years of life and that their early behaviors have a lasting impact on their development, thereby shaping their character later in life. The opposite also holds true—that twigs (children) can grow into crooked trees (adults) if appropriate interventions are not introduced early in the lifespan. If parents understand the importance of their children's early learning experience, they would be more inclined to capitalize on the first 5 years of their lives, laying the foundation for not only their children's academic success but also their social development.

The majority of child development experts assert the principle of the "window of opportunity" to describe the first 5 years of a life, but what does that mean for parents and early childhood caregivers? Most importantly, every parent should know that by the time a child reaches age 5, 90% of their brain is developed, which has occurred at a pace never to be repeated again (Bipartisan Policy Center, n.d.). This reaffirms the importance of the quality of a child's early experiences because it makes a critical difference in the formation of either a strong or a weak foundation for learning, health, and behavior throughout life. Sadly, despite the wealth of child development studies available over the past 6 decades, there still seems to be a gap between what the experts say and what parents know or understand about child development and early brain development. Some of these gaps are highlighted later in this essay, as I focus on three concurrent concepts to bolster the "window of opportunity." The overall goal is to show that when parents become more cognizant of their role and impact on their children's lives, these gaps will be reduced as they learn on the job.

The first of these concurrent concepts that I address is that of parents being their children's first and most important teacher and playing a key role in helping them attain their full potential (Benveniste, 2023). This takes some getting used to because parents often only see themselves as caregivers. However, it is critical for them to understand this significant principle because this can enhance or impede their ability to help their children succeed in life. To help them do this, parents will need to understand that everything they do with their children can teach important lessons about their world—things as simple as play, singing to them, playing music and games, and responding verbally to their cues. Once parents begin to see these everyday activities as opportunities for learning and the hours spent with their children as teaching in a real-world classroom, they begin to make the connections. In addition, parents need to know that infants and toddlers learn faster than they may realize—that they are the world's best "copycats"; as such, parents will now acquire a new position, that of being role models. This seems like a lot for any parent to absorb, so it is important for them and those who support them to ensure they are connected to community resources necessary to remove barriers.

Now, if we believe that parents are their children's first and most important teachers, then it naturally follows that "home is the child's first school" and rightfully so because this is the place where children first learn, grow, socialize, and develop important life skills to shape their world for a lifetime (Rowcliffe, 2012). This is the second concept I discuss. A word of caution: This concept should not be confused with homeschooling but should be understood as the first resource place, where a child's initial academic and social development occurs. It is also for this reason that parents need to understand that their "little bundle of joy" enters their home environment packed with potential, is curious and ready to learn, thrives in loving and respectful environments, and has an innate ability to process and use language. Every parent should also learn that by helping their children master language skills, along with impulse control, they are giving them the ability to communicate meaningfully with the world as they develop. So how do parents prepare the home to model a classroom? For one, they can begin by having stimulating, age-appropriate toys for exploration; books for reading; and lots of great materials and colors for arts. Parents should be actively engaged with their children in the activities to help them develop building blocks for their well-being.

Finally, "parental perception" refers to how parents understand and interpret their child's growth, behavior, and educational needs. A lot rests on this concept when it comes to child development outcomes; in fact, one researcher (Parker, 2021) found that "parental beliefs and child development outcomes go hand-in-hand and can be shifted to positively impact their level of investment in their children during the early years of life." Other studies show that parental perception is influenced by various factors, such as cultural values, religious beliefs, or children's physical or mental disabilities; this often leads to parents forming inaccurate perceptions that have a negative impact on parent–child interactions, parenting practices, and support for their children. This issue is important for parent educators and other service providers because it will inform the level and types of intervention they provide for caregivers regardless of the roles they play in children's lives.

As mentioned earlier, the old adage "as the twig is bent, so grows the tree" implies that children are born to grow straight and strong like healthy trees; however, certain conditions can bend the "little twigs" and disrupt that growth process; unfortunately, some parents unintentionally contribute to that bending. How does this play out in real time? Let us examine two common illustrations that are directly connected to inaccurate parental perceptions. In some cultures, for example, parents believe that responding to their infants in loving and supporting ways can spoil a child. When a child cries, several things could happen; the child could be wet, hungry, or hurting, but what happens when a parent says something like, "Let him cry, he'll have a good singing voice"? What if that same parent is encouraged to understand that infancy is a perfect time for them to bond with their babies through loving behaviors? What a difference it would make for both the parent and child. When addressing parent responses, Fredrickson (in Abdullah, 2019) shared that "this is more about shared positivity in connection, and when that occurs in a caring way with synchrony, those moments of positive emotions seem to be especially nutritious for our growth and development." Studies also show that positive bonding between a parent and child can serve as a model for future intimate relationships and foster healthy self-esteem, while enhancing the child's cognitive development.

Another example of parents exhibiting an inaccurate perception occurs when they perceive their toddlers "pitching a fit" as an attempt by the child to avenge themselves. If you have been a parent, certainly you understand; however, as challenging as these behaviors are for some parents, this presents a truly teachable moment, and parent educators can help parents learn that when toddlers throw tantrums, they are experiencing a conflict between what they want to do versus what they are capable of doing. It is also a perfect time to explain developmental milestone theories, allowing parents to understand that between certain ages, children will exhibit certain behaviors. What if in this case, a parent understood that between the ages of 2 and 3 years, children experience a flood of emotions for which they have no reference point based on experience or their language development (Byrd, 2022)? Here educators could also introduce parents to emotional charts to help them teach their children how to express their feelings appropriately and ultimately redirect the behavior. Although these are only two of the most common examples, they clearly indicate that parental practice is heavily influenced by what parents believe and what they know and why practitioners should endeavor to help bridge the gap between theory and practice.

Finally, you have heard it said that parenting is one of the most difficult jobs, if not the most difficult, a person can have; consider how ironic it is that parenting requires no prior training, no degrees or license, and has no term limits attached. We need to teach, and we need to encourage parents and caregivers to recognize that the importance of the early years cannot be underestimated. If their children have passed age 5, explain that just because a child is no longer within the so-called window of opportunity does not mean all is lost, but only that they will have to work harder to accomplish the outcomes mentioned in this chapter. Nobel Prize–winning poet Gabriela Mistral captured this best when she said, "Many of the things we need can wait. The child cannot. Right now is the time his bones are being formed, his blood is being made, and his senses are being developed. To him, we cannot answer 'tomorrow;' his name is 'today.'" Investing in the early years of children's lives not only benefits parents; well-developed and well-educated children benefit society as a whole.

Discussion Questions
1. How do the experiences of caregivers/parents affect children's lifelong outcomes?

2. How are current policies, systems and practices helping or hindering families' efforts to succeed as caregivers?

References

Abdullah, M. (2019, June 18). "With kids, love is in the little things." Interview with Barbara Fredrickson. *Parenting and Family.* https://greatergood.berkeley.edu/article/item/with_kids_love_is_in_the_little_things

Benveniste, L. (2023, November 20). *Parents: A child's first teacher.* World Bank Blog,

Bipartisan Policy Center. (n.d.). *The science of early childhood development.* https://bipartisanpolicy.org/download/?file=/wp-content/uploads/2021/05/C.-1-The-Science-of-Early-Childhood.pdf

Byrd, F. (2022). Preschooler emotional development. *WebMD Health & Parenting Guide.* https://www.webmd.com/parenting/preschooler-emotional-development

Parker, A. (2021, October 4). Parental beliefs on child development and child outcomes go hand-in-hand and those beliefs can be shifted. *University of Chicago Health & Science News.* https://www.uchicagomedicine.org/forefront/research-and-discoveries-articles/2021/october/parental-beliefs-child-development

Rowcliffe, J. A. (2012, August 31). *Home is the first school, and parents are the first teachers.* Slow Parent Movement. https://slowparentingmovement.wordpress.com/2012/08/31/home-is-the-first-school-parents-are-the-first-teachers/

Chapter III
Guidance, Discipline, and Parenting Aproaches

"In a Minute"

Rebecca A. Adams, Ph.D.
Associate Professor Emeritus, Ball State University,
Muncie, IN

My husband and I used the following bit of wisdom with our daughter. Now that she is a parent, we have observed her and her husband using the technique with their 4-year-old son. Their results continue to be positive and once it becomes part of the parenting routine, daily or weekly, transitions can be less stressful than they might otherwise be. The technique involves giving children a "1-minute heads-up" to adjust to a change that parents have planned in the near future. For example, when it is time for children to stop an activity because it is bedtime or because it is time to come inside, give children a "1-minute heads-up." Instead of saying, "Bryce, it's time for you to pick up your toys, because it's your bedtime," say, "Bryce, in a minute, it will be time for you to pick up your toys, because it will soon be your bedtime." In the second scenario, the additional time gives children the opportunity to make the cognitive transition from playing to getting ready to end their play. Because they initiated the change, parents already have had the opportunity to process the upcoming transition.

This approach is very similar to that used by the Guerneys in their filial play therapy (Rye, 2008). During play, when needed, the child is cautioned as to what is, or is not, expected to be done. It has been found that when children are aware ahead of time as to what is expected they are far more cooperative. They usually seek to follow what they know is expected of them.

By allowing time for the children to modify their thought processes, parents demonstrate respect for their children. They acknowledge that their children are separate individuals and may need their own time to adjust to change. It may be unfair to expect them not to be frustrated when they are asked to make an immediate behavioral change. In many respects, their experience can be compared to an adult situation in which two people are watching television and one is in charge of the remote control. The person without the remote can develop "cognitive whiplash" if she is concentrating on a television show when her partner changes the channel. Children, too, may experience whiplash and demonstrate it through whining, crying, or angry outbursts when they are confronted with immediate change without prior notification.

As with other behavioral techniques used with children, consistency and follow-through are important. Parents need to be consistent with the timing (although, the minute does not need to be precisely 1 minute). When the time is up, parents should expect their children to begin picking up their toys, come inside, or whatever their expectation might be. If this does not happen, a time-out, or, better yet, a logical consequence of their behavior may be appropriate.

Logical consequences are the costs to children as a result of their actions. The consequences need to relate to the current problem, be respectful of the child, and be reasonable, as stressed by Dreikurs and Soltz (1964) in their classic book, Children: The Challenge. They should not humiliate or induce suffering but teach the child proper behavior. For example, Bryce may decide that he does not want to come inside after his parent has given him an "In a Minute" getting-ready-for-bedtime message. A logical consequence might be to say to Bryce that if he does not come in now, he will not be able to play outside tomorrow morning, or that you will only read one bedtime story to him tonight instead of the usual two. An unfair consequence may be to say, "Bryce, if you don't come in this moment, you will not be able to ride your bike for a month." Here the consequence is far greater than the misbehavior. It is also important for a parent not to become angry while using "In a Minute" because it is likely to exacerbate the situation.

We introduced the "In a Minute" technique to our daughter when she was a toddler and continued to use it throughout her childhood. Most daily transitions were less stressful when the technique was used.

Discussion Questions
1. What is an example of how you might use the "In a Minute" technique in your own life?
2. What can be done if a child resists the "In a Minute" technique?

References
Dreikurs, R., & Soltz, V. (1964). *Children: The challenge.* Hawthorn Books.

Rye, N. (2008). Filial therapy for enhancing relationships in families. *Journal of Family Health Care, 18*(5), 179–181.

Parenting Using "While Activities"

Jerica Berge, Ph.D., LMFT, CFLE
Professor, Department of Family Medicine and
Director, ACCORDS;
University of Colorado Medical School
Anschutz Medical Campus, Aurora, CO

Teaching children values, morals, and interpersonal relationship skills is often high on parent's list of important things to do, yet knowing how to do so is often elusive (Garcia, 2024). Parents usually easily identify with parenting techniques that use external motivators to alter children's behaviors, such as disciplining through rewards/punishment, natural/logical consequences, and time-outs (Li & Guo, 2023). However, they have a harder time relating to skills used to impart intrinsic, or internal, motivators to guide their children's behaviors, so that they wish to "do the right thing" for reasons or values that they have taken on as their own. Parents say that they typically approach the task of teaching values, morals, and interpersonal skills through lectures or discussions with their children (Garcia, 2024; Li & Guo, 2023). For some, after this approach fails, they hope that their example alone will be enough to influence their children's behaviors. It is known that observational learning through modeling has an impact on children's behaviors; however, we also know that enacting the behaviors themselves with the child have an even more powerful effect on future repetition of the behaviors and eventual internalization of the behaviors (Bahr, 1996; Garcia, 2024; Li & Guo, 2023). This is somewhat similar to the adage "it is easier to act yourself into right thinking than to think yourself into right acting."

"While activities" include any activity that most people would consider mundane, such as chores (dishes, laundry, gardening), driving in the car, shopping, or making dinner. Such activities simultaneously provide an opportunity to model and enact behaviors that facilitate interpersonal relationship skills and also have a values or moral position that is either inherent to them or that can be spontaneously created "while" engaging in them (Bahr, 1996). These seemingly uneventful activities can provide a context for improving family interactions, as well as nurturing and teaching children values and morals. "While activities," such as household chores, are typically thought of as necessary and often go unnoticed or uncounted as relational activities (Bahr, 1996). For instance, many parents want their children to have a good work ethic, believing that it will enhance the future job opportunities available to their children and secure their career longevity. Household chores provide an optimal setting for modeling this characteristic (Bahr, 1996). The key is that parents must engage in the chores with their child. This doesn't mean that the parent hovers over the child to make sure they do the job correctly; instead, the parent joins in or does a complementary job alongside the child. In the act of "doing," the parent will be modeling and teaching what it means to have a strong work ethic. This activity then becomes a relational activity in which the parent and child have social interaction, develop a value, and complete a necessary task. Chores also provide, at times, opportunities to gain conflict resolution and communication skills. Children may have differing opinions about who should do what or how to do it. This is a crucial moment in which parents can model and teach conflict resolution skills. Values such as love, unselfishness, and cooperation are also acquired during such encounters.

There also is a considerable amount of downtime during "while activities" because they may not require a lot of intellectual capacity to perform them. This provides yet another optimal moment for interpersonal relationship skills, such as problem-solving, to be taught and modeled. For example, while gardening together, a daughter may have a conversation with her father about whether she should continue to be friends with girls who have started to engage in risky behaviors. Or a mother and son could have a conversation about drinking and smoking as they listen to a radio program discussing these issues on their way to dropping the son off at soccer practice. In both of these situations, the father and mother have the opportunity to use problem-solving skills with their child, while imparting their values during the conversation.

Parents who use "while activities" as part of their parenting repertoire will be able to influence their children's values, morals, and interpersonal relationship skills through everyday, mundane activities. In addition, research shows that when parents spend time with their children, they have better emotional well-being and academic success (Li & Guo, 2023). Children may even wonder how they acquired their intrinsic or internal motivators without any noticeable effort.

Discussion Questions
1. What is an example of a "while activity"?

2. Can you think of "while activity" that you model for your children in daily life or that your parents modeled for you?

References

Bahr, K. S. (1996). More than clean windows: The unrecognized value of housework. In K. S. Bahr, A. Hawkins, & S. Klein (Eds.), *Readings in family science* (pp. 211–216). Kendall/Hunt Publishing.

Garcia, H. (2024). *9 ways to spend quality time with your kids.* https://www.parents.com/parenting/better-parenting/positive/quality-time/

Li, D., & Guo, X. (2023). The effect of the time parents spend with children on children's well-being. *Frontiers in Psychology, 14*, Article 1096128. https://doi.org/10.3389/fpsyg.2023.1096128

Rewards to Encourage: Spark an Interest in Reading

Mary Bold, Ph.D., CFLE
Financial Planner
Abacus Financial Planning, LLC

Long summer breaks between school years have a reputation as "the brain drain," also known as "the summer slide" (Kulfeld & Lewis, 2023). Analysis of multiple studies confirms that learning loss occurs for Grades 3 through 8, and math is affected more than reading. What has not been confirmed is that the drops are greater for students who experience poverty; this was reported in the past but has been found to be incorrect.

Although testing data are sometimes contradictory about summer learning loss, there is evidence that remediation and enrichment during summer breaks is helpful for students who were already behind in academics before the break (Pappas, 2023). For all students, a general conclusion is that if one summer of programming helps prevent or slow loss, then consecutive summers of programming provide even more protection. Educators report benefits of both formal and informal programming.

Research has long questioned what motivates people (including children) to take on a new task or learn something new. Intrinsic motivation, meaning that the individual acts because of internal rewards, has typically been studied as separate from achievement motivation, but some research suggests these two constructs may be connected (Puca & Schmalt, 1999). For example, the child who receives recognition for achievement may be stimulated to pursue the next level or skill, and that the reward may be internalized. In general, research tells us that self-determination, or making choices, leads to more creativity in children (Deci, 1992). More specific to children's reading, research suggests that motivation and reading skill are related, so that an increase in one can spur an increase in the other (Morgan & Fuchs, 2007). Also, parents' beliefs about their children's reading can influence how children develop as readers (Lynch et al., 2006).

To create interest in summer reading for my school-age children, I announced an ancillary reward system to the local library's program for individual reading. My children had participated in the library program in previous years and the reward of pizza coupons was, by then, routine. To create new interest, I offered cash. The bounty was a penny a page. My children made a dash for the thickest books on the library shelves. One hundred pages? No problem: Come collect your dollar. Two hundred pages? Impressive: Your reward is $2. When the novelty wore off, the reading habit did not. The money launched the summer's reading, and the sheer joy of reading became reward enough or the reading simply became habit.

The length of the typical summer break from school supports the idea that a reading habit was created. Despite a long-standing myth that a habit is established in 21 days, research puts the span at 18 to 254 days, with an average reported at 66 days (Solis-Moreira, 2024). The biggest factor in creating a habit is consistent daily repetition.

And the next factor is whether the task is familiar or requires a big change. My children's summer break was about 90 days, and reading was a daily activity. Because they already knew how to read, there was not a learning curve.

Our culture has cautioned parents against rewarding children for desired behavior. But sometimes we all need an incentive, and the wise parent knows when to use a small reward to spark an interest or initiate a new behavior. Some parents worry that children will later request payment for doing something else that is asked of them. That kind of a response can easily be turned off by merely saying, with a smile, "Wouldn't it be nice if we all got paid for every little thing we do? Now, please go ahead and take out the trash."

Discussion Questions & Activities

1. What creative activity or new habit might your child be encouraged to discover by the short-term use of an incentive?

2. How might an incentive backfire?

3. What are examples of internal motivation and external motivation?

References

Deci, E. L. (1992) On the nature and functions of motivation theories. *Psychological Science, 3*(3), 167–171. http://www.jstor.org/stable/40062779

Kulfeld, M., & Lewis, K. (2023). *Is summer learning loss real, and does it widen test score gaps by family income?* Brookings Institution. https://www.brookings.edu/articles/is-summer-learning-loss-real-and-does-it-widen-test-score-gaps-by-family-income/#:~:text=Children%20might%20lose%20a%20third,%2C%20or%20they%20might%20not.%E2%80%9D

Lynch, J., Anderson, J., Anderson, A., & Shapiro, J. (2006). Parents' beliefs about young children's literacy development and parents' literacy behaviors. *Reading Psychology, 27*(1), 1–20. https://doi.org/10.1080/02702710500468708

Morgan, P. L., & Fuchs, D. (2007). Is there a bidirectional relationship between children's reading skills and reading motivation? *Exceptional Children, 73*(2), 165–183. https://doi.org/10.1177/001440290707300203

Pappas, S. (2023, July 10). School's out. Should you worry about the "summer slide"? *Scientific American.* https://www.scientificamerican.com/article/schools-out-should-you-worry-about-the-summer-slide/#:~:text=Scores%20from%20the%20widely%20used,series%2C%20show%20basically%20no%20loss

Puca, R. M., & Schmalt, H.-D. (1999). Task enjoyment: A mediator between achievement motives and performance. *Motivation and Emotion, 23*(1), 15–29. https://doi.org/10.1023/A:1021327300925

Solis-Moreira, J. (2024, January 24). How long does it really take to form a habit? *Scientific American.* https://www.scientificamerican.com/article/how-long-does-it-really-take-to-form-a-habit/

Taking (Digital) Candy From Strangers

Mary Bold, Ph.D., CFLE
Financial Planner
Abacus Financial Planning, LLC

When my children were young, I was confident in addressing "stranger danger," what we now also call "tricky people" to emphasize awareness of personal safety even when the person is not a stranger (Covel, 2023). My first line of defense was close supervision. My second was the promise that "If a stranger tells you there's candy for you someplace, you must come straight to me, because I will give you DOUBLE candy." Years later, my daughter told me she was grateful for the double candy promise. She remembered it as being something her Mama had in reserve for her. Much later, she added that she felt loved, knowing that a parent had given her a strategy for leaving a temptation. One review of attempted abductions found that 80% of children who escaped would-be abductors did so by running away or yelling (National Center for Missing and Exploited Children, 2018)—in short, by doing something. Thus, taking action has become the cornerstone of guidance to children, with focus on the surroundings, not just whether a stranger is there.

As children grow older, the supervision and supports change, especially in light of their use of electronic communication and digital media. In fact, the dangers in the digital world challenge most of our strategies and warnings about stranger danger. Physical abduction and abuse by people known to the child have always outnumbered similar crimes committed by strangers (National Center for Missing and Exploited Children, 2020). But in the online world, strangers outnumber everyone—and their identities can be shaped to best advantage for manipulation: A 40-year-old sexual predator can pretend to be 14 and friendly. Maybe a law enforcement officer or other trained personnel can spot that person online, but most of us cannot. And if we cannot, what chance does a 13-year-old have?

Over time, children can learn to protect themselves in the online world. That doesn't happen with one magical stranger danger lecture but hopefully it can develop without too many errors along the way.

The first lesson is privacy of personal information. "Don't share your name, age, or address." We find pitfalls immediately: screen names are highly individual because a game permits use of a name only once. After MissKitty is taken as a screen name, the next person may be assigned MissKitty2, and so forth. Thus, a player can be tracked in that online environment very efficiently. Technically, the screen name does not disclose identity, but it does permit repeated observation or interaction and it can create a sense of familiarity among players. Similarly, online chatting about age and location is one way that a predator builds familiarity and presumed friendship. Even teens who would never share a home address can be tricked into sharing details about their hometown or school. For some kids, location sharing by phones may become a threat. Our first line of defense online is still to keep personal data private, but we should also educate and empower children.

The second lesson is recognizing a scam. Luckily, children relate to the unfairness of scams. They spot the fake ads for free game currency, and they learn quickly enough that a subscription or award in a digital world represents huge profits with little or no new production cost. Contests rarely produce rewards and even young children find satisfaction in declaring an offer to be fake. In gaming, such growing cynicism can be helpful. We can point out that fakers and scammers must be detected and avoided. Admittedly, some of the child's allowance, or even the family budget, may be spent in gaining this education. The real payoff comes as children learn that offers of friendship may be fake and any person online could be a scammer.

The third lesson is the hardest one: helping children and teens realize that if they fall for a scam, there is always a way out but they must tell us what is going on. Emotional turmoil can arise from online bullying, but it may be invisible to the family. Bullying that spills over to school can escalate to bodily harm or severe trauma. Parents and caregivers can step in to help, but there is no doubt that children will be upset, embarrassed, and angry. Communicating the lesson of "tell" is crucial to avoid the tragedy of suicide when a person feels shame at an extreme exploitation. When Brandon Guffey was elected to the South Carolina legislature, he performed a public service in telling us of his son's death after a documented case of sextortion when predators threatened to publish nude photographs of the 17-year-old (Karimi, 2024). As the Federal Bureau of Investigation (n.d.) explains, the crime of sextortion involves threatening and coercing children and teens into sending explicit images through online communication. The crime may then become financial sextortion if cash or gift cards are demanded to avoid the publication of the images.

Open discussion about personal safety is advised for all ages of children and many of the same concepts apply across the ages, but the language must be appropriate to the child's developmental stage. Young children may be able to process "tricky people," but adolescents may respond better to terms such as "predator" and "criminal." Even then, teens may feel they are not likely to be threatened and therefore react negatively to a warning of vulnerability. Researchers of Internet security behavior found that males experience more security incidents than females, and the reason appears to be a greater sense of invulnerability paired with more visits to untrusted websites (White & Hewit, 2023). The findings are consistent with long-standing research into adolescents' sense of invulnerability.

How families address Internet use varies widely. Some households limit screen time, whereas others impose few rules. Yet the concern for child safety while online crosses all households. Open communication is our best course for helping children understand the dangers. The strongest strategy is delivering the clear message that adults can intervene when necessary, and there is no shame in needing such help.

Discussion Questions

1, Considering today's digital world, what media platform do you think is most concerning for young children and why?

2. What kind of limits or rules did you have growing up regarding access to smartphones, social media, etc.?

3. What type of rules or limits do you think are necessary for Internet safety/smart phone use today?

References

Covel, D. (2023, January 30). *Is "stranger danger" still relevant to teach kids?* Health News. https://healthnews.com/family-health/family-relations/is-stranger-danger-still-relevant-to-teach-kids/#:~:text=Instead%2C%20teach%20kids%20what%20to,caution%20around%20people%20they%20know

Federal Bureau of Investigation. (n.d.) *Sextortion*. https://www.fbi.gov/how-we-can-help-you/scams-and-safety/common-scams-and-crimes/sextortion

Karimi, F. (2024, January 30). A South Carolina lawmaker is suing Instagram after his son died by suicide. *CNN*. https://www.cnn.com/2024/01/30/us/rep-brandon-guffey-instagram-lawsuit-cec/index.html

National Center for Missing and Exploited Children. (2018). *Analysis of attempted abduction trends.* https://www.missingkids.org/content/dam/missingkids/pdfs/Attempted%20Abduction%20trends%20with%20talking%20points_2018.pdf

National Center for Missing and Exploited Children. (2020). *Analysis of nonfamily abductions.* https://www.missingkids.org/content/dam/missingkids/pdfs/analysis-of-nonfamily-abductions-reported-to-ncmec-2016-2020.pdf

White, G. L., & Hewit, B. (2023). Lewin's behavior equation to explain the differences in internet security incidents. *Proceedings of the ISCAP Conference, 9*(5928). Information Systems and Computing Academic Professionals. https://iscap.us/proceedings/2023/pdf/5928.pdf

Blame the Folks: A Strategy for Handling Peer Pressure

Mary Bold, Ph.D., CFLE
Financial Planner
Abacus Financial Planning, LLC

The pressures of social conformity are not limited to the young, but often, young people have a challenging time escaping peer pressure. Teenagers may not want to go along with the crowd but may find it difficult to excuse themselves from group activities. Although this difficulty creates a problem, it is solvable. Researchers have found that peer pressure is not necessarily tied to a teen's self-esteem (Bano et al., 2024); we do not have to worry about a lifetime of following the crowd. A strategy for the short term is to invite teens to blame the folks when they want to separate from the crowd. With an agreed-upon code word, teens can let their parents or caregivers know it's time to "play the bad guy" and spare teens from having to challenge the peer group's expectations.

When my kids called me from a friend's house to ask for permission for an extension or an outing, they knew they could count on me to say no, by uttering our code word. The message was in the greeting. If my kids said, "Mother, I want to go to the movie tonight" that meant they *didn't* want to go to the movie and needed me to say, "No, you have to come home." On the other hand, if the greeting was the usual, "Hi, Mom ...," I knew that the request was genuine. And I could answer the way I needed to, which was usually "OK." The alternative would be that my kids had to tell their peers they wanted to separate from the group or that they had to go along with the group and be in an uncomfortable or unsafe situation.

The pressure to conform has been well documented by research (Asch, 1956), and studies suggest that young people, especially when experiencing social anxiety, strive not only to fit in but also to avoid negative emotions (Bică, 2023; Lashbrook, 2000). While parents are sometimes frustrated by the power of their children's peer groups, they also can see that the parent–child relationship is not completely excluded from peer interactions. At least when playing a support role (as in the example of the code word), parents can provide a socially acceptable means of escape for their teen.

The influence of family on children's development has been assumed with little debate. A modern challenge to that assumption is group socialization theory (GST; Harris, 1995, 1998; Tice & Baumeister, 2024), which posits that the child's peer group has the greatest impact on the child's adult personality. (Harris excluded infant, toddler, and preschool years from the theory and acknowledged that abusive parents had the greatest impact.) GST addresses the long span of childhood, when children are part of a peer group, known as the school years. With just a few exceptions (such as food consumed at home), GST predicts that peers, not parents, are the primary influence on development. Harris identified that the peer group was larger than the friend set, demonstrating that influence came from a large number of people. Harris also pointed out that some adults can have direct influence on children—the adults who oversee the activities of the peer group. Thus, teachers, coaches, mentors, and some peers' parents have an impact greater than the child's own parents. Parents' influence on socialization is indirect, largely through the selection of community and school where the child will then be socialized by the group. Harris suggested that parents' main focus in family life should be building supportive relationships that can be enjoyed for decades after childhood ends.

GST was not warmly received by parents nor by child and family professionals. Most did not agree with Harris's conclusion that nature accounted for about 50% of development (citing twin studies and adoption studies as evidence) and nonfamily nurture accounted for the other 50%. But the wise parent admits that we humans are group-oriented and our recognition of that permits us to be tolerant when our children place highest value on peer group standards.

As adults, we also conform to our social groups. The difference is that we have an easier time of excusing ourselves from the group. We get to say "No, thanks" and not lose a friend. Eventually, teens will reach that point but, in the meantime, their folks can help out.

Discussion Questions & Activities

1. When can young people be expected to advocate for themselves without family support?

2. What factors, such as social anxiety, differ among young people? How might anxiety be exhibited in adherence to peer group expectations?

3. How does group socialization theory (GST) help to explain why teenagers cannot break from group norms?

4. One of Harris's examples of GST is the "credit" or blame assigned to parents. If the peer group is the greatest influence, then the parent may be absolved from responsibility when the child misbehaves. That also means the parent cannot take credit when the child excels at something. How does that strike you?

5. Do you bristle at GST, or are you intrigued by it?

References

Asch, S. E. (1956). Studies of independence and conformity: A minority of one against unanimous majority. *Psychological Monographs: General and Applied, 70*, 1–70. https://doi.org/10.1037/h0093718

Bano, S., Kamal, S. S., Shah, I., & Gul, S. (2024). Role of peer pressure in enhancing self-esteem and pro-social behavior among adolescents. *International Journal of Contemporary Issues in Social Sciences, 3*(1), 1488–1494. https://ijciss.org/index.php/ijciss/article/view/476

Bică, A. (2023). Peer pressure: Conformity outweighs reciprocity in social anxiety. *Current Psychology, 42*, 18142–18149. https://doi.org/10.1007/s12144-022-03021-1

Harris, J. R. (1995). Where is the child's environment? A group socialization theory of development. *Psychological Review, 102*(3), 458–489. http://dx.doi.org/10.1037/0033-295X.102.3.458

Harris, J. R. (1998). *The nurture assumption: Why children turn out the way they do.* The Free Press.

Lashbrook, J. T. (2000). Fitting in: Exploring the emotional dimension of adolescent pressure. *Adolescence, 35*(140), 747–757. PMID: 11214212

Tice, D. M., & Baumeister, R. F. (2024). The changing social world that children make: Reflections on Harris's critique of the nurture assumption. *Developmental Review, 72*, Article 101123. https://doi.org/10.1016/j.dr.2024.101123

Discipline — "To Teach"
Dawn Cassidy, M.Ed., CFLE Emeritus
Retired Director of Family Life Education
National Council on Family Relations

When my daughter was a toddler, I came across an article in a parenting magazine about discipline. The article explained that the root of the word discipline is "to teach." That simple clarification had a profound impact on my parenting. Before that, I had always associated the word discipline with punishment. If a child needed to be disciplined, it meant they needed to be punished.

After reading this article I began to see discipline in a very different, and much more positive, way. When my daughter displayed a behavior that I wanted to change, such as having a tantrum, disobeying, or not listening, I found myself stepping back and asking, "What is it that I want to teach her in this situation?" rather than, "How should I punish her?" That simple approach made a huge difference in how I parented her and resulted in much more positive outcomes for most situations.

Instead of punishing her, I began talking to her, explaining to her what it was that I wanted or expected from her, and why. Times of discipline became moments of teaching. Instead of seeing hurt feelings and crying, I began to see the kinds of behavior I hoped for. Instead of moments of stress, there were moments of calmness and a feeling of cooperation between us.

Discussion Question
1. How can you use a moment where your child won't listen as an opportunity to teach them rather than as a situation in which they are punished?

2. Are there situations where punishment is appropriate? What does that look like?

Suggested Reading
Bettelheim, B. (1987). *A good enough parent.* Knopf.

Which Way? Giving Toddlers Agency

Dawn Cassidy, M.Ed., CFLE Emeritus
Retired Director of Family Life Education
National Council on Family Relations

We want our children to grow up with a sense of self-efficacy—that is, a belief in their own ability to control their functioning and events that affect their lives (Bandura, 1982). That sense of control is enhanced through the development of agency—the ability to make wise decisions and to put those decisions into action (Mom Enough, 2022).

When my daughter was a toddler, I discovered how to help her develop a sense of control or agency. On our way home from preschool, I would allow her to decide which way the car would turn. I also used this technique when we would be out for a walk with her in her stroller. "Which way?" I would ask. "That way!" she'd shout and point right, or left, or forward. We even turned around on occasion! It sometimes took us a bit longer to find our way home, but it made her so happy to get to be the one in charge. My daughter is now an adult, but occasionally, I will ask, "Which way?" A big smile will come across her face as she decides and points!

References
Bandura, A. (1982). Self-efficacy mechanism in human agency. *American Psychologist, 37*(2), 122–147.

Mom Enough. (2022). *Supporting your child's development of agency.* https://www.momenough.com/wp-content/uploads/2022/03/Supporting-Your-Childs-Development-of-Agency.pdf

Resources

Carey, M. P., & Forsyth, A. (2009). *Teaching tip sheet: Self-efficacy.* American Psychological Association. https://www.apa.org/pi/aids/resources/education/self-efficacy

Transformingeducation.org. *Importance of self-efficacy.* https://www.youtube.com/watch?v=VW5v6PQ5PEc

SimplyPsychology
https://www.simplypsychology.org/about-us
https://www.simplypsychology.org/self-efficacy.html

A Small World Families Live In: Six Degrees of Separation

Kristie Chandler, Ph.D., CFLE
Chair, Department of Human Development and Family Science
Samford University, Birmingham, AL

The notion of "six degrees of separation" evolved from social network theory research (meaning how people are connected to each other), such as Stanley Milgram's small world experiment (Department of Psychology, Harvard University, n.d.; see also Blass, 2004; Kirvan, 2022; Morse, 2014). Although there is some debate about the actual number of connections, the theory suggests that any two people are connected to each other using six or fewer relationship links, thus indicating that it is indeed a small world. This idea has been incorporated into various formats, including the "Six Degrees of Kevin Bacon" game, a play, a film, a television production, and a website (https://www.sixdegrees.org/) launched in 2007 and designed to create a socially conscious charitable network. (Fowler, 2020)

My children used to play a game based on a version of this concept. While in the car, one of the children would need to go to the bathroom—of course! One child would say something like, "I have to go to the bathroom, so please don't say anything that will make me think about it. Let's discuss something else to keep my mind off it." Then the other child would say something like, "OK. Let's talk about our vacation to New Mexico." Then the child who needed to go to the bathroom would connect New Mexico to deserts, deserts to thirsty plants, and thirsty plants to the lack of water, reminding them of the need to go to the bathroom. The topic chosen to distract from nature's call did not matter; it was always connected to water and the need to go to the bathroom. What is it about children and bathroom humor?

Most things in this world seem to be interconnected, and parenting is no exception. The family serves as the primary socializing agent for children. Social network theory helps us understand the dynamics within family networks, including parent-child relationships, sibling interactions, and extended family connections. These relationships play a crucial role in transmitting cultural values, norms, and behaviors to children (Benokraitis, 2021).

To understand the functioning of families, it is necessary to examine the individuals in the family, as well as the society influencing those individuals and their relationships (Garbarino & Bedard, 2002). I use a version of the "six degrees" concept in my Marriage and Family class to help college students understand this interconnectedness. For example, a student will bring up a current news topic, an advertisement, a magazine article, a television show, a recently passed law, and so on. Then, I will legitimately connect that topic to a concept in the marriage and family textbook, using six or fewer links. For instance, a student might comment that a local news show segment was on self-defense. I then connect the self-defense topic to dating violence or family violence, whether or not there is a biological or social reason that men usually abuse women, the fact that violence occurs frequently within the family, and so forth. Most topics are usually pretty straightforward.

On a slow news day, one of the students said that the new T.M. Elmo (Tickle Me X-treme Elmo) was just released. I stood there for a minute, trying to think of a connection to the Marriage and Family class. Then I remembered the topics in the class that related to the socialization of children. This led to a great discussion regarding television and toys' impact on children. We discussed whether Elmo was male or female and how you determine through clues such as name, voice, and actions. We discussed what makes a toy appropriate for boys, what is appropriate for girls, and whether there should be any differentiation. The conversation evolved into a discussion about parenting authority, instilling values, and raising children. All of this evolved from the announcement that T.M. Elmo was now available.

One of the primary functions of the family is to socialize their children. Although parents are still the primary socializing agent, some parenting experts believe there are other such agents, including advertisers, toy and video game manufacturers, and social media, hoping to influence your child's desire for a particular toy, snack, or television program (Benokraitis, 2021). Although this societal influence may seem more evident to some, other ways may be less noticeable. Through this discussion about Elmo, I was reminded how we sometimes defer the privilege of shaping our children to television, toys, peers, and other sources. Often, we are unaware of the influence some of these issues can have on our children. An issue can seem so far removed from our personal families that we don't make, or want to make, the connection that this may affect our family. So far, I have been able to relate every issue to the family using six or fewer connections. It reminds me, as a parent, that it is indeed a small world families live in and that I need to become more aware of this impact on my children.

Not all societal influences are necessarily bad; nonetheless, they are still influences. Our job, as parents, is to become aware of how our children are socialized and make conscious decisions that will sway their socialization process positively. Without this awareness, parents may be unable to fulfill one of their primary responsibilities.

When it comes to families and society's influence on families, the concept of "six degrees of separation" illuminates the connections that bind individuals, ideas, and experiences in our world. From Stanley Milgram's small-world research to the playful games of childhood and classroom discussions, this notion underscores the profound interconnectedness of human existence. As parents and educators, we are reminded of the influences shaping our children's lives, steering them toward positive socialization and growth.

Discussion Questions

1. What are some ways parents can maintain their role as the primary socializing agent while acknowledging the impact of other societal factors?

2. What are some potential positive and negative influences of societal agents (such as advertisers, toy manufacturers, and social media) on children's socialization, and how can parents mitigate the negative impacts?

3. How do family interactions and relationships transmit cultural values, norms, and behaviors to children?

References

Benokraitis, N. V. (2021). *Marriages and families: Changes, choices, and constraints (9th ed.).* Pearson.

Blass, T. (2004). *The man who shocked the world: The life and legacy of Stanley Milgram.* Basic Books.

Fowler, B. (2020, September 22). Famous "joke" that embarrassed actor. *The New Zealand Herald.* https://www.nzherald.co.nz/entertainment/the-exact-history-of-six-degrees-of-kevin-bacon/NCVVAU73UZ4TNCZAK726ENOBBQ/

Garbarino, J., & Bedard, C. (2002). *Parents under siege: Why you are the solution, not the problem, in your child's life.* Free Press.

Department of Psychology, Harvard University. (n.d.). *Stanley Milgram.* https://psychology.fas.harvard.edu/people/stanley-milgram

Kirvan, P. (2022, July 18). What is six degrees of separation? *TechTarget: WhatIs?* https://www.techtarget.com/whatis/definition/six-degrees-of-separation

Morse, G. (2014, August 1). The science behind six degrees. *Harvard Business Review.* https://hbr.org/2003/02/the-science-behind-six-degrees

"Did You Have Fun?"

Jean Illsley Clarke, Ph.D., CFLE †
Author and parent educator
Minneapolis, MN

"Did you have fun?" the parent asks when the child comes home from the playground, school, or friend's house. It is the question often asked to children by adults who care about their children and want them to be happy. When young Charles comes home from school, his mother may ask, "Did you have fun today?" If Charles says, "No!," his well-meaning mother may stop her activity and take him to the park so he can have fun. She wants him to be happy.

Happiness is a worthy wish, but the path from pleasurable activities to happiness is not always straightforward. Exposing children to a constant stream of entertainment may provide some fun, but it may not lead to the happy state for the child that the parent intended. In fact, it can potentially have adverse effects on their overall well-being.

Many adults who were overindulged as children and indicated that their parents made sure that they were highly entertained reported the following (Clarke et al., 2014):
- *On the whole, I am not satisfied with myself.*
- *At times, I think I am no good at all.*
- *I certainly feel useless at times.*
- *I do not feel that I'm a person of worth.*
- *I wish I could have more respect for myself.*

This outcome is probably not what the parents intended. Why doesn't constant entertainment lead to happiness? Writing about the phenomena in *What Happy People Know*, Baker and Stauth (2003) said:

> Once we become accustomed to any pleasure, it no longer has the power to make us happy. … Neurologically, it overloads the brain's pleasure centers, prohibiting further sensations, and depletes the feel-good neurotransmitters serotonin and dopamine. Psychologically, it creates inflated expectations and a sense of boredom (p. 62).

These are the detrimental effects of constant entertainment that we must be aware of as parents.

If fun and pleasure are not the basis of happiness, what is? One crucial component of happiness is accountability, the act of holding ourselves accountable or responsible for how we respond to our world and nurture ourselves. This vital lesson is learned when children are accountable for their own feelings and entertainment; the well-being of others; and experiencing the feeling of boredom (Dalai Lama XIV et al., 2016; Miller, 2023).

As a high school junior, Charles, whose mother made sure he had fun every day when he was little, was surprised that she was upset about his "D" in French. He explained that the class wasn't interesting, and the teacher was boring and not fun, so he couldn't be expected to learn from her. Charles's mother had not only presented having fun as a value but also that it was someone else's responsibility to provide it. Charles did not believe he was accountable for his learning.

Instead of asking "Did you have fun today?" Charles's mom might have encouraged accountability by saying the following:
- Tell me about something you did today.
- How did you do that?
- Tell me one thing that happened to you.
- What feelings did you have when …?
- Did you play games (or do things) that you already knew how to do?
- Did you play any new games (or do new things)?
- Tell me about one thing you did for someone else.
- Tell me about something someone else did for you.

- Tell me about one thing you did well today, and I'll tell you one thing I did well.
- Tell me one thing you could have done better today, and I'll tell you one thing I could have done better.
- How did you take care of yourself? (If something was distressing.)
- Was there a way that you could help others?

Consider Dan who tells his child how to be competent. As she leaves for school, instead of saying, "Have fun today," Dan encourages her to be accountable or responsible by saying:
- Be smart.
- Do something kind today.

The directive to "be smart" includes not only learning classroom lessons but keeping yourself safe on the bus and handling yourself responsibly on the playground. *Do something kind today* encourages an empathic attitude and signals the parent's expectations about the child's developing social skills. These two directives offer the child her parents' assessment of how to be competent, or even how to survive in her time and place, thus telling her how to succeed in her childhood world. It does not tell her to have fun or how she is expected to feel. She may like it or not; she may feel competent or inadequate; she may feel happy or sad, and she might even have fun. But she is not obligated to have fun. She is not a failure if she does not have fun. She would not have to defend herself if she did not have fun. She will not need to find a way to blame someone else for not "making it fun."

If we have not been encouraging accountability, we can start today. Of course, we want our children to have fun. But pleasure is an outcome, not an activity. We need to remember that not everything can be fun. Sometimes "Life hurts. If it doesn't hurt some of the time, it's not life" (Baker & Stauth, 2003, p. 159).

Our job is to teach children how to be accountable and to handle hurt responsibly. They can have fun without our making that a priority or a job or even a burden.

Discussion Questions

1. ***Accountability in Everyday Conversations:*** In what ways can shifting our questions from "Did you have fun?" to those suggested in the article encourage children to become more accountable and reflective about their daily experiences? How might this shift influence their approach to challenges and responsibilities?

2. ***Balancing Pleasure with Reality:*** Considering the statement "Life hurts. If it doesn't hurt some of the time, it's not life." How can we prepare children to embrace life's challenges alongside its pleasures? Discuss the importance of teaching children to find satisfaction and joy in accomplishments and resilience in the face of difficulties.

For more information about the Overindulgence Research Studies, see www.overindulgence.org.

References

Baker, D., & Stauth, C. (2003). *What happy people know.* St. Martin's Press.

Dalai Lama XIV, & Tutu, D., with Abrams, D. (2016). *The book of joy: Lasting happiness in a changing world.* Avery.

Clarke, J. & Dawson, C., & Bredehoft, D. (2014). *How much is too much? Raising likable, responsible, and respectful children-from toddlers to teens in an age of overindulgence.* Da Capo Press.

Miller, G. (2023). *The benefits of boredom: What kids can learn from handling more free time.* Child Mind Institute. The Benefits of Boredom—Child Mind Institute.

Thank you to Lisa Krause, M.A., CFLE, Jean's colleague and friend who reviewed the entries and provided updated references.

Is "Good Job!" Enough?

Jean Illsley Clarke, Ph.D., CFLE †
Author and parent educator
Minneapolis, MN

"Good job!" has a nice ring to it. It was frequently used as a compliment in the Zeb family. However, Mother and Father Zeb noticed that it does not necessarily encourage children to "do better." When their teenage son passed his driver's test, and the family shouted, "Good job!," his response was to start telling how often he will *need* the car. When their fourth-grade daughter passed her spelling test and the reward was "Good job!," she thought, okay, that was good enough. I don't need to study more and get a higher score. When the 2-year-old puts three crayon scribbles on his paper, big sister said, "Good job!" But little brother threw the paper aside, put two marks on the next paper, looked up for his reward, and reached for another clean sheet.

So why doesn't "Good job!" motivate children to achieve? Probably because it tells them that *we like* what they did instead of telling them what *they did well* or finding out what *they* think.

"But" you tell me, "I say 'good job' all the time because I want to encourage my child." Certainly, you do, because you care, you love your children, and you want them to be successful. Your intentions are good but try reading each of the following pairs of responses aloud. Say each of them with pride and pleasure in your voice and think about how they might strike a child.

Teenager:
"Good job!" Or
"You must be learning how to set priorities to get that long-term paper done so well."

School-age:
"Good job!" Or
"Hey, you got an A on that paper. Tell me how you did that."

Four-year-old:
"Good job!" Or
"I like the way you colored the flowers in your picture. What do you like?"

Two-year-old:
"Good job!" Or
"You brought three books to me. Which one shall we read first?"

One-year-old:
"Good job!" Or
"You got out from under the table all by yourself!"

How was that? Did it help you understand that a constant barrage of "good jobs" can create praise junkies where children perform to get praise rather than to enhance their own skills and learn to develop their own internal reward system?

Other Thoughts About "Good Job!"
- "Good job!" is appropriate if we are teaching specific standards for a specific skill. Even then we need to point out specifically *how* the task was well done.
- "Good job!" is a way of telling children to feel good about what they did. What if they don't feel good? Do they need to act like they do to please us?
- Too much praise can program children to expect to be praised for everything they do. That is debilitating for them and boring for the rest of us.
- "Good job!" is well-meaning but lazy parenting.
- We can say we like something without telling the child she must like it. "I love the valentine you made for me. How did you guess I would like a lace border?"

Over nurture
Adults who have been overindulged as children (i.e., participants in the first three overindulgence studies reported in the *How Much Is Too Much?*; Clarke et al., 2014) told us their parents had given them "too much love." This is called over-nurture. What parents meant to have been helpful has turned out to be a liability, not an asset. So, let's remember that saying "Good job!" is for our needs, not the child's.

Whenever we want to say, "Good job!" let's hold fast to our good intentions, describing exactly what was well done or asking what the child liked about it, and remember that our job is always to encourage growth and, only when appropriate, to evaluate.

Discussion Questions:
1. ***Reflecting on Praise and Motivation:*** How does using "Good job!" as generic praise affect children's motivation and self-perception, as illustrated in the examples provided in the article? Can you think of instances where you've observed similar responses in your own children or those you interact with?

2. ***Alternative Approaches to Encouragement:*** What are some alternative ways parents can offer praise and encouragement that promote intrinsic motivation and self-awareness, as suggested in the article? Share your thoughts on how these approaches might foster a deeper connection with your child's achievements and experiences.

3. ***Balancing Praise and Overindulgence:*** How can parents strike a balance between providing positive reinforcement and avoiding overindulgence or excessive praise, as discussed in the article? Reflect on your own parenting practices and consider adjustments that align with encouraging growth and self-evaluation.

4. ***Considering Cultural Differences:*** How might cultural differences influence parents' approaches to praise and encouragement? Explore how cultural values and norms regarding praise might shape parenting practices and children's responses to praise.

Activities

Reflective Recognition
Objective: To practice specific and meaningful praise, encouraging self-reflection and acknowledging effort and achievement.

Procedure:
1. As a family, discuss the concept of meaningful praise and its impact on motivation and self-esteem based on the insights shared in the article.
2. Choose a recent achievement or action by each family member to recognize.
3. Instead of saying "Good job!," provide specific praise that highlights effort, progress, or unique qualities related to the achievement.
4. Encourage each family member to reflect on how the recognition makes them feel and what aspects of their effort they are proud of. (Open AI, 2024).

Praise Reflection Journal
Objective: To create a reflective practice for parents to observe and adjust their praise habits based on the principles discussed in the article.

Procedure:
1. Start a praise reflection journal where parents can record instances of praise given to their children throughout the week.
2. For each entry, note the specific praise given and reflect on whether it aligns with the principles of meaningful praise discussed in the article.
3. Identify opportunities for improvement or adjustment in praise habits, focusing on providing specific, descriptive, and encouraging feedback.
4. Discuss findings and reflections with your partner or support group to share insights and accountability for implementing positive change (Open AI, 2024).

References

Clarke, J., & Dawson, C., & Bredehoft, D. (2014). *How much is too much? Raising likable, responsible, and respectful children-from toddlers to teens- in an age of overindulgence.* Da Capo. (For more information about the Overindulgence Research Studies, see www.overindulgence.org.)

OpenAI. (2024). Activities created with *ChatGPT* (3.5) [Large language model]. https://chat.openai.com

Thank you to Lisa Krause, M.A., CFLE, Jean's colleague and friend who reviewed the entries and provided updated references.

Making Choices and Using My "One": A Toddler's Bedtime Routine

Rebecca A. Cobb, Ph.D., LMFT
Clinical Professor
Master of Arts in Couples and Family Therapy Program
Seattle University

I hear from a lot of parents who struggle with their child's bedtime routine. Many of my 4-year-old son's friends require that a parent lay in bed with them until they fall asleep, or they come out of their room 18 times before they finally settle in for the night. This may be an exaggeration, but it's not for some! I too have experienced that struggle and know how hard it is to be ready to have a few minutes to myself but be unable to because of a strong-willed toddler who refuses to go to bed. Luckily, through trial and error, we finally found something that works for him: choices and "ones."

Toddlers typically do well when they are provided with a consistent routine and simple choices that allow them to have a sense of control in a world in which they are typically told what to do. Although the goal is to go to bed and there is no choice in the matter, there are choices that parents can offer around bedtime routines that let children feel as though they have some say in the process. The following describes our nightly bedtime routine and provides examples of choices that we give along each step of the way: (1) bedtime announcement, (2) pick a book, (3) brush teeth, (4) lotion, (5) pajamas, (6) "Baby Emperor," (7) book, (8) slip-slide and potty, and (9) hug, tuck, kiss, and cover. It concludes with an explanation of the (10) "one," an addition to our bedtime routine that changed everything for the better.

1. *Bedtime announcement.* "Bedtime in 5 minutes! Finish whatever you are doing!"

2. *Pick a book.* If he takes a long time, we tell him that he has 2 minutes left to pick a book or we will pick two that he can choose from. Then, even if it comes to us picking, he's still allowed a choice, but a simpler one.

3. *Brush teeth.* We know that our son prefers mint toothpaste, and our daughter prefers strawberry. Yet every night when their dad brushes their teeth, he asks, "Mint or strawberry?" On rare occasion, our son will say, "Both!" although it's almost always mint.

4. *Lotion.* Our son has eczema, so he needs to put on lotion every night. Typically, I put it on for him, but when I notice that he's struggling, I ask, "Do you want to put it on or should I?"

5. *Pajamas.* I choose two and ask which one he wants, "Sesame Street or dinosaurs?" This allows him a choice without providing so many options that he feels overwhelmed.

6. *"Baby Emperor."* When our son was a baby, we made up a silly song that we sang him every night before bed. We held him up above us and sang about how tall and strong the baby emperor was. Four years later, we're still singing the same song, but it has evolved into an even sillier dancelike routine where we swing him

around or his dad puts him up on his shoulders. We let him choose who holds him while we sing, although this is usually dad's job.

7. *Book.* I usually read his book, but sometimes he asks Dad to read it, especially if Dad has the best voices for that book. We typically oblige.

8. *Slip-slide and potty.* I'm not sure how this made its way into our routine, but it serves as a playful way of getting our son to go potty as his dad guides his body and fuzzy socks "slip-slide" him across the floor on the way to the bathroom. On the way back to the bedroom, they make a pitstop to chase me around the kitchen. Although sometimes I turn the tables and chase them with the threat of tickles until they reach the safety of the bedroom.

9. *Hug, tuck, kiss, and cover.* Dad is the best tucker and coverer, so he's usually the one to help settle him into bed. After our son is tucked and covered and we leave his room, we will not tuck and cover him again. In fact, we won't step foot in his room again unless there's an extenuating circumstance. We tell him that the only reasons we'll come into his room after tuck and cover are if he's sick, there's an emergency, or we forget to do something like give him his cup of water, turn on his noise machine, or put on his socks. If we forget any of these things, he can call us back into his room and we'll do whatever we forgot to do. He loves it when we forget something. And we don't mind going back for this now that we've implemented the "one."

10. *"One."* After his final hug, tuck, kiss, and cover, our son is allowed to come out of his room one time and do whatever he wants (within reason) for 3 minutes. Sometimes he wants an extra book. Sometimes he wants to cuddle on the couch. Sometimes he watches with bewilderment as we do whatever chores we do after he goes to bed at night. Sometimes he helps with them. As soon as the 3 minutes are up, we give him an extra hug and kiss, ask him to go potty one last time, and tell him that it's time to go back to bed. We don't go into his room with him. We simply keep doing whatever we were doing and send him on his way.

He's allowed to use his "one" at any time, although he almost always uses it immediately after "going to bed." We prefer it this way because it only prolongs the bedtime routine by a few minutes and then we can get on with the night. On occasion, he'll save his "one" for later in the evening. For example, if his dad is at a work-related dinner and missed the bedtime routine, he'll wait to use his "one" when his dad comes home, if he hasn't fallen asleep by then.

If he comes out of his room more than once, we lock his door until we go to bed. We make it very clear that (a) if there's an emergency, he should let us know and we'll come to his room right away; (b) he's always allowed to come out of his room to go potty; and (c) we'll always unlock his room before we go to sleep.

The first few times that we tried this were a challenge. We explained the process and encouraged him to save his "one" for when he really needed it. He seemed excited about the opportunity to come out of his room at first, but when it came to locking his door and not being able to come out of his room as often as he wanted, he was upset. It took him a while to understand the boundaries of the "one." It took a while for us to understand the boundaries of it too. We are good at it now, but it was hard for all of us at first.

Now, on occasion, he will call us into his room. We remind him that if we come in, his door will be locked. Sometimes, he does not follow through with asking us in. And sometimes he weighs his options and chooses to have us come into his room in exchange for locking his door until we go to bed. But he is okay with this because it is his choice.

Discussion Questions

1. In what ways does setting clear expectations and having a consistent routine support young children in going to bed at night?

2. How might parents create their own bedtime routines for younger children that incorporate the use of choices?

3. How might playfulness on the part of parents facilitate bedtime routines for children?

4. Some parents don't feel comfortable locking their child's bedroom unless there is a clear safety risk (e.g., the child goes outside in the middle of the night). What are other ways of setting boundaries around bedtime that might work?

Screen Time: Whose Problem Is It?

Karen DeBord, Ph.D., CFLE
Professor Emeritus
North Carolina State University
Raleigh, NC

For years, medical and educational professionals were concerned about the amount of time parents allowed children to spend watching television (Huston & Wright, 1989); now parents and professionals are additionally concerned with screen time associated with the Internet, smart phones, and video games. Parents today say that parenting in harder than it was 20 years ago, with many citing smart phones and social media as reasons. It is a turn of the tables, however, as parents realize that it is not only children who are distracted with social media and smart phones; it is the parents themselves. More than half (56%) of parents with at least one child under 18 indicate that they spend an inordinate amount of time on social media or playing video games, and 68% say that they are distracted by their phones when they should be spending time with their children (Auxier et al, 2020).

Children indeed are born into the digital age, and there are many positive uses for technology. However, the age at which children engage with media on a regular basis has fallen from 4 years old to 4 months old (Radesky & Christakis, 2016). This is of real concern because the first year of life is when children learn to focus their eyes and brains on their caregivers, learning to trust and depend on their parents or a primary person who cares for them. Human interaction and even preverbal social exchange is the foundation for all relationships.

Research has shown that academic development is compromised with excessive reliance on screen media. First, language and social interactions are impacted, then there are the secondary effects of obesity, low physical activity, sleep disorders, anxiety, depression, and resulting mental health conditions (Muppalla et al., 2023).

Is screen time addictive? Many say yes. Screen time releases dopamine, the same neurotransmitter released by some drugs such as cocaine. The brain begins to crave it. The pleasure–reward cycle then may cause a parent–child power struggle as parents attempt to limit screen time. Children can become aggressive over these limits, which leads to difficulties at home and school.

According to research from the Centers for Disease Control and Prevention (2018), children aged 8 to 10 years spend 6 hours per day using screens, children aged 11 to 14 spend 9 hours, and teenagers/young adults aged 15 to 25 spend seven and a half hours per day using screens (including television). Setting boundaries and using parental controls while modeling acceptable amounts of screen behaviors are all key to reducing the negative effects.

Handing a child a device or turning on the TV may seem convenient for parents. It keeps children busy, may reduce conflict, and avoids boredom. Some parents say their children have anger fits when the TV is turned off or limited (Walsh, 2006). Parents who are tired or stressed with work tasks and home chores may turn to television or other devices for themselves or their children to provide a break. But later parents may find that using "screen time to buy time" gets out of control.

Time spent with devices could be time spent in building a foundation for relationships that will benefit the child and their well- being throughout their lives. When large amounts of time are devoted to social media or playing games online, children have limited opportunities to experience a supportive family that values open communication and warm connections.

Setting limitations on screentime must start in the early years. This includes keeping a television out of the child's bedroom and parking devices during family time and before bedtime.

What to do instead of depending on screen time?
Instead of learning to depend on media to help raise children, consider the influence parents can have. First stop and ask, "What do I hope for my child? What values do I want to convey? How can I convey those values?"

Start by making family time special and fun. Such times may include family meals, planned and impromptu family outings, and playing outside.

If you view television, watch it together, then talk about the life lessons in the program. Select programs that are consistent with your values or the values you hope to build in your children. If you wish to spend time with your child together with a device, ask him or her to explain what they are doing online and to show you their favorite games or sites.

Young children want time with their parents. Children under 2 years old should not be exposed to devices or television. Sit on the floor or stoop to their eye level and play with them. Activities such as stacking blocks, putting things together, scooping, pouring, scrubbing, rearranging, and putting in order are all skills they will need to understand science and math in school. Make it fun! Talk together. Ask how things work and use your imagination to create stories.

Other Ideas

Toddlers: Allow kitchen play in one designated drawer or cabinet that holds plastic ware, read together, take stroller walks, put music on to bop about the house as you do your chores at home, look through family photos, look at picture books, and stack blocks. Don't hand them a device!

Preschoolers: Allow safe kitchen help, read together, take a walk with a collecting container, go to the library, tell stories where they name the characters and the setting to get started, use extra-large drawing paper on the floor to draw together, play dress-up, and erect a puppet stage with a sheet and table.

School-agers: Play outside, bike, take walks, read together, or tell stories and record them, make things in the kitchen or with miscellaneous things in the house (egg cartons, cardboard tubes, tape, glue, clay), plant a garden together, or get a pet.

Teens: Play ball, bike, work on the car, work together to learn to pay bills and understand banking, learn to change a tire, learn how to check the oil, take photographs, create a family video channel, plan a vacation or a weekend for the family, allow teens to plan the meals, or go to the grocery store together.

As children become more verbal, ask them open-ended questions, which require more than a yes or no answer. Challenge them to think. Go online together to find answers to "what if" questions. Brush up on conversation starters. Keep the lines of communication open in the early years so that they will be more likely to communicate with you in their teen years when social issues get much tougher to manage. Social media, television, and video games will not hold the answers.

Discussion Questions and Activities

1. When you are in a park or a social setting with other families, notice how parents are using or not using devices for child entertainment. Reflect on your thoughts.

2. Select a family-centered program and watch it with your child. Have a meaningful discussion about the program.

3. Consider having a family meeting to discuss the use of devices. Together, form a new rule about parking devices at a particular time in the evening.

4. Did your family have rules/guidelines regarding screen time when you were growing up? If so, how did these rules or guidelines affect you? If there were no rules or guidelines regarding screentime, discuss how the absence of them impacted you.

References

Auxier, B, Anderson, M., & Nolan, H. (2020). *Parenting children in the age of screens.* Pew Research Center.

Centers for Disease Control and Prevention. (2018). *Screentime vs lean time.* https://www.cdc.gov/healthyschools/physicalactivity/getmoving.htm

Huston, A. C., & J. C. Wright. (1989). The forms of television and the child viewer. In G. Comstock (Ed.), *Public communication and behavior: Vol. 2* (pp. 103–159) Academic Press.

Radesky, J. S., & Christakis, D. A. (2016). Increased screen time: implications for early childhood development and behavior. *Pediatric Clinics of North America, 63*(5), 827–839. https://doi.org/10.1016/j.pcl.2016.06.006

Muppalla, S., Vuppalapati, S., Pulliahgaru, A., & Sreenivalulu, H. (2023). *Effects of excessive screen time on child development: An updated review and strategies for management.* National Library of Medicine.

Walsh, D. (2006, November). *Media use.* Plenary Session presented at the annual conference of the National Council on Family Relations, Minneapolis, MN.

The Struggle Is Real for Parents at Bedtime

Lori Elmore-Staton, Ph.D.
Associate Professor, Mississippi State University
Mississippi State, MS

Pediatricians indicate that sleep concerns are some of the most discussed issues parents raise during routine checkups. Infants come into the world with their sleep schedule, and preschoolers often fight the need for bedtime and sleep, leaving parents stressed and sleep deprived. As you enter the teen stage, youth tend to stay up all night and sleep all day! Adjusting to these sleep changes and knowing how to address them at each stage is important because sleep infiltrates every aspect of your life (see Walker, 2017). Since my training started examining children's sleep and their environment, I thought I would share some tips and tricks I learned that parents may find helpful.

Infants come into the world without a circadian rhythm and may have their days and nights confused for the first few months. If this is the case, it can be challenging for parents because our bodies are most likely in tune with the rising and setting of the sun. But there are some steps you can take that can help your infant's body find its rhythm. For example, you can help give their body cues by using natural daylight and lights around the home to stimulate the baby and their brain. Play with them when they are awake during the daylight hours and offer less physically stimulating activities, such as reading a book, at night when you want them to rest. In the evening, draw the curtains and use lamps instead of overhead lights to help the body recognize that it is time for sleep. This scheduled light and dark pattern will assist in setting their sleep pattern. It will take some little ones more time to adjust to the world than others, with most adjusted to a day–night pattern by 6 months of age (Meltzer & Westin, 2011). Parents should also heed the advice of *sleep when the baby sleeps.* It is estimated that parents lose an average of 6 months of sleep in their baby's first year of life, so take naps when you can, and don't forget to find self-care practices (for examples, see Hardman & Braddock, 2020) that work for you.

Parents of *toddlers and preschoolers* often struggle with bedtime resistance—the act of refusing to go to bed or stay in bed—because they are afraid that they are missing out on something or because they want to be with family members. Bedtime resistance can be an exhausting and frustrating experience for parents. As a sleep researcher, one of the most important tips that I can give is for parents to set a bedtime routine that is calming and consistent from the beginning. For example, after dinner, you bathe her, put on her pajamas, offer her a small drink of water and a small snack (e.g., part of a banana), brush her teeth, read one story, then move her to the bed and sit next to her to read the last story. By implementing this type of routine, you have given her body time to calm down from the bath and engage her in a peaceful bedtime activity (e.g., reading). If you do this each night, it will train her body to this bedtime schedule. I included offering a drink and snack in the routine because one of the common requests of children when they get out of bed is "I'm thirsty" or "I'm hungry." My family dealt with the requests by making some rules around bedtime. One was that there was no more food after we had brushed our teeth. They learned that if they wanted a snack after dinner, they had to ask for it before brushing their teeth. I also would put a small paper cup with just a little water in it next to their bed; that way, they had something if they were thirsty but not enough to cause an accident in the night. We decided how many stories we could read before we started reading because they would often try to delay bedtime by saying, "Just one more!" and it is hard to say no when a child asks you to read a book. Just remember that you must be consistent and stick to the rules you create for it to work.

School-age children may have challenges adjusting to school start times and/or after-school activities that disrupt their previous bedtime routines. Knowing how many hours of sleep your child needs to function well is important. The National Sleep Foundation (Hirshkowitz et al., 2015) provides sleep recommendations by developmental age, which can be a helpful tool when deciding a bedtime for your child. As you are making this decision, consider what time they must get up to arrive at school on time, keeping in mind if they are slow to warm up in the mornings. As they become more involved in activities, it will become harder to be consistent in the bedtime schedule. One way my family helped manage this issue was by limiting our children to one extracurricular for each season. Although this still got hectic at times, it allowed us to have some days of the week where we could stay in routine and have more downtime together at home.

Teens experience a natural shift in their circadian rhythm during puberty that can delay their need to sleep by about 2 hours. That means that melatonin, the hormone responsible for sleep onset that typically starts around dusk, begins to be released later. This later release delays their sleepiness and can influence when their body is ready to wake, resulting in problems going to bed at their usual time or difficulty getting up for school in the mornings. Some schools have started to acknowledge this shift and have altered school start times for teens because they recognize that youth will not do as well in school when they are not getting enough sleep. Another rising concern for teen sleep is technology-based activities, which are related to reduced quality and quantity of sleep (de Sá et al., 2023), and combined with the natural shifts in sleep, can lead to health (Short & Louca, 2015) and academic problems (Curcio et al., 2006). Helping your child set limits around screen time, especially in the evenings, is important for their health and well-being. In my house, we decided the best route was to leave our phones charging in the kitchen so none of us are tempted to be scrolling in bed or are woken up by alerts.

Regardless of what stage of life your family is in, sleep schedules and routines can be challenging. As a parent, check to make sure your child is receiving the amount of sleep that is recommended. If not, consider making changes to their sleep-wake schedule, their sleep environment, and/or the activities and nighttime entertainment they are involved in that might be impacting their ability to get the sleep they need.

Discussion Questions

1. Are you and your family members consistently meeting the recommendations for sleep need as noted by the National Sleep Foundation?

2. Are there changes that you could make to your family's sleep routine or sleep environment that might help everyone obtain better sleep?

References

Curcio G., Ferrara M., & De Gennaro L. (2006). Sleep loss, learning capacity and academic performance. *Sleep Medicine Reviews, 10*(5), 323–337. https://doi.org/10.1016/j.smrv.2005.11.001.

de Sá, S., Baião, A., Marques, H., Marques, M. D. C., Reis, M. J., Dias, S., & Catarino, M. (2023). The influence of smartphones on adolescent sleep: A systematic literature review. *Nursing Reports (Pavia, Italy), 13*(2), 612–621. https://doi.org/10.3390/nursrep13020054

Hardman, A. M., & Braddock, A. (2020). *Tips for taking care of yourself: Self-care practices.* Mississippi State Extension, Publication 3516 (9-20).

Hirshkowitz, M., Whiton, K., Albert, S. M., Alessi, C., Bruni, O., DonCarlos, L., Hazen, N., Herman, J., Adams Hillard, P. J., Katz, E. S., Kheirandish-Gozal, L., Neubauer, D. N., O'Donnell, A. E., Ohayon, M., Peever, J., Rawding, R., Sachdeva, R. C., Setters, B., Vitiello, M. V., & Ware, J. C. (2015). National Sleep Foundation's updated sleep duration recommendations: Final report. *Sleep Health, 1*(4), 233–243. https://doi.org/10.1016/j.sleh.2015.10.004

Meltzer, L. J., & Westin, A. M. L. (2011). Impact of child sleep disturbances on parent sleep and daytime functioning. In M. El-Sheikh (Ed.), *Sleep and development: Familial and sociocultural considerations* (pp. 113–131). Oxford University Press. https://doi.org/10.1093/acprof:oso/9780195395754.003.0006

Short M. A., & Louca M. (2015). Sleep deprivation leads to mood deficits in healthy adolescents. *Sleep Medicine, 16*(8), 987–993. https://doi.org/10.1016/j.sleep.2015.03.007.

Walker, M. (2017). *Why we sleep: Unlocking the power of sleep and dreams.* Scribner.

Positive Discipline Strategies

Lori Elmore-Staton, Ph.D.
Associate Professor, Mississippi State University
Mississippi State, MS

Alisha M. Hardman, Ph.D., CFLE
Associate Professor, Kansas State University
Manhattan, KS

Parents are their child's first and arguably most influential teacher, yet parenting does not come with a manual. Any parent with more than one child can attest that parenting strategies are not a "one size fits all" situation. What works effectively for a 3-year-old will not work the same for a 13-year-old. Parents must equip themselves with as many parenting tools as possible to meet the needs of different ages, personalities, and situations.

A colleague and friend shared this acronym years ago, and we have found it to be an excellent resource for reminding parents of positive parenting strategies.

D = Distraction
I = Ignore some behaviors
S = Soothe
C = Choices
I = Involve children in the behavior plan
P = Positive reinforcement
L = Logical consequences
I = Increase consistency
N = Natural consequences
E = Example—Be a good one!

Distraction, especially for young children who have short attention spans, can be a valuable parenting strategy to get your child's behavior back on track. One day as we were leaving the child development center, my (A.M.H.) 3-year-old daughter demanded that I pick her up and carry her to the car. When I told her that she needed to use her "walking feet," she got upset and sat down on the concrete. I sat down next to her and noticed a dandelion "puff" nearby. I drew her attention to the puff and asked her if she wanted to help me blow the seeds off it. We took a couple of blows and once the dandelion seeds had all been blown away, she stood up and walked to the car herself. Distracting her with the dandelion took her mind off being upset, and after a few minutes she happily walked to the car, the exact behavior I wanted to see.

You have probably heard the phrase "pick your battles," and that is similar to *ignoring* some behaviors. One behavior that I (L.E-S.) have a hard time with is whining. My children learned early on that if they spoke to me in a whiny voice asking for something, they were not going to get it until they used their "big kid" voice. Ignoring whiny requests was one way I helped resolve that unwanted behavior. (Of course, you do not want to ignore something that could be dangerous.)

Big emotions can be challenging, so teaching children how to soothe themselves is key to keeping the peace in your home. Years ago, I (L.E-S.) was giving a workshop at a conference where I was providing teachers with calm-down strategies for their classroom. As one of the activities, participants were making calm-down jars. I had my daughter (a 4-year-old) and niece (a 3-year-old) assist me in creating some examples to use during the workshop. While away at the conference, I received a call from my sister-in-law saying that the girls had been in an argument and came to her asking for the calm-down jars they made. She said that they both shook the jars up and did deep breathing while the glitter settled. She was shocked they had used the tools they learned in that one short interaction.

Giving voice and *choice* to your children does not mean they are in control, but it can often help you avoid a power struggle while building your child's self-esteem and critical thinking skills. Two main components to keep in mind when offering choices are (1) you create the choices, and you must be okay with whatever selection the child makes, and (2) you have to consider the number of options you offer because having too many things to choose from can be overwhelming, especially for a younger child. Some choices can be proactive (e.g., what to wear), having the potential to prevent a meltdown, whereas other choices can be in response to a specific situation (e.g., put away the dishes now or after you finish your homework).

Involving your child in establishing house rules and/or the consequences for not following the rules can help them develop an understanding of the connections between behaviors and consequences. When children have a say in the rules, they are more likely to abide by them. When they help determine the consequences, there is less pushback on the punishment. Outside of behavior changes, involving them in these decisions can help them build their critical-thinking and problem-solving skills.

Positive reinforcement is used to reward behavior that we want our children to repeat. By recognizing children's positive behaviors, we give them our attention and encourage them to act in positive ways. Positive reinforcement may be as simple as offering verbal praise or a smile. When praising children, it's important to emphasize the behavior and/or child's effort. For instance, when my (A.M.H.) toddler has helped a friend at school, I'll exclaim, "It was very kind of you to help your friend when they were scared." Positive reinforcement can also include giving rewards or special privileges. For instance, maybe your child can pick out the game for family game night. Avoid using food and sweets as positive reinforcement because this can lead to poor eating habits and make an unhealthy connection for children between food and feeling good.

Logical consequences help children make the connection between their behavior and the consequence. In other words, the consequences match the behavior. For instance, my (A.M.H.) toddler started throwing toys, so the logical consequence was that the toys were taken away. The message is, "If you don't play nicely with your toys, you cannot play with them." My (L.E-S.) college-age son was pulled over for speeding, and the consequence was that he had to pay for the ticket with his own money. He was a college athlete then, so he didn't have a paying job. Us not stepping in to pay the fine for him made him think twice about speeding.

Children thrive when they have consistent rules and consequences. *Increasing consistency* means that expectations and consequences should be consistent from one parent to the next and from one situation to the next. Parents need to make sure they are on the same page, so children do not pit the parents against one another. For instance, it is common for children to ask both parents the same question to see if their answers differ. Additionally, the same rules should apply when you are at home, in public (e.g., grocery store or school), or at a family member's house. Parents' mood and circumstances also influence consistency. When parents are tired or distracted, we sometimes give in or allow children to do things they normally are not allowed to do. Although consistency can be a lot of work for parents, it helps children understand that expectations for their behavior is the same across settings and situations.

Sometimes people must learn lessons the hard way, with the only thing that makes that lesson stick being the *natural consequence* that comes from the experience. When natural consequences for disobeying are not dangerous, like not carrying an umbrella with you in case of rain, sometimes it is just better for that natural outcome to happen. A great example of this could also be a child not picking up their toys and someone stepping on one and breaking it. In this case, a parent can reiterate that when you are finished playing, toys need to be put where they belong or they could get broken.

Children learn from watching us! They watch how we handle emotions and respond to situations. For instance, one day I (A.M.H.) heard my toddler yell from the backseat, "Go people!" which I instantly knew she had heard me say while driving. Although this could have been much worse (at least it was not a curse word!), as parents, we need to be a good example for our children so that we practice what we preach. If we do not want our child to yell, we should not yell. If we want our child to learn how to self-soothe, we need to model these practices (e.g., deep breaths) when our emotions are high. If we want our children to be polite, we need to say please and thank you in our interactions with our child, but also with others. If we want our child to apologize, we need to model saying "I'm sorry" to our child, partner, and others.

Discussion Questions
1. What parenting strategies were used in your childhood that you want to model? Why?

2. What parenting strategies were used in your childhood that you want to avoid? How did those practices make you feel?

3. Which of these strategies are you already using? Which strategies would be easy to implement in your home? Which strategies might be more challenging for you to use?

Further Reading
Grubbs, E., Hayes, A., DeBerry, T., & Elmore-Staton, L. (2020). *Tips for parents: How to effectively use positive discipline strategies.* Mississippi State Extension Publication 3512 (09-20).

"I Gotta Be Me": Every Child Is Special
Cynthia Garrison, M.S., CPE, CFLE
Home-Based Program Manager
ChildCareGroup, Dallas, TX

Each child comes into the world special and unique. The revered psychotherapist Carl Rogers theorized that every person has the ability to grow, develop, and realize their full potential. This theory is called *actualizing tendency* (Rogers, 2012). This means that everyone has an innate sense of who they should become. It means that a tiger will never try to be a monkey, and a rose will not strive to be a daisy. Our job as parents is to help our children discover their natural personal tendencies without imposing our own hopes or desires on them. Children have a sense of what they like, want, and desire, and as difficult as it may be, as parents, we need to set our thoughts and wishes aside to encourage them to go through the actualizing tendency process (Motsching-Pitrik & Lux, 2007). As parents, we sometimes impede this natural process by interjecting our thoughts and desires, being too intrusive, or thinking we know better or more than the child. Most parents mean well and think they are being helpful by guiding their children. They are often oblivious to the possibility that they are hurting their child by pushing them into an activity or profession that doesn't suit them. The child begins to view their own desires in a negative way or may feel "there is something wrong with me."

Wait—did you hear that? If you listen carefully, you can hear it. I've heard it from my own children, and I heard it from my clients when I was in private practice. Now I hear it when working with parents of children in their early childhood years. It's the voice of the child saying, "Listen to me." It is that same voice saying, "I gotta be ME!" They may not say it with their voice, but their actions say it loud and clear. We must not only listen with our ears but also use our eyes—and especially our hearts—to hear them. This is the first step in helping our children *become*.

I worked with the mother of an 8-year-old girl who loved to write poetry. Mom came to see me because her daughter had started to change, and mom didn't know why. Among other things, we discussed her daughter's poetry. She brought in several examples to show me and expressed her pride. I looked at the poetry and noticed lots of red markups on the paper. I asked her who made these. Mom admitted that she had corrected the poem for her daughter and then gave it back to her. I began asking more questions: How long ago was this poem written? Why did she feel the need to correct something daughter wrote that was not related to school? How did she feel about the poem herself? And so on. The most striking answer to me was that this poem was written more than 6 months ago. I asked if her daughter had written more poems lately. She said no and that was why she was visiting me. Her daughter had stopped creative writing altogether. After more questions, mom concluded that her interference in "correcting" the papers had hurt her daughter and made her feel as if her work was not good enough. Perhaps she had begun hiding her work so mom would not "butcher" it. Her daughter had used this word once, asking mom to stop "butchering" her work. We then went into problem-solving mode. Mom decided to talk with her daughter, apologize for "butchering" her creative work, and promise not to interfere again. A few weeks later, mom called and said her daughter was sharing her poems again. The relationship was healing.

Jenny McFall (2023, p.21) wrote about the importance of listening to our children even when they are very young, noting how even then the brain and cognitive development are far more advanced than what we as parents tend to imagine. Her poem from her book says it all:

> Your unselfish love creates courage and strength in me. / With these,/ I get ready to conquer any difficulty./Your love puts solid ground under my feet./ Your guidance gives me wings to fly./ Please do not worry about me;/ I will find my own way/ sooner or later./ I will achieve my goals.

When you fail to listen to your child as they express their desire to try something or explore new territory, it can break the child's spirit. We learn more when we listen than when we do most of the talking. Active listening, a purposeful involvement in the communication process (Garraway, 2023), is even more important to practice, especially with our children. When we listen and really hear their ideas or desires, it just feels good. Think about how you feel when you find someone who really listens to you. It feels good, doesn't it?

My son dressed uniquely for his age. When others in high school wore T-shirts and jeans or shorts, he wore khakis and button-down shirts. I once asked him why he chose these clothes to wear. He simply said, "Because I like them, and they make me feel comfortable." Enough said.

When my daughter was in ninth grade (she is now 30), she was obsessed with K-Pop music. I didn't understand the music but loved the dancing. I considered this a teenage phase. She was invested—joined the fan clubs, went to concerts, watched the videos. She wanted me to watch the videos with her. I honestly thought it was a waste of my time; however, I knew it was important to her, so I begrudgingly but regularly watched a few videos and commented positively on the dancing. Her obsession translated into a study abroad opportunity in Seoul, South Korea.

So often, when a child tries something new or different, it evokes strong reactions from parents. If you continue to have negative thoughts about your child's behaviors or decisions, your thoughts will become actions, resulting in negative comments and hurtful words. And this will end up damaging the relationship. Research is clear (Sharf, 2000): When we embrace our children's original, creative, and unique attributes, they will show us a whole new, nonjudgmental world where we don't always have the right answers or have to know everything. This type of thinking and acting brings about a more harmonious home—and ultimately a more harmonious world.

Discussion Questions

1. What does listening look like in a parent/child relationship?

2. What characteristics make a good listener?

3. How can being a good listener to children help them with their future relationships (friends, work, personal relationships) as adults?

References

Rogers, C. (2012). *On Becoming a Person*. Houghton Mifflin Company

Garraway, R. (2023). *Effective communication and empathy*. Independently published.

McFall, J. (2023). *Mum and dad, please listen to me: A little book filled with big thoughts for parents*. Balboa Press, pp21

Motsching-Pitrik, R., & Lux, M. (2007). The person-center approach meets neuroscience: Mutual support for C.R. Rogers and A. Damasio's theories. *Journal of Humanistic Psychology, 48*(3), 287–319.

Sharf, R. S. (2000). *Theories of psychotherapy & counseling* (2nd ed.). Brooks/Cole Publishing Company.

Compassionate Parenting: A Case Study

H. Wallace Goddard, Ph.D., CFLE
Retired Professor of Family Life
University of Arkansas Cooperative Extension Service
Little Rock, AR
Editor of *Between Parent and Child*

There is a nationally syndicated columnist who regularly gives advice that commonly encourages parents to be tough with their children. Many parents appreciate his no-nonsense approach; some do not.

The columnist and I agree that the failure to regulate bad behavior has serious consequences for our society. Parents must let their children know that they are serious about the rules they make. The way children know we are serious is that we set reasonable rules and enforce them appropriately.

Yet I believe that there is a danger in focusing primarily on doling out consequences for misbehavior. If we are not careful, we will throw out the baby with the bath water. It takes more than consistent consequences to teach goodness, character, and compassion. Consequences are especially unhelpful when delivered with irritation and rejection. We should strive to replace our frustrations and annoyance when children break a rule with a feeling of compassion. Also, we need to realize that for any given situation, there usually are several alternative ways of dealing with it, which may get lost or not considered if we too quickly seek to exact a consequence for a broken rule.

A Case Study
To move this from an abstract discussion to a practical one, let us look at an example from the columnist's published column and contrast his approach to some alternatives that I believe would probably be more acceptable to scholars who study childrearing.

A mother wrote to the columnist that her 4-year-old daughter at some point during a meal would sometimes decide that she wouldn't swallow her food (Rosemond, 2002, p. E3). When told that she cannot spit it out, she would hold the bite for hours. The mother reported that they had tried many things to get the daughter to swallow: having her remain at the table for hours, skipping the next meal, returning the unswallowed food to her at the next meal, removing toys and privileges for weeks, banishment to her room without toys, spanking, praising (on those rare occasions when she swallowed), and withholding dessert.

Almost parenthetically, the mother noted that the girl was adopted internationally a year previous to her writing to the columnist. The problem began about 4 months after the adoption. The mother also mentioned that there were other children in the family.

Given this information, what do you think should be done to solve the problem?

One Recommendation
Let's begin with the columnist's recommendations. He first suggested that it was not useful to look for a psychological cause for the behavior. "This is one of those weird, strange, inexplicable things that some children sometimes do, for no obvious reason at all." Further, "some of the things children do defy explanation. Some of the

odd stuff in question is harmless to the point of being funny. What your daughter is doing is funny (to me, at least), but it's also a very clever, subtle form of defiance" (Rosemond, 2002, p. E3).

One might wonder if all of this is funny to the child who doesn't swallow or to the parents perplexed by the behavior. It seems doubtful.

The columnist confidently gives a solution, offering to chew his hat if it doesn't work: "You simply tell your slyly defiant and highly intelligent little princess that you called her doctor and he/she said that not swallowing happens because a child is tired and doesn't even know it. Your doctor said that from now on, if you take a bite and you are so tired that you can't swallow, you have to go to the bathroom, spit it out and go to bed. If she balks at swallowing, and you begin the procedure, and she suddenly decides to swallow, you must still put her to bed. Just tell her the doctor said that even having problems swallowing means she's tired and doesn't know it. I predict that in a week or two, it will be a thing of the past, and I will still have my hat."

Testing the Counsel
Does this counsel sound helpful to you? If you were the child, would it seem helpful to you?

Certainly, there are many possible ways of responding to the child who doesn't swallow. I don't believe there is only one "right" answer. But if I were responding to the parent's question, my recommendations would be quite different from those of the columnist.

A Different Starting Place
First, I would recommend the kind of compassion and humility that comes from seeking to understand the child's experience. What were the first 3 years of the child's life like? How was she nurtured and nourished in those years? Did she have consistent and caring attention during those 3 years before she was adopted, or did she experience chaotic or stressful conditions? Was availability of food a grave concern for the girl during this time? Under what circumstances was she adopted? How has this little girl integrated with the other children in the adoptive family? Does she have friends? What is the child's personality or temperament like? Is there a certain food that she refuses to chew? Are there foods she enjoys? What kind of food did she have before the international adoption? Was there unusual stress in her life at the time the problem behavior began? How have siblings reacted to the non-swallowing? Has this girl been teased previously about her eating? How affectionate and appreciative do the parents feel about this child when not at the dinner table? Does the little girl have friends and activities she enjoys? All these questions suggest the merits of considering alternative solutions.

To recommend a certain remedy confidently without knowing the child's history is not wise. Given the scant information provided by the parent, some sensible actions can be suggested, but humility seems to be a wiser stance than dogmatism.

The Limits of Power
Apart from the limited information issue, there is another issue. Any parent who has ever been a child knows that the "put-the-child-to-bed" prescription is a power technique that can lead to long-term conflict. The power technique may have a smile on its face, but it is unmistakably a power play. No child will be fooled no matter how big the smile. Research on guiding children recommends against the raw use of power (Maccoby & Martin, 1983).

The behavior recommended by the columnist may work in some narrow sense. It is likely that the child will start swallowing the food rather than be put to bed. Yet in my opinion, the real problem will go untreated. Does this child feel desperately confused in her new country? Does she feel stupid and helpless (maybe even picked on) in a family that already knows the rules of American life? Does she feel lonely and unloved?

The Magic Cure
The most important factor in determining how well a child develops is nurture. Children who have people who understand, support, love, and teach them are likely to become strong and able adults. By turning up the use of power on the annoying but harmless behavior, in my view, the columnist could be guaranteeing a lifetime of trouble.

Might using power to control the child almost guarantee that the root problems will get worse? Today's dinner battles may become tomorrow's eating disorder, anxiety problem, learned helplessness, or depression.

Based on the scant information provided by the parent, I would recommend minimizing the swallowing issue by unceremoniously providing a "discharge" bowl for the little girl while encouraging family members not to worry about the swallowing issue. She is welcome to eat as much as she is inclined to eat and may stop at any time. At the same time, I would look for ways to strengthen the parent–child relationship away from the dinner table. The Number 1 question for her parents is: "What is life like for this 4-year-old?" I recommend that the parents monitor the child's food preferences while noticing the child's areas of connection, expression, and joy as well as any particular difficulties.

The child is trying to tell us something. From the compassionate viewpoint, we will get the message best if we have the patience and wisdom to hear and interpret her message. As a side note, the best writing on the subject of families and eating is probably Ellyn Satter (2008), who underscores that we should not turn eating into a battleground. Many of us are still struggling with irrational eating because of ill-advised eating rules in our childhood homes.

Two Ways or More to Consider
The columnist's recommendations have a certain natural appeal. I wonder if that is because the natural instinct in each of us is to be in control and to be obeyed. We do not even want to be inconvenienced. "Things should be done my way—and done promptly."

Yet we probably realize that there are ways that are more sensitive to the child. A loving parent might take the little girl on his or her lap and hum to her. He might ask her what foods from her native country were her favorites. I can imagine him making a bear out of peanut butter balls for her—if he knew that she liked peanut butter. Or raisin ants on a cheese and celery log. A compassionate parent will take time to discover what the girl likes and will do it in the context of a loving relationship.

How do we know what will help the child feel loved? When we see an earnest, struggling child behind the imperfect behavior, when we feel compassion for the child, we are likely to act in ways that are loving.

Clearly, there are children's misdeeds that need "consequences" and teaching. But if we lead with correction rather than compassion in our responses to children, we may not be helpful to many children. An overriding feeling of love, even when correcting a child, is what distinguishes effective parents from all others.

We adults have far more power than children do. The question for all of us who guide children is whether we will choose to act in ways that are sensitive to the child or whether we will demand compliance at all costs—even at the expense of the child's well-being and development.

Of course, there is more than love and compassion to effective parenting. Another article in this text, "First Compassion, Then Teaching," will expand on this theme.

Discussion Questions
1. What examples of power struggles have you observed between a parent and a child?

2. While parents commonly act with the best of intentions, they may not fully understand the child's perspective. In the power struggles you observed, why might the child be resisting the parent's influence? How might the parent work with the child more effectively?

References
Maccoby, E. E., & Martin, J. A. (1983). Socialization in the context of the family: Parent–child interaction. In P. H. Mussen (Ed.), *Handbook of child psychology, Volume IV* (pp. 1–101). John Wiley & Sons, Inc.

Rosemond, J. (2002, October 23). Obstinate daughter won't swallow food. *Arkansas Democrat Gazette*, 3E.

Satter, E. (2008). *Secrets of feeding a healthy family.* Kelcy Press.

First Compassion, Then Teaching

H. Wallace Goddard, Ph.D., CFLE
Retired Professor of Family Life
University of Arkansas Cooperative Extension Service
Little Rock, AR
Editor *Between Parent and Child*

Compassion is the first law of parenting. Nothing matters as much as compassion in helping children develop into healthy adults. What's more, the quality of love has an impact on the effectiveness of all other parenting efforts.

In dealing with parenting dilemmas, it is hard to tease apart loving compassion and disciplining or guiding. Many issues we think of as control issues are really, at their root, relationship issues.

There is far more that can and should be said about effectively loving children. It is worthy of our most devoted and patient attention. But in this article, I focus on the other key dimension in parenting. It goes by several names: control, guidance, or structure. I like to think of it as *teaching*.

The Control Dilemma
This discussion can begin with another bit of counsel from the same parent columnist (Rosemond, 2002), described in my other article in this publication, "Compassionate

Parenting: A Case Study"). There are two parts of his counsel on which I would like to focus. First, he said that children should not be allowed to complain about the food they are served. It is rude, he said. Second, he took to task a parent who would create an alternative meal for a child who was not happy with what had been offered.

Before discussing his counsel, let's set the stage for thinking about control. What is its purpose? Is it primarily intended to prevent problems? To keep children out of trouble? To make life run smoothly?

The Purpose of Control

I believe that there is one primary purpose for parents to exercise control in their children's lives: to teach them to make good decisions. Certainly, control also should be used to keep children safe from threats for which they are not prepared. But this fits within the larger purpose of parental control—helping children learn to make good decisions. We want them to make good choices long after they have left our homes.

There are many ways to abuse parental control, but these can be classed into two broad categories for the sake of this discussion: too much and too little.

Too Much Control

Those who exercise too much control may be trying to prevent their children from making mistakes, but in the process, they hamper their children's development.

Progressive Choosing

The solution to the control problem is not to allow children total freedom. The solution is progressive opportunities to make choices. We honor a baby's preference for one toy or another. We allow a preschooler to pick a book to read at bedtime, but usually not the time for going to bed. We allow a school-age child to pick the clothes to wear to school—providing subtle coaching along the way and holding our complaints when they are not welcome. Most adolescents are allowed to make many decisions, under wise and gentle parental guidance.

Progressive choosing is much like helping a child learn to ride a bike. As children are almost ready to ride, we provide a bike with training wheels. As they get more experienced, we might adjust the training wheels up or even remove them. For a short time, we run alongside children as they learn, coaching on steering, braking, and balancing. Eventually they learn to ride on their own. Along the way, most children get some bumps and bruises. But wise parents provide just enough guidance to prevent damaging or discouraging accidents. We give children all the freedom for which they are prepared. We even coach them to help them be ready for more freedom.

Examples of Control With Progressive Choosing

Children should be given choices within the bounds set by loving and wise parents. And we do not have to become unpleasant as we set limits. One of our parenting mottoes has two vital parts: It is our job to (1) help our children get what they want (2) in a way we feel good about. We care deeply about our children's preferences. But we set some boundaries based on their readiness. We did not let our young children decide whether they wanted Hershey bars or green beans for dinner. But we might offer a choice between green beans and peas.

Another example: When 17-year-old Andy asked us if he could go to the lake with his friends on an upcoming Friday night, we took seriously our responsibility to help him make a good decision. But we also honored his good sense and maturity.

So I asked, "How do you feel about going?"

"I think it will be fine. We'll play ball and have snacks."

"So you don't see any problems with the gathering?"

Andy paused. "Well, I do have a question. I know some of the guys will be bringing marijuana, but I won't be using any, so it shouldn't be a problem, right?"

I managed my surprise. We had a calm discussion about potential problems. I encouraged him to think about it for another day or two. He ultimately decided that he didn't need to be at a party with drugs. In fact, he offered an alternative gathering at our house.

The Gentle Art of Progressive Choosing

Progressive choosing is an art. It requires wisdom to provide children abundant opportunities to make decisions while not setting them up for failure.

When does setting boundaries become too controlling? Perhaps the answer is when we fail to be sensitive to both their abilities and their limitations. But this is not a tidy answer. It is only when we have love, concern, and compassion in our hearts that we can set boundaries wisely. Compassion must guide the purpose and enlighten the practice of progressive choice with wisdom as her fair companion.

Back to the Food Issue

So, when we look at the question about food preferences, I disagree with the parenting columnist about children expressing their dislike for foods. Why? I do not consider it rude within a family for a person to express that he does not have a taste for a certain food. The expression can be phrased with consideration for the people who provide and prepare the food. But a child should be able to express feelings.

And we can model civility ourselves. We do not need to shame them. We can set a standard that seems reasonable: "I ask that you try one bean. Then, if you do not want more, you may have a carrot" (or some other reasonable choice).

Even in making such simple requests, we can avoid stark confrontation. Psychology teaches us to minimize power as a relationship issue. It tends to get in the way of helpful guidance. As the insightful psychologist Wendy Grolnick (2003) has observed, "[Humans] simply do not do well (or feel well) when we are made to feel like pawns to others, whether at work, at school, or in our personal relationships" (pp. 32–33).

The best tools for effective parenting include persuasion and patience. Please note: A capable parent is not afraid to set and enforce reasonable limits. Yet this is done with the abilities and needs of the child in mind.

In the eating arena, we provide lots of nutritious foods and let children make choices. Yet I agree with the columnist (Rosemond, 2005) that a parent probably should not jump to prepare an alternate meal for the child. And I would not allow the child to eat just anything. I would probably have an alternative in mind that was acceptable to the child, which he or she might help prepare. That would set appropriate bounds.

So having discussed the exercise of excessive control, with the introduction of progressive choosing, let's turn our attention to insufficient control.

Too Little Control

Many parents cannot tolerate children's displeasure. They are not willing to set boundaries. They may lecture and threaten but they do not deliver on their threats. What do children learn from such parenting? They learn that the key to getting what you want is to keep your parents constantly on the horns of your displeasure. They learn to be tormentors.

Most of us have seen parents caving in. In fact, most of us have done such caving ourselves. For example, we likely have all seen a parent insist to a child in the supermarket that he cannot have a candy bar under any circumstances. But, after some whining, nagging, and maybe even a tantrum, the child gets the candy bar. What did the child learn? A little persistence pays handsome dividends. So children learn to become efficient tormentors.

Children learn just what combination of whining and demanding will get them what they want. And many parents learn to be endless lecturers. Both sides lose. Both parent and child lose dignity in the battle over a candy bar. We teach children to surrender character and become tyrants. And we become chronic grouches.

There are other ways of exerting too little control. One of them is to use threats as a control technique. Frustrated parents may threaten to withhold treats or to keep a child home from a party. Both parent and child know that the threat is unlikely to be enacted. It is merely a stick swung threateningly in the air. Feeling insulted by the unjust attack on his or her dignity, the child resists. The parental anger and threats escalate. Childish indignity grows.

This can't possibly be the best way to teach children how to use their ability to make choices. The drama would be comical if it were not so damaging.

Guidelines for Guidance

Sensible rules for guidance include at least the following:
1. **Be careful about the rules you make.** Avoid idle threats. Do not make big issues out of little behaviors that should be ignored.
2. **Consistently enforce the rules you make.** The action behind the promise is the only way children learn that we—and nature—are serious about the rules we make.
3. **Use consequences.** Let nature, rather than angry diatribes, teach the law of the harvest. When we do not sow, we do not reap. If we do not finish our chores, we do not go out and play.
4. **Keep the relationship positive.** We should probably deliver at least five positive experiences for each negative one. And even the negative encounters should be done with persuasion, gentleness, meekness, patience, and genuine love.
5. **Give children lots of real choices.** It takes regular practice for them to learn to use their decision-making capacity well. (For more details on these five principles, see Goddard, 1994.)

A Concluding Example

My wife and I once attended a birthday party for a graduate student. The hostess was greeting all her guests even as she tried to finish preparations for the party and manage her two children. We tried to help as we noticed trouble brewing. Four-year-old Ellen (not her real name) was standing at the kitchen table, nose-to-nose with the cake. She clearly had designs on the frosting.

This is a crossroads in parenting. The mother may choose to do nothing. She may menace her with threats. Or she may set Ellen up for success.

In this case, Mom followed her poorer instincts of control. She threatened. "If you touch that cake, you're in trouble!" and shot the little girl a threatening glare. Ellen returned the glare with the hidden message: "I can make you suffer for treating me this way."

Having offered her threat, Mom returned to preparations for the party. Ellen returned to frosting-lust. Obviously, the maternal injunction had not created an effective deterrent for Ellen.

Ellen lingered near the cake and Mom continued to glower at Ellen. When Mom got busy taking snack items to the party area, Ellen snatched a frosting-rich corner of the cake. When Mom returned and spotted the telltale signs of the crime, she screamed, "I told you not to touch that cake!" Ellen felt mistreated, and Mom judged Ellen to be a bad child. This approach did not lead to growth for Ellen or peace for the family.

Some would say that Ellen should be obedient. Some would say that she should be punished. An alternative: Parents can set children up for success. When the mom spotted the high-risk situation, she might have done any of several things:

1. She might have gotten Ellen a snack. This would be especially appropriate if Mom knew that Ellen was hungry; yet maybe just giving her some of the leftover frosting might suffice.
2. Mom might have explained to Ellen that for a party like this, it is important to keep the cake looking nice and "whole" for the guests to see.
3. Mom might have gotten Ellen busy helping, inviting her to take supplies and snacks to the table.
4. Mom might have cut a slice of cake for Ellen to eat right away.
5. Mom might have moved the cake to a higher plane, minimizing the temptation.

Which is the best response? It depends. It depends on Ellen's disposition and current state of hunger. It depends on Mom's need to deliver an uncut cake to the party. It depends on how long it will be before the cake is cut and served. That is the unique challenge of parenting. There are no simple, pat answers. There are just sensible, compassionate considerations.

Ideally, Mom wants to help Ellen get the experiences she wants. In addition, Mom wants to help Ellen learn to make good decisions. We don't want to set her up for failure. We don't want to punish her into resentful submission for being a normal child. We want to help Ellen learn to make good decisions.

No Simple Answers
Hundreds of thousands of words have been written about parenting. Parenting does not have a simple formula. Ultimately, good parenting requires us to have kind hearts and wise minds. It also helps if we are feeling peaceful and purposeful.

There are clear principles. Grolnick's (2003) summary is compelling: "Providing rationales and clear consequences for behavior in the context of choice, acknowledgement of feelings, and minimization of pressure should facilitate the active process of [helping children do right things for right reasons]" (p. 64).

While each parent has different strengths and limitations, a few parenting books find the balance between compassion and control—such as Ginott's (2003) classic *Between Parent and Child* or Gottman and DeClaire's (1997) *Raising an Emotionally Intelligent Child.*

In the process of becoming better parents, we should remember that we are forming relationships that can equip our children for a lifetime of good decisions and can bless generations to come.

Discussion Questions

1. What are your thoughts about the idea that the purpose of parental control is to teach children how to make good decisions? Would you modify that objective in any way?

2. Describe examples of progressive choosing that you have witnessed in parenting.

3. How can a parent tell if they are using too much or too little control?

References

Ginott, H. (2003). *Between parent and child.* Three Rivers.

Goddard, H. W. (1994). Something better than punishment (HE-687). In *Principles of parenting*. Alabama Cooperative Extension System.

Gottman, J., & DeClaire, J. (1997). *Raising an emotionally intelligent child.* Simon & Schuster.

Grolnick, W. (2003). *The psychology of parental control.* Lawrence Erlbaum Associates.

Rosemond, J. (2005, March 2). Catering to children creates spoiled brats. *Arkansas Democrat Gazette*, 3E.

Parenting With Style

Sharon M. Ballard, Ph.D., CFLE
Professor and Department Chair
Human Development & Family Science
East Carolina University, Greenville, NC

Kevin H. Gross, Ph.D.

Parents have a style, which is to say that all parents have a particular style of parenting. How we choose to raise our children often is related to whom we want them to be when they grow up. And while some parents spend a considerable amount of time thinking and learning about and shaping their own parenting style, others simply do mostly what their parents did. There are four basic parenting styles, discussed here, which scholars have studied, based on two primary dimensions: **responsiveness** and **demandingness** (Baumrind, 1971, 1991; Maccoby & Martin, 1983).

Responsiveness refers to the amount of warmth or acceptance that is characteristic of the parent–child relationship. It also is about respect for a child and his or her rights as an individual. **Demandingness** refers to the rules or expectations we parents have for our children's behaviors and the amount of structure we have provided for them.

Authoritative parenting, the first parenting style, is characterized by both a high level of responsiveness and a high level of demandingness. Authoritative parents have a clear set of reasonable expectations for a child's behavior, and they take the time to explain to the child why it is important to behave in such a way. For example, when faced with a preschool-age child who will not eat their green beans at dinner, an authoritative parent may say to the child, "It is important to eat your vegetables so that you can stay healthy and play with your friends." Or they might say, "You may either eat your green beans or your salad, but you need to eat one to be healthy." However, the child is not allowed to leave the table until they eat some sort of vegetable. Although this sounds easy enough, in practice, authoritative parenting tends to take more time and energy, especially with young children. The payoff is that as they become older, they become more autonomous or independent in their decision-making and tend to make better choices for themselves.

In contrast, the **authoritarian parenting** style is characterized by parents who have a high level of demandingness but a lower level of responsiveness. With an extremely authoritarian parent, a child is not allowed to question why they are to behave in a particular way, nor is any explanation usually given. Often an authoritarian parent will rely on physical punishment to teach a child what is expected of them. They tend to place a higher value on following the direction of an authority figure than they do on independent thought. An authoritarian parent may say to a preschool-age child, "You eat your green beans because I said so" or "because that is what we have to eat tonight." Often authoritarian parents are overly critical of their children, focusing only on what they have done wrong or on their failures. To the child, it may seem as if no matter how well they do something, it is never good enough, and so they may give up even trying. Children of authoritarian parents often have a difficult time forming their own identity and are more susceptible to negative peer influences. They tend to have trouble deciding for themselves between right and wrong and thus rely on others to tell them.

A **permissive parenting** style, in contrast to the authoritarian parenting style, is characterized by a high level of responsiveness but a low level of demandingness. Thus, there is a strong, warm emotional connection between the parent and child, but there is little in the way of rules and expectations. Sometimes the parent seems more like a friend than a parent, especially as the child grows older. Using the green bean eating example again, a permissive parent is likely to say, "You don't have to eat your green beans if you don't like them" and let the child leave the table without eating any vegetables. Although these children tend to have good social skills and sometimes may seem more mature than their peers, they often struggle with forming a clear identity or purpose in life, and so they spend a lot of time exploring different identities. They may drop in and out of college, change majors frequently, or try several careers before they finally settle on something. At times they may seem lost and unsure about what do to next, and they may not be sure where to look for guidance or even recognize that they might need some. Generally, children who experience one of these three styles do well in life; however, there are some differences, as discussed subsequently.

Lastly, it should not be surprising that we refer to parents who are low in responsiveness and demandingness as having an **uninvolved or neglectful parenting** style. Children who grow up with this fourth parenting style tend to have a much more difficult time. It's not that these children are doomed to a life of misery, but the challenges they face seem to be more difficult to overcome when there is no one there to help. When they do succeed, it is often due to another adult in their lives stepping in the take on a parenting role.

There has been a considerable amount of research on parenting styles, and the general consensus is that authoritative parenting works as a protective factor in reducing the likelihood of a young person participating in any of a number of "undesirable" behaviors. Regardless of sex, ethnicity, socioeconomic status, or family structure, children who are raised in homes characterized by warmth, structure, and high but reasonable expectations are more likely to experience positive outcomes and fewer behavior problems (Kuppens & Ceulemans, 2018). Reasonable expectations can be shaped by a basic understanding of child development that in turn can help interpret children's behaviors. Authoritative parents often understand that the way a child sees and interacts with the world around them is very different from the way adults see things. They do not expect their child to behave like an adult, nor do they expect them to understand their environment from an adult perspective.

However, there has been increasing research on the cultural relevance of parenting styles (Mowen & Schroeder, 2018; Pezzella et al., 2016). Overall, recent research has shown support for authoritative parenting in reducing future delinquency across race; however, factors such neighborhood disadvantage play a role. It may be that higher levels of demandingness and control, as found in authoritarian parenting, serve as protective factors for Black youth with higher levels of disadvantage and risk (Mowen & Schroeder, 2018).

Parenting is difficult, and there are many factors in today's world that influence the ways in which we parent. Thus, what worked for children a generation or two ago is not necessarily what is best for them today and what works for a child growing up in one setting may not be best for a child growing up someplace very different. And adopting an authoritative parenting style does not guarantee that your children will not experience any problems along the way. But high levels of warmth and responsiveness can increase the chances that our children will experience the sort of positive outcomes that we want for them. And when your children make mistakes, whether big or not so big, they may be better equipped to move on from those mistakes in a positive way.

Finally, to lump all parents into these seemingly simple four styles may seem like an oversimplification of the many ways in which parents, at times, parent. Depending on the circumstances some parents may switch from one style to another. For example, when it comes to keeping the child's bedroom clean, a parent may be permissive, but they may be authoritative when it comes to how that child behaves when there is company over for dinner; however, most parents tend to emphasize one style over the others. It also may be that in two-parent households, one parent has one style, and the other parent has a different style. Research suggests that gender influences parenting style, with mothers more likely to be authoritative and fathers more likely to be authoritarian, but this may vary with the child's age and the family's culture (Yaffe, 2023). In such a situation, differing parenting styles might lead to confusion for the child, so it is beneficial for parents who have differing styles to be aware of this and learn ways in which their parenting styles can complement each other. Ultimately, what is most important is that parents be thoughtful about what style they use most and why and that they make thoughtful decisions about the way in which they parent.

Discussion Questions & Activities

1. What style of parenting do you think you use with your own children? Or what style of parenting do you think your parents used in raising you?

2. In what ways does parenting style impact children? Why do you think authoritative parenting has been found to have positive effects on children?

3. What are examples of situations or cultural contexts that may call for a particular parenting style?

This online quiz can be used to help you further understand your parenting style. *Parenting Style Quiz: What's Your Parenting Style?* (verywellmind.com) https://www.verywellmind.com/parenting-style-quiz-7562663

References

Baumrind, D. (1971). Current patterns of parental authority. *Developmental Psychology, 4*(1, Pt. 2), 1–103. https://doi.org/10.1037/h0030372

Baumrind, D. (1991). Parenting styles and adolescent development. In J. Brooks-Gunn, R. Lerner, & A. C. Petersen (Eds.), *The encyclopedia on adolescence* (pp. 746–758). Garland Publishing.

Kuppens, S., & Ceulemans, E. (2018). Parenting styles: A closer look at a well-known concept. *Journal of Child & Family Studies, 28*(1), 168–181. https://doi.org/10.1007/s10826-018-1242-x

Maccoby, E., & Martin, J. (1983). Socialization in the context of the family: Parent–child interaction. In E. M. Hetherington (Ed.), P. H. Myssen (Series Ed.), *Handbook of child psychology: Vol. 4. Socialization, personality, and social development* (pp. 1–101). John Wiley & Sons.

Mowen, T. J., & Schroeder, R. D. (2018). Maternal parenting style and delinquency by race and the moderating effect of structural disadvantage. *Youth & Society, 50*(2), 139–159. https://doi.org/10.1177/0044118X15598028

Pezzella, F. S., Thornberry, T. P., & Smith, C. A. (2016). Race socialization and parenting styles. *Youth Violence and Juvenile Justice, 14* (4), 448–467. https://doi.org/10.1177/1541204015581390

Yaffe, Y. (2023). Systematic review of the differences between mothers and fathers in parenting styles and practices. *Current Psychology, 42,* 16011–16024. https://doi.org/10.1007/s12144-020-01014-6

Harnessing the Power of Failure

Alisha M. Hardman, Ph.D., CFLE
Associate Professor, Kansas State University
Manhattan, KS

Lori Elmore-Staton, Ph.D.
Associate Professor, Mississippi State University
Mississippi State, MS

As parents, it is often hard to watch our child struggle, experience setbacks, or be disappointed. Many parents step in to protect their children from unpleasant experiences. For example, parents rush to school to deliver forgotten permission slips, assignments, or practice clothes. Additionally, it is often faster for us to do things ourselves than it is to be patient as we let our children figure out how to do something on their own. For instance, it may be faster and easier for us to get our toddler dressed or put on their shoes than it is for the toddler to dress themselves. Or we may want chores done "our" way and criticize our children for doing them their own way—that is, your teen doesn't load the dishwasher the way that you want it done. Parents also tend to over incentivize our children using external motivators in exchange for behaviors, such as "if you do your homework without being asked every night this week, I'll buy you the video game you asked for." When helping children with homework or with a problem they encounter—say, church camp and soccer are the same week," parents often provide solutions or answers before the child has had a chance to struggle with the problem. Similarly, many well-meaning parents do not allow their children to make their own decisions and instead make decisions for them.

The problem is our overprotection, lack of patience, and need for control have resulted in children who are not given an opportunity to experience failure. In our society, failure has become a dirty word. We like to use an acronym to remind parents and children that to FAIL, is the First Attempt In Learning. Failure affords children and youth the opportunity to learn to solve their own problems. Problem-solving is a critical skill that children and youth need to learn to become well-functioning adults. From our experience as college professors, it is much better for children to be given opportunities to fail when they are young and the stakes are relatively low (e.g., failing a quiz or test) than for them to learn those lessons when the stakes are higher (e.g., failing out of college). How can we parent in such a way that our children become less dependent on us and successfully navigate their own failures? We use strategies that *support* our children as they struggle, experience setbacks, or disappointment. In doing so, we will promote their *autonomy* and their ability to deal with the failures that are inevitable in life.

Jessica Lahey, author of *The Gift of Failure*, outlined five strategies that parents can employ to support and promote the autonomy of their children. First, guide children toward solutions. Parents should look for teachable moments to lead their children toward answers. The discoveries that children make with your support will stick with them longer and more deeply than any answers you give them. For instance, if your child comes home complaining that their friends did not play with them at school, pose the question: "Why do you think your friends didn't want to play with you?" Or if your child mentions that their tummy is growling, ask, "What do you think you should do to make it stop growling?" Allowing your child to produce their own solutions to problems—both big and small—builds their independence.

The second strategy is to allow your child to make mistakes and help them understand the consequences of those mistakes. It can be hard to keep our composure when our child spills milk all over themselves and the kitchen floor, but if we remain calm and model patience during these incidents, we show our children that mistakes are part of the process of learning. Doing so will make it easier for them to bounce back from mistakes in the future. In response to your child spilling milk you could say, "Oops! It looks like you made a mess. Let's clean it up and get you changed into dry clothes, and next time you can remember to sit still in your chair when you want a drink." Responding with patience rather than scolding makes it more likely that your child will come to you when they make mistakes in the future.

The third strategy parents can use is to value mistakes as much as successes. Parents sometimes need reminders that children will make mistakes. Give them grace when they mess up. Empathize with your children and make sure they know you love them as much when they make a mistake as you do when they succeed. Help your child find the lessons in the failure and help them learn from their mistakes so they can do better next time! For instance, ask your child, "What do you think you could do differently next time?" Or remind them some things are difficult and need practice, but if you keep trying, you will eventually succeed.

The fourth strategy is to acknowledge children's feelings of frustration and disappointment. Tell your child that you understand what they are feeling. Normalizing, validating, and empathizing with your child's challenging feelings lets them know that they are not alone. This is a powerful opportunity to connect with your child. Once their feelings have been validated, it is typically easier for them to move past the emotion and begin problem-solving. "I get upset too when I feel like I am not being heard or understood. Do you remember when I was frustrated after work last week because my colleagues did not listen to my ideas during our meeting? I had to remind myself that it was not personal, and I developed a strategy to make my ideas heard in our next meeting. What do you think you could do next time to make sure that the teacher hears your idea?" You may think they are overreacting to a situation, but their emotions are real and might feel overwhelming to them. Validating their feelings and sharing your own experiences can help children navigate disappointment.

The final strategy is to give effective feedback that supports your child's effort and guides them to resolve their mistakes. Rather than giving your children specific directions, provide them with supportive observations that encourage them to solve their own problems. Children feel accomplished and proud when they can solve their own problems. For example, if your child puts their shoes on the wrong feet, you might say, "Look down at your feet. Something looks off—can you figure out what is wrong?" Guiding children to a solution rather than solving the problem for them empowers them to resolve their own issues.

It takes time and practice to use new parenting strategies. You will make mistakes, and that's okay. It is a perfect opportunity for you to model ways to learn and grow from failures. Be honest with your child when you make a mistake so that they see you are human, and you make mistakes too. We have found that admitting when we are wrong and apologizing to our children is a great way to strengthen your bond. We can always "err and repair." If they see you handle failure with grace, it will be easier for them to do the same.

Discussion Questions

1. Do you immediately jump in and help your child, or do you allow them to struggle?

2. Do you complete tasks for your child to avoid their frustration?

3. Do you encourage them to keep trying, even when they are frustrated?

4. What do you say and/or do to help motivate your child to keep trying? Does it work?

Reference

Lahey, J. (2016). *The gift of failure: How the best parents learn to let go so their children can succeed.* Harper.

Intentional Parenting: What Are Your Goals for Your Child and Your Relationship?

Cameron Lee, Ph.D., CFLE
Professor of Family Studies
Fuller Theological Seminary
Pasadena, CA

You're at the grocery store with your child, ready to check out at the register. Wide-eyed, she spies her favorite candy, and asks for some. You refuse, but she insists, and is starting to get upset. It's clear you won't be able to keep saying no without a struggle.

What do you do? And more importantly, why?

If we tune in to them, we may notice that multiple and possibly competing goals are passing through our minds. *I don't want to be the bad guy. But I also don't want her to spoil her dinner. I want her to learn to eat things that are good for her. I want her to learn self-control; nobody gets to have everything they want, and money doesn't grow on trees. And I wish she would just enjoy being with me, whether she gets candy or not!* If the situation dissolves into a tantrum, many parents would have another major and immediate goal—*I want this to stop right now, because it's embarrassing me!*

Notice how the goals differ. Some are more immediate and short term, while others are more long term. Moreover, some are about what we want for ourselves. Hastings and Grusec (1998) called these *parent*-centered goals, distinguishing them from *child*-centered goals. Thus, in the preceding example, stopping the tantrum because we don't want to be embarrassed is a *short*-term *parent*-centered goal. Helping our children learn self-control and good eating habits are *long*-term *child*-centered goals.

Beyond what we want for ourselves or our children, however, there are also *relationship*-centered goals (Hastings & Grusec, 1998). For example, we don't want to have a fight every time we go to the grocery store. Negatively stated, that's what we *don't* want to happen. But what *do* we want, positively stated? Perhaps we want to be able to enjoy each other's company at the store—a very different goal than just getting the shopping done. Or we want her to accept our decision because she trusts that we always have her best interests at heart. Pondering relationship-centered goals means reflecting on what we want our relationship to look like, not just in this moment but over the long haul of parenting. What will it take right now, to help us get there?

It's common wisdom in the business world that successful organizations need to have clear and achievable goals, with short-range goals serving long-range ones. These goals are often embodied in the mission and vision statements that guide strategic decisions. Without this kind of intentionality, precious energy and resources are squandered needlessly.

Something similar can be said of families. As therapist Bill Doherty (1997) has recognized, modern life poses many challenges to keeping a family together. We are so busy and fragmented that we can't take family life for granted. If we want our families to be a certain way, we will need to be *intentional,* putting thought and effort into the pursuit of family goals.

To do this, of course, we must first know what our goals are. Long-term goals are particularly important because they embody the larger vision that gives shape and context to shorter term goals. Some parent educators even advocate having a 10-year plan (e.g., Christopherson & Mortweet, 2003)

Here's an example of a relationship goal as part of a long-term vision. In teaching communication skills to parents of younger children, I often ask: "What kind of a relationship do you want to have with your child when they are 15 or 16 years old?" Imagine your teenager in trouble, having made some bad decisions. Wouldn't we want them to come talk to us? Wouldn't we want them to think, "I know I can depend on Mom and Dad. They might get really mad, but they'll listen." If we want that kind of relationship in 10 years, then what are we doing now to build the proper foundation of trust? What are we doing to show them that they can depend on us to love and help them in even the most difficult situations? How we respond in the present is one step toward that future goal.

Here's another example. I have had the privilege of speaking to a large group of parents in a first-generation immigrant church. Raising their children in the United States, with its decidedly more individualistic values, was a confusing challenge. Communication grew more tense as their children got older, went to school, and soaked in more and more of American culture. Part of the difficulty stemmed from the parents' implicit goals: they wanted to keep things the same as they would have been in their home country, where the norms were more collectivistic and hierarchical. They instinctively resisted the idea of "active listening" and similar recommendations.

What I did was to first affirm their values and normalize the struggle of raising kids in a culture different than the one they took for granted growing up. Then I began helping them recast their goals accordingly. Many had come to the seminar asking, "How can I get my children to obey me?" I nudged them toward this goal instead:

"How can I keep a connection with my children as they grow, so I'll still have some influence even when they're teenagers and beyond?"

Long-term child-centered and relationship-centered goals can be particularly helpful in those situations where we are most tempted to overreact emotionally. When our goals are more parent-centered, we're more likely to use power to impose our goals and get our own way. But when we stop to think about what's best for the child or for the relationship, we tend to be more understanding, and rely more on gentler methods of persuasion (Hastings & Grusec, 1998).

This is one facet of what is known as emotional intelligence, which includes the ability to manage our own emotions. When we are upset with our children, stopping to consider our goals, short and long term, helps slow us down and access our higher brain functions. We can be more intentional about what to do next, rather than simply reacting without thinking. And this in turn will help our children learn to do the same, which is itself a valuable long-term and child-centered goal! Indeed, more and more parenting guides are using neuroscience to help parents respond more constructively for the sake of their children's emotional and brain development and long-term success (e.g., Amen & Fay, 2024; Siegel & Bryson, 2011).

Goals can also be shared as a family. Maurice Elias and his colleagues (1999), for example, suggested that families can have *mottos, mission statements*, and *constitutions*. A family motto is a short and memorable phrase that defines a core value of the family: "We are a family who ... cares about others." A mission statement is a somewhat more detailed sentence that helps parents keep their most valued long-term goals in mind. A constitution is a simple set of principles and rules, embodying the motto and mission, usually posted somewhere for all to see and follow—including (especially?) the parents. Making goals explicit and shared in this way helps everyone to commit to a mutual vision of who we are and want to be (Lew & Bettner, 1999).

Researchers have demonstrated that our goals as parents shape how we converse and interact with our children (e.g., Rowe & Casillas, 2011). Thus, it's important to take some time by ourselves, when we're calm, to consider what goals we have as parents. Don't wait until there's a problem with your child to try to figure it out. Think about your goals, write them down, and keep them in mind. What kind of a parent do you want to be? What qualities do you want to help foster in your child? What do you hope for your relationship? Then, when thrust into a situation with your child that provokes an emotional response in you, don't just react. Be an intentional parent. Stop and ask yourself: "What should be my goal?"

Discussion Questions and Activities
1. Think about the last argument you had with one of your children. If you can, write down two or three short-term and long-term goals you may have had in the moment. Decide which ones are parent-centered, which are child-centered, and which are relationship-centered.

2. Evaluate each one. Ask yourself, "Are these the goals I want to have?"

If you haven't come up with any child- or relationship-centered goals, consider constructing some now. Ask yourself, "Looking back on that situation, what would have been good short- and long-term goals to have for my child? What would have been good short- and long-term goals for our relationship?"

Now consider what you could have done differently to serve one or more of these goals, and how you will remind yourself to pursue those goals intentionally next time. Write down whatever you come up with and make it a point to revisit these ideas periodically.

References

Amen, D. G., & Fay, C. (2024). *Raising mentally strong kids.* Tyndale.

Hastings, P. D., & Grusec, J. E. (1998). Parenting goals as organizers of responses to parent–child disagreement. *Developmental Psychology, 34*(3), 465–479. doi:10.1037/0012-1649.34.3.465

Doherty, W. J. (1997). *The intentional family: How to build family ties in our modern world.* Addison-Wesley.

Christopherson, E. R., & Mortweet, S. L. (2003). *Parenting that works.* American Psychological Association.

Elias, M. J., Tobias, S. E., & Friedlander, B. S. (1999). *Emotionally intelligent parenting.* Three Rivers.

Lew, A., & Bettner, B. L. (1999). Establishing a family goal. *The Journal of Individual Psychology, 55*(1), 105–108.

Rowe, M. L., & Casillas, A. (2011). Parental goals and talk with toddlers. *Infant and Child Development, 20*, 475–494. doi:10.1002/icd709

Siegel, D. J., & Bryson, T. P. (2011). *The whole-brain child.* Random House.

Teaching the Right Lesson: What Do Our Kids Learn From Our Behavior?

Cameron Lee, Ph.D., CFLE
Professor of Family Studies
Fuller Theological Seminary
Pasadena, CA

Seven-year-old Adam is lying on his stomach on the living room carpet. His crayons are scattered about him as he happily makes bold red swirls on a piece of paper. As he reaches for the purple crayon, 5-year-old Hannah comes running through the room. She accidentally steps on some of her brother's crayons, breaking them in two. Suddenly, Adam is furious. He flies into a rage at his sister.

You come running at the commotion, just in time to see Adam push Hannah to the floor. Horrified, you immediately cross over to Adam and give him a firm and angry smack on his behind. And with the smack comes the rebuke: "That'll teach you not to hit your sister!"

As parents, we're confronted with questions of discipline when our children misbehave. But discipline is about more than just stopping unwanted behavior. It's about teaching our children values and molding their character. The word *discipline* comes from the same root as the word *disciple* (Bettelheim, 1987). Just by being around us, they are learning from us all the time, even when we aren't consciously trying to teach them anything. What might change if we thought of our children as our disciples?

If we were the parents in the preceding story, we would want Adam to stop hurting his sister. That's the immediate change in behavior we would want. But beyond this, we also want him to learn better ways to deal with his anger, so he can stop *himself* from hurting her in the future. And we want him to do this because he knows it's right, not merely because he's afraid of being punished.

In other words, we don't just want our kids to endure discipline. We want them to develop *self*-discipline. That's part of growing up. We cannot chase them around for the rest of their lives, telling them what to do. Instead, we hope that they will internalize some of our values as their own, not just put up with our rules until they can get out of the house.

Parenting is complicated. We as parents have our own worries and stresses, and this can lead to our being less patient and harsher with our children. But research (e.g., Jackson & Choi, 2018) suggests that harsh parenting can result in *more* behavior problems, not fewer, as well as difficulties adjusting as teens. Punishing Adam, in other words, may make him stop what he is doing, but it will not help him learn the self-control he needs to succeed in life.

In fact, he may be learning an entirely different lesson, one we didn't intend to teach. He may learn that the "normal" way adults handle anger (at least with their kids) is by hitting. Our intended goal may be to teach our child not to hit. But if we do that by hitting, ironically, we might accomplish the opposite.

This doesn't mean we can never show anger as parents. Anger is a natural part of any close relationship. Kids will inevitably do things that make us angry, and we will do things that anger them. The question is what we teach them about how to handle anger from the example we set. How well do we as parents *self-regulate,* that is, constructively handle our own anger and other negative emotions? Contemporary brain-based approaches to parenting (e.g., Siegel & Hartzell, 2013) encourage parents to understand how their own emotional history and relationship to their parents have shaped their own development and their response to their own children in the present. Moreover, as some researchers have suggested, parents' ability to regulate themselves is the key to understanding harsh discipline and its negative effects (e.g., Lunkenheimer et al., 2023).

Thus, we can force Adam to stop hitting his sister—at least when someone is looking—but we cannot stop him from *wanting* to hit. He may learn that hitting brings consequences, but that is different from learning to deal with his anger. And who will teach him that ongoing lesson, if not his parents? If we calm ourselves and then take the time to try to understand what Adam is feeling, we will be better able to help him find other ways to deal with his emotions.

So we can be firm with Adam and set limits on his behavior; he needs to know that pushing and hitting are not OK. If we set those limits calmly, he is more likely to internalize them. More than this, if we want him to learn self-control, he will first need to see that quality in us. We must be good examples of the kind of behavior we expect to see in our children.

The moral of the story is that "Don't do as I do, do as I say" won't get the job done. Discipline is more than punishing bad behavior. We can force children to comply with our demands. But good behavior is not the same thing as good character. What do we really want our children to learn? Discipline is about teaching, in the context of a close relationship with our children. Sometimes, they learn much more than we intended. We must pay close attention to how we discipline if we want to teach the right lesson.

Discussion Questions and Activities

1. Think back to the last time you disciplined your child. Try to recall what your child said or did, and how you responded.

2. What were your emotions in that moment? How might those emotions be related to your experience as a child and to your own parents?

3. What, if anything, did you want your child to learn from your response? Viewing the situation from their perspective, what might they have learned that you did not mean to teach?

4. What do you want to do differently next time, and how can you help ensure that happens?

References

Bettelheim, B. (1987). *A good enough parent.* Knopf.

Jackson, A. P., & Choi, J.-K. (2018). Parenting stress, harsh parenting, and children's behavior. *Journal of Family Medicine and Community Health, 5*(3), Article 1150. https://doi.org/10.47739/2379-0547/1150

Lunkenheimer, E., Sturge-Apple, M. L, & Kelm, M. R. (2023). The importance of parent self-regulation and parent-child co-regulation in research on parental discipline. *Child Development Perspectives, 17*(1), 25–31. https://doi.org/10.1111/cdep.12470

Siegel, D. J., & Hartzell, M. (2013). *Parenting from the inside out* (10th anniversary ed.). Penguin.

Imperfection Is Perfectly Fine

Margaret E. Machara, Ph.D., CFLE
Professor of Human Sciences
Tennessee State University,
Nashville, TN

When I played sports in high school, my coach, probably like many coaches, used to say, "Practice doesn't make perfect, perfect practice makes perfect." In reflection, this idea isn't really very helpful in the ever-changing world in which most families are trying to survive. In fact, parenting is a realm where the game keeps changing. Once you feel confident in being the parent of a toddler—Boom! You now must parent a preschooler; and so on. Therefore, instead of recommending becoming a perfect parent, imperfection is not only tolerable but completely fine. In fact, imperfection will nurture better kids.

First, take care of yourself and stop trying to be the "perfect parent." Daily news recounts stories about neglectful or abusive parents, yet some parents have the opposite problem—they are so attentive, trying to be perfect parents, that they feel guilty for taking care of themselves. Parents need time for themselves and should not feel bad about taking it. When parents focus all their attention on their children, several negative things happen. First, the children start to feel like the center of the universe—not a good belief to encourage—and the children don't learn how to be empathetic to other people's needs. Second, children start internalizing the pressure to be perfect (Elkind, 2001). Instead of getting to be kids, they have the added weight on their shoulders of having to be good for the sake of the family. Third, kids have stressed parents who are not taking good care of themselves (Edwards, 1999). Therefore, consider hiring a babysitter occasionally and go shopping without a stroller or schedule a manicure. Take time to work out at the gym after work or plan a night with friends. But most of all, do these self-care activities without feeling guilty. You can be a better parent if you take time for yourself and don't feel like you need to be a perfect parent.

Taking time for yourself is especially essential during stressful times. Parenting always has some layer of stress by nature, but additional aspects such as parental work stress, situations in other relationships, or even factors in the wider environment create new dynamics. One extreme example of such an overarching phenomenon was the COVID-19 pandemic in 2020. Parental stress compounded stress in their children, especially in families with impaired parent–child functioning (Hu et al., 2024). Other institutional or historical pressures can add yet another dimension to parental pressure. Black families were disproportionally impacted by COVID-19. However, when mental health support was coordinated with daily tasks, it enabled parents to take care of themselves while meeting their other responsibilities (Coates et al., 2023).

In addition to self-care, make mistakes. Since everyone does, give yourself permission to make mistakes without guilt or remorse. Although there have been some good trends in recent generations, parents are losing ground in at least one critical area. Parents have become more involved and responsive to the needs of their children, but some studies have found that parental self-efficacy is lower (Glatz & Buchanan, 2023). Children do not need perfect parents. To develop and thrive, children need loving and consistent care but not perfection (Berk, 2018). Parents tend to feel like they have ruined their children if they lose their temper, break a promise, or make an occasional mistake. Rather than feeling like a failure when you make a mistake, use it as a teachable moment. No child is perfect, so use your mistakes to show them how to recover gracefully. It will not lower you in the eyes of your children to admit that you were wrong and apologize to them. You have just shown them how to take responsibility, apologize to others, and try to make things better. By making mistakes gracefully, you show your child that it is not the mistake but how you handle it that matters.

Therefore, imperfection is perfectly fine. Keep teaching kids that they do not have to be perfect and show them that it is important to take care of themselves. When parents model how to take responsibility for their mistakes, imperfection can even be superior to perfection.

References

Berk, L. (2018). *Development through the lifespan* (7th ed.). Pearson Education, Inc.

Coates, E., Katherine, H., de Heer, R., McLeod, A., Curtis, L., Domitrovich, C., & Biel, M. (2023). "It was good to have an outlet for other parents to talk to": Feasibility and acceptability of integrating mental health and wellness services into predominantly Black early childhood education centers during the COVID-19 pandemic. *Child Psychiatry & Human Development.* Advance online publication. https://doi.org/10.1007/s10578-023-01563-4

Edwards, C. D. (1999). *How to handle a hard-to-handle kid: A parent's guide to understanding and changing problem behaviors.* Free Spirit Publishing, Inc.

Elkind, D. (2001). *The hurried child: Growing up too fast too soon* (3rd ed.). Perseus Publishing.

Glatz, T., & Buchanan, C. (2023). Trends in parental self-efficacy between 1999 and 2014. *Journal of Family Studies, 29*(1), 205–220. https://doi.org/10.1080/13229400.2021.1906929

Hu, Y., Russell, B., Wu, R., Adamson, K., Horton, A., & Tambling, R. (2024). Relationship factors in the longitudinal spillover of stress between parents and children during COVID-19. *Journal of Family Issues.* Advance online publication. https://doi.org/10.1177/0192513X241236559

Discussion Questions and Activities

1. Discuss the following question: Do all groups of parents (i.e., fathers versus mothers, parents of different races/ethnicities or socioeconomic groups) feel the same pressure for perfection in parenting?

2. In pairs or groups, play act a scene where a parent makes a mistake and discusses it with their child as a teachable moment.

3. Make a list of free or low-cost ways parents can practice self-care.

Additional Resources

Fiegel, T. (2017). *Present moment parenting: the guide to a peaceful life with your intense child.* Beaver's Pond Press, Inc.

Kruenegel-Farr, D. (2021). E.N.R.I.C.H. *Your relationship with your child.* Best Publishing by Farr.

Want Smarter Kids? Try a Little Roughhousing

Julie K. Nelson, CFLE, MFHD, SFHEA
Associate Professor in Family Science
Utah Valley University
Orem, UT

One of my favorite childhood memories was a bedtime routine involving a pillow fight. Feathers and laughter filled the air and bonded us. We didn't always entice my dad to join, but when he did, it was magic. There's a special bond created between parents and their children physically playing together in open-ended, active fun. It's quite common to see this in a public swimming pool with parents throwing their kids in the air in a "rocket launch" or swinging them in circles in the "motorboat" chant.

Research positively correlates healthy and appropriate "rough-and-tumble play," or "roughhousing," with several benefits to children. It appears that men do this intuitively (StGeorge et al., 2018). If I'm in a room with adults and a baby appears on the scene, it takes only minutes before that baby turns into pigskin and the men are tossing it around like a quarterback and wide receivers on the 49ers. Moms stand aghast, their eyes and mouths wide open, trying to run interference. What's going on here? Why are we evolutionarily wired to play differently with kids? Is wrestling with kids reserved for just the dads, or should moms participate also? No matter the parental role or gender identification, whoever is the more nurturing parent tends to be more protective and not engaged in rough-and-tumble play. This doesn't need to be so. Actively playing with kids should be shared by both parents because of the unique relationship it fosters. If the household is headed by one parent, the parent can be both nurturer and play-giver.

Self-Reflection: If you grew up in a home with two parents, was one more nurturing and the other more oriented to physical play? If you were raised in a single-parent home, did that parent nurture and play? How can you integrate both nurturing and playing into your role as parent?

The books by DeBenedet and Cohen (2011) and DeBenedet et al. (2023) are great resources for parents who want ideas and benefits from physical play with kids. "Play—especially active physical play, like roughhousing—makes kids smart, emotionally intelligent, lovable and likable, ethical, physically fit, and joyful" (DeBenedet & Cohen, 2011, p. 13). Let's look at each benefit more carefully.

1. Roughhousing fosters smart kids.
This is fascinating: Roughhousing fertilizes our brain. This kind of physical play releases a chemical called brain-derived neurotrophic factor (BDNF), which is like fertilizer for our brains. Roughhousing stimulates neuron growth within the brain's cortex and hippocampus regions, which are responsible for memory, learning, language, and logic. Animal behaviorists have found that the youngsters of the smarter species engage in physical play, so it isn't surprising that roughhousing boosts school performance.

2. Roughhousing builds emotional intelligence.
Roughhousing prepares a child to navigate the emotional adult world successfully by allowing them to practice reading the emotions of others (*"Is he going for my gut? Or is he going to grab me over the head?"*) and manage their own emotions (*"I am not going to hit him in the gut or grab him over the head"*). These skills transition well into reading a boss's mood, knowing how to challenge a coworker, or being able to hang out with the family during the holidays. The unpredictability of rough-and-tumble play prepares children for the unpredictable world and how to pivot, adapt, and regain self-control, which makes them more confident in their emotional lives.

3. Roughhousing correlates with being more likeable.
In research done by Pellegrini (1988), popular children on schoolyard playgrounds had a positive correlation between rough-and-tumble play and social competence. This is

true for four reasons. First, physical play builds friendships and other relationships. Roughhousing can be a declaration of friendship or affection when it's harder to come out and say, "I like you. Let's be friends." Second, kids who roughhouse can distinguish between innocent play and aggression; therefore, it helps children develop social and problem-solving skills. Third, youngsters who physically play learn how to take turns. If they are playing right, each person will get a chance to chase and to be chased. No one person should be "it" the entire time. Finally, roughhousing teaches kids the concept of leadership and negotiation. Think about the rules that go into physical games. Everyone needs to agree on the rules before the game starts, which is wonderful preparation for professional success as well as committed relationships.

4. Roughhousing provides opportunities for children to practice ethical and moral behavior.

Animals with the highest level of moral development also engage in the most play. One way we can measure moral behavior in animal play is by observing "self-handicapping." This occurs when the stronger animal holds back her strength, such as a lioness with her cubs, when playing with a weaker or smaller opponent. Humans do this too, and especially parents, when physically engaging with their children. Parents regulate the appropriate kinds of healthy play that become a framework for life. For example, they don't allow someone to pin their opponent to the ground until they cry "Uncle!" or tickle them mercilessly. Rather, they model roughhousing as a mutually satisfying, win–win activity. When the child crosses the line, the parent pulls them back and warns them to stay within the emotional and physical safety zone. DeBenedet and Cohen (2011) wrote:

> When we roughhouse with our kids, we model for them how someone bigger and stronger holds back. We teach them self-control, fairness, and empathy. We let them win, which gives them confidence and demonstrates that winning isn't everything. We show them how much can be accomplished by cooperation and how to constructively channel competitive energy so that it doesn't take over. (p. 21)

5. Roughhousing makes kids physically fit.

This one is obvious. However, physical fitness isn't just about body strength; it involves complex motor learning, concentration, coordination, body control, cardiovascular fitness, and flexibility. Free play offers different benefits from organized sports. The latter is adult controlled; the former is child-centered. Children need both the gym class and the playground for a well-rounded, physically healthy development.

6. Roughhousing brings joy.

According to studies in neuroscience, when the play circuits in the brains of mammals are activated, they feel joy. As a species, humans are hardwired for playful roughhousing, so the body and mind are happy when we engage in this activity. Adrenaline released through active play causes the heart to beat faster, pupils to dilate, air increase to the lungs, and emotions such as happiness and excitement to surge. When roughhousing is combined with laughter and positive touch, oxytocin, also known as the "cuddle hormone," is released. This should signal to parents that hugs and cuddles are a good way to end the play period and calm the child down.

Rough-and-tumble play is good not only for kids and the parent–child relationship, but also for adults. Parents can be so enmeshed in the role of caregiver and protector that they forget to play. When my dad softened his "Get to bed!" face and let down his guard, he became one of us in a pack of playful puppies. When I play as a parent, I revive my inner child and get in touch with the pure joy that is so instinctive for children.

Discussion Questions and Activities

1. Think for a minute of when you wrestled, chased, or had a pillow fight with one of your parents. Jot down a few of your favorite memories. Describe how you felt at that moment. If you didn't do this kind of play, when did you see other parents actively playing with their kids? What did you see in their relationship through that activity?

2. Are you ready to get outside your comfort zone and play like a child and with a child? What daily rituals, such as bedtime or after dinner, lend themselves to some active play? Look for additional opportunities for spontaneous play. When your children are playing on the playground or in a park, rather than sitting on the bench scrolling your news feed, consider the invitation to join. You may be surprised at how different—even joyful—you'll feel.

References

DeBenedet, A. T., & Cohen, L. J. (2011). *The art of roughhousing: Good old fashioned horseplay and why every kid needs it.* Hardie Grant.

DeBenedet, A. T., Cohen, L. J., & Tognola, M. (2023). *Unplug and play: The ultimate illustrated guide to roughhousing with your kids.* Quirk Books.

Pellegrini, A. D. (1988). Elementary-school children's rough-and-tumble play and social competence. *Developmental Psychology, 24*(6), 802–806. https://doi.org/10.1037/0012-1649.24.6.802

StGeorge, J. M., Goodwin, J. C. & Fletcher, R. J. (2018). Parents' views of father–child rough-and-tumble play. *Journal of Child and Family Studies, 27*, 1502–1512. https://doi.org/10.1007/s10826-017-0993-0

Why Kids Lie: How to Teach Children Truthfulness and Respond to Lies Helpfully

Jody Johnston Pawel, LSW, CFLE, CTSS, CEO
Relationship Toolshop® International Training Institute, LLC
Springboro, OH

Lying can be a *big* trigger button for many parents. Parents want honest children, but sometimes unintentionally model dishonesty or react in unhelpful ways to children's lies. As science discovers more about brain development and subconscious processes, it's revealing new perspectives on why children might tell lies. Here's a summary with practical tips for preventing and responding to lies.

What Is a Lie?
When asked to define a lie, most parents start with "a false statement." Some add what dictionaries say: "made with a *deliberate intent* to deceive." Others include passive forms of lying, such as not telling the whole truth or omitting information.

The medial anterior prefrontal cortex manages "reality monitoring" and it does so on an individual basis. Remembering an event can cause the same reaction as experiencing it. This creates the individual lens through which a person interprets what's real and true (Buda et al., 2011).

The prefrontal cortex manages spontaneous lies triggered by fear. When children are afraid due to past trauma, it can trigger fear in the present. Children's development influences self-regulation, executive functioning, perceptions, and behavior, like lying. When chronic stress becomes toxic, it has similar effects as trauma (Harvard Center for the Developing Child, n.d.). The symptoms often present as mental health issues and problematic behavior—like lying.

A LIE *MUST* INCLUDE ALL the of the following factors:
A lie is a FALSE statement a person KNOWS IS UNTRUE and is told with the INTENT TO DECEIVE.

So, it's not a lie to make a false statement if you believe it's true, accidentally give incorrect information, or believe a lie someone tells you and repeat it. Those are unintentional.

If a child makes untrue statements due to a medical condition that affects their perceptions or behavior, like trauma, it's not a lie but is a problematic behavior that needs exploration.

"White lies," lies told to spare others' feelings, many excuses, and fictional stories like the Tooth Fairy and Santa Claus are all lies, although some think they are "okay" to tell.

When Do Children Understand Lying?
Children learn to lie. First, they must understand social rules and consequences, which can vary among families and settings like home and school. They also must be able to imagine what others are thinking, which is a function the brain does not develop until after age 6.

According to Ekman (1991), there are five developmental stages of understanding truthfulness and lying:

1. By age 4, to get their way, get rewards, and avoid punishment.
2. By age 5 or 6, to please adults.
3. Around ages 6 to 8, based on what's in it for them.
4. Around ages 8 to 12, so others will think well of them.
5. Children aged 12 and older are either honest to be good citizens or lie out of habit.

Two age periods are especially important: around age 3 or 4 when children can tell a deliberate lie and in adolescence because teens can understand that lying destroys trust. Not everyone reaches the last stage, and many adults never go beyond Stage 3.

Preventing Lies
Preventing lies is a continual process of catching and creating "teachable moments." (Pawel, 2000)
- Teach truthfulness consistently, not only after a lie.
- Teach the value of truthfulness by pointing out the benefits.
- Handle mistakes calmly.

- Question children in ways that encourage them to be truthful, rather than trying to trap them in a lie.
- Reassure children that you won't be as angry if they tell the truth.
- Acknowledge the difficulty of telling the truth and the courage it takes.
- Avoid punishing children, which imposes suffering. Help them learn from the situation in ways that feel safe and supportive. If they feel threatened, they are more likely to lie.

Are We *Really* Good Role Models?

It's hard to preach honesty to children when misinformation surrounds them and they see adults, including public leaders, being openly and even proudly dishonest. Children absorb these unspoken lessons and notice hypocrisy, so let's practice what we preach.

Research shows that children who lie most often have parents who frequently lie. We need to tell the truth even when it's inconvenient or makes us "look bad." Find ways to be honest *and* tactful. Be honest when getting incorrect change, stopped for speeding, or getting discounts based on children's ages, for example.

Also avoid using lies to get children to behave, like saying you'll leave them in a store if they don't come right away. Scaring children might work in the short term but breeds insecurity and can be traumatizing.

Be selective when sharing information about adult issues or upsetting events that could be traumatizing. Only tell children truths they can developmentally understand and handle *now, if* they ask or *need* to know. Then tell them more later if they ask. You aren't lying if your intent is to protect the child and what you say is true.

Truth or Consequences?

Even if you do all the above, most children lie at some point. How you respond can determine whether the child continues lying.

IF it *is* a lie, there is not one perfect response, but you can **follow this three-step formula** (Pawel, 2000):

1. **Identify the goal of the lie.** While there are infinite reasons why children lie, each reason will fit one of Rudolf Dreikurs's "Four Goals of Misbehavior" (Dreikurs & Stoltz, 1964; see also https://parentstoolshop.com/children-misbehavior/):

    a. For **Attention**, such as telling a whopper of a story or to get a laugh.

    b. For **Power**, to see if they can dupe others or to get something forbidden.

    c. For **Revenge**, because they feel they were lied to.

    d. As a **Display of Inadequacy.** They've given up on telling the truth because no one believes them anyway.

2. **Teach children how to meet that goal without lying.**

3. **Tell children that if they lie, they will be in "double trouble."**

    a. One discipline is for the actual offense.

    b. The other is for lying, and it relates to the breakdown in trust.

For example, if children ride their bikes beyond the allowed boundaries, they might lose their bike privileges for a short time. When reinstated, the parent may double-check that the children are where they said they'd be.

When you understand what lying is and why children might lie, you can prevent and respond to lies in ways that encourage truthfulness. By teaching truthfulness not only in words but by your deeds, you can raise children who are honest, moral, truthful, tactful, and trustworthy.

Discussion Questions and Activities

1. What is a lie?

2. How might others define or perceive lying differently if they have different life experiences than you?

3. Is it ever okay to lie? If so, when?

4. After teaching the 3-step response formula, apply it to examples, focusing on whether the child is really lying and, if so, why and how to respond. Notice how the answers are unique to each situation and child, yet you can apply the formula to each one.

Resources

For more than 30 years, I've trained thousands of parents through hundreds of workshops (from 1 to 6 hours) on this subject. Here are some recordings:

- A 1-hour recorded webinar with a certificate: https://parentstoolshop.com/lying

- A 1-hour audio of a lively discussion among parents and professionals on thought-provoking questions. https://parentstoolshop.com/lying-tele

- A 2-hour video of a live trauma-informed training for foster-adoptive parents. Certificate available. https://parentstoolshop.com/fapt-lying

References

Buda, M., Fornito, A., Bergstrom, Z. M., & Simons, J. S. (2011). A specific brain structural basis for individual differences in reality monitoring. *Journal of Neuroscience, 31*(40), 14308–14313. https://doi.org/10.1523/jneurosci.3595-11.2011

Dreikurs, R., & Stoltz, V. (1964). *Children: The challenge.* E.P. Dutton.

Ekman, P. (1991). *Why kids lie: How parents can encourage truthfulness.* Penguin Books. (See the updated teachings at https://www.paulekman.com/deception/children-lying/)

Harvard Center for the Developing Child. (n.d.). *What are ACEs and how do they relate to toxic stress?* https://developingchild.harvard.edu/resources/aces-and-toxic-stress-frequently-asked-questions/

Pawel, J. J. (2020). *The Parents Toolshop: The universal blueprint for building a healthy family.* Ambris Publishing.

Stop the Sibling Self Comparison

Elizabeth A. Ramsey, Ph.D., CFLE
Assistant Professor
Tennessee Technological University, Human Ecology
Cookeville, TN

The virtue of competence can be built by providing children an opportunity to excel at various activities that help them build a sense of industry. According to Erik Erikson's psychosocial theory of development (Erikson, 1963; Martorell, 2023), school-age children, aged 7 to 11 years, need opportunities to be industrious, which is the feeling of being productive and contributing members of society. Otherwise, if children don't achieve that sense of industry, a feeling of inferiority can develop. During this stage of development, children will naturally compare themselves to their same-aged peers and evaluate their own abilities. It is so important that parents help build a sense of industry by ensuring that they have positive experiences in which they can see themselves as successful and contributing members of the family and society.

When our four children were school age, they were involved in several activities, including different types of sports, dance classes, music lessons, and theater. For the most part, the children's interests varied, but on occasions, their interests overlapped with their siblings. I noticed an unhealthy tendency of one of our younger daughters to compare herself to her older sister, who was 4 years her senior. In particular, she compared herself in playing the piano. She was beginning to express a feeling of inferiority because she was looking at the older sister and comparing herself to big sister's piano abilities. She was saying things like she wasn't good at piano or that her older sister was better at it. In fact, she got to a point where she was feeling very defeated and not sure that she wanted to continue playing.

Thankfully, she expressed her feelings, and I was able to talk to her about them. Little sister was a very gifted musician, and she was picking up the piano at an extraordinary rate. Yet big sister was better than her at playing the piano; but do you know why? She was an entire 4 years older than little sister, and she had been playing and practicing the piano for a much longer time. I remember the day that I explained all this to the little sister. I told her how wonderful she was at playing the piano and that she was younger and had only been playing for a few years. I explained that when big sister was her age, she was playing the piano just like her. I told her that she could not judge herself or compare herself to big sister because she has had piano lessons 4 years longer than her. It was not a fair comparison.

Siblings will compare themselves to each other, and many times, younger siblings will feel like they don't measure up to older siblings. Here's the secret: They aren't supposed to. Considering their age and stage of development, they are thriving. Encourage them where they are, and recognize their gains, just as much as you recognize those older children's gains.

Discussion Questions
1. Discuss how parents can build the virtue of competence in school-age children.

2. From your own childhood, discuss something that helped you feel competent, or perhaps something that made you feel that you lacked competency.

3. Do you think this approach to parenting could help prevent sibling rivalry. If so, why or why not?

References

Erikson, E. H. (1963). *Childhood and society.* W.W. Norton & Co.

Martorell, G. (2023). *Child* (3rd ed.). McGraw-Hill.

The "Mom, I Need You" Touch

Elizabeth A. Ramsey, Ph.D., CFLE
Assistant Professor
Tennessee Technological University, Human Ecology
Cookeville, TN

When my kids were young my husband and I worked in ministry—he was senior pastor of our church, while I worked as Director of Outreach, Children's and Women's ministry. Most people don't take their children to work with them, but in ministry, children are often present while parents are working. I found this especially challenging as a young mother because my husband was often out of reach on Sunday mornings due to his demands from the pending service. Parenting on Sunday morning often fell squarely on my shoulders because of his teaching schedule.

I knew that our children needed me—they needed me to take interest in what they learned in their class, the friends they played with, and how their morning went. Yet I had a steady flow of people approaching me before and after service with problems or concerns; all those people needed my help and attention too. This presented unique challenges for me as well as our four children. Many times, I felt pulled in different directions. Early on, I noticed that my children interrupted my conversations frequently; they would come out of their children's program with things they wanted to share with me or with various needs. I also noticed that some congregants had very little patience with my children's interruptions, making it even more challenging for me.

I began sensing my children's frustration and knew that I needed to do something. So, I got an idea. I taught my kids that when they needed me, instead of interrupting me, I asked them to put their hand on me. I explained to them that when I felt their hand, I would respond because they are important to me and their needs mattered to me. I told them that when I felt their hand, I would help them as soon as I could.

So, we started the "Mom, I need you" touch. I remember talking with people and feeling a little hand on my leg. Sometimes, I would be sitting with congregants praying, and I would feel a touch on my shoulder. As soon as I felt their hand on me, I would gently lay my hand over theirs. We didn't need to say a word to each other because they knew they mattered, their turn to talk to me was coming, and I was going to respond. As soon as I could, I would look at the person I was talking to and say,

"Excuse me, please, my child needs me." I would then bend down on my child's level, look them in the eye, smile, and ask what they needed. It was typically something easy and fixable in the moment. However, every now and then it was a big enough issue that I might need to excuse myself altogether from the congregant and tend to my child, because after all, they needed to know that above all else, I was their mom and that they were most important to me.

People matter—we loved our church family, but at the end of the day, it was important that my children knew they came first. When my kids needed me, all they had to do was to touch me, and I would respond. Every now and then, I feel a big hand on my shoulder from one of my emerging adult children, and I know I'm needed. It is my joy to stop and listen with love.

Discussion Questions and Activities

1. Describe another scenario where the "Mom, I need you" touch might be implemented.

2. Discuss examples like this that you have seen illustrated in other parents or your own life.

3. Besides learning that they matter, what else are children learning when using an approach like this?

Life Lessons From the Pandemic: Children Are as Parents Do

Jim R. Rogers, M.Ed., CFLE Emeritus
still learning, inc.

The worry list is long and complex. As we continue to recover from years of the pandemic attack on our lives, our days are still filled with concerns that can impact our well-being in many ways. With unsettling and controversial governments and social conditions, foreign wars, domestic instability, and much more, our challenges loom bigger and harder, with potential feelings of futility and hopelessness knocking on our psyche. There is magnified grief from a deep sense of loss—of lives both personally and globally—and opportunities have disappeared for many.

And yet, we as a country of decent, caring, and concerned peoples are making valiant efforts to move on, believing that the days ahead will be better. Smart people are making plans to lead us toward those better days. But all of us must be smart and not hurry toward a desire for our "normal," whatever that might be, before it is time, before it is safe. Patience is still needed, as is understanding of the issues that will only grow more complex and more difficult to keep untangled.

Some families say they are not sure they want to return to "what was" prior to the pandemic. Mothers, fathers, and their children liked living closely in the family. Many felt being with each other encouraged them to find common ties, using more patience and understanding because days were less hectic due to schedules being realistically simple.

Of course, there are many who did not feel this way and could not wait to get back to work outside the home, reestablishing chaotic and even unhealthy lives. If you wonder about what you might do, ask yourself, what do I really miss? What would you like to keep that was learned from the isolation? Change? Why not, if it adds more meaning to our lives.

What a great learning opportunity for all the partners raising our children to demonstrate concern, kindness, and just being human. All parents in the community can encourage family members to be aware of others, their concerns and practices, respecting their rights to make decisions that are best for them. It is a challenging time for human beings to test their true humanness. How should we feel about our fellow humans?

Anthropologist Margaret Mead offered this incredible definition as to who we can be. Mead said that the first sign of civilization in an ancient culture was a femur (thighbone) that had been broken and then healed. She explained that in the animal kingdom, a broken leg means you die. You cannot run from danger, get to the river for a drink, or hunt for food. You are meat for prowling beasts. No animal survives a broken leg long enough for the bone to heal.

A healed broken femur is evidence that someone had taken time to stay with the one who fell, had bound up the wound, had carried the person to safety, and had tended the person through recovery. Helping someone else through difficulty is where civilization starts, Mead said.

We are at our best when we serve others. This is the lesson I hope our parenting community is giving our next generations. Caring about others—what better way to heal!

A major concern is the health of our children, some suffering in ways that even they may not know, and more importantly, that the parents may not know. Mental health is a rising issue for our youth, especially since they may not understand that what may seem overwhelming is not a permanent state of being. They have a future with promise and potential success, and they need wise and loving people to help them see that truth—parents, who must stop, look, and listen.

There is no perfect parenting. Even the best parents can have moments when everything comes crashing down, and they lose their temper. We are human, and there are limits. Self-blame will not help, but knowing what to do after the crash might. Try apologies for losing it, making sure children do not think it is about them, and have a discussion of what could have gone differently.

Parents, what kind of adult do you want your children to become? During these post-covid times, with many pushes and pulls and challenges still surrounding us, it is critical that parents work even harder to make sure their children are not experiencing damage that will haunt them for a lifetime. According to social learning theory, children are copycats, so to speak. They emulate behaviors they see around them; adults often behave in ways that they do not want to teach their children. Parents perform their critical roles more effectively when they discuss what they see around them. Unacceptable behaviors must be pointed out, named, and explained, making sure children know the difference between peaceful disagreement conducted through respectful exchanges and overt, planned acts of senseless violence. We adults are modeling the behaviors we want children to have. So, what do we want? What kind of memories are we creating for them?

Following is some great advice I'll share with you, recommended by *Dr. Neha Chaudhary*, child, adolescent, and adult psychiatrist at Massachusetts General Hospital and Harvard Medical School. Her advice is some of the best.

1. Create the space to ask questions. The first step in opening a dialogue is creating a safe space, remaining calm and nonjudgmental, and approaching the conversation with your ears and heart wide open.

2. Limit media/screen time based on age. Shield your children and do not expose them to inappropriate content. By setting media/screen time limits, you can avoid a flood of information that may overwhelm your child.

3. Reassure your children that they are safe. Assuring them that they are safe and you will keep them safe should be a priority. When stress and fear are high, emotions cloud judgment, cognition, and rational thinking.

4. Be open and honest.

5. Talk about bad actions, not bad people. Labeling people as "bad" or "good" can be confusing. But naming bad actions or behaviors can highlight what you do not condone without frustrating your child.

6. Highlight the helpers and any positives. Look for good helpers. Spotlighting them can instill hope for your children and encourage them to become involved.

7. Help children name their feelings. *You* are not stressed, *you* are *feeling* stressed.

8. Parents keep their own feelings in check. Be real, yet stable. This helps parents teach emotional literacy—the ability to recognize, read, and name your emotions.

9. Create good coping skills. When children see parents in distress, it is scary, no matter how old they are. Manage your feelings and emotions so that children will learn to manage theirs.

10. Use these suggestions as a foundation for future and continuing discussion. We can use breaking news as a springboard from which to have conversations on tough topics, including observing how they are handling their concerns and what you notice about their usual behaviors.

Stay well and engaged. Model the behaviors you want to see. Children are as parents do!

Empowering Children

Dorothea M. Rogers, D.Min., LMFT, CFLE

A common definition of power is the ability to influence another person. "Most research on the use of power in the family has focused on a person's attempting to influence or control the behavior of another" (Balswick et al., 2021, p. 15). Empowering, on the other hand, attempts to establish power in someone else: "empowering is an active, intentional process of helping another person to become empowered. The person who is empowered has been equipped, strengthened, built up, matured, and has gained skills because of the encouraging support of the other" (Balswick et al., 2021, p. 15). This occurs by giving someone a growing sense of self-control and the ability to determine their own future.

Cloud and Townsend (2017) asserted, "Children need to have a sense of control and choice in their lives (p. 182). Choices empower children. Parents can help their children find options, yet children should not be overwhelmed with more choices than they can handle. When children can make choices, they learn to feel secure and more in control. "Learning to make age-appropriate decisions helps children have a sense of security and control in their lives" (Cloud and Townsend, p. 182). Additionally, empowering children will help them be aware of their strengths and how best to use these strengths. The affirmation of children through empowerment gives them the ability to learn, grow, and become all that they can be. There are several ways in which parents can help empower their children:

- Showing children love, concern, and respect at all times.
- Giving children choices when possible, such as deciding between different outfits for school or selecting menu items for a family meal.
- Having rules that are understood and allowing children to be part of the rule-making process. If consequences are involved, children can help determine what might be the most effective deterrents for them.
- Helping children express their feelings and listening to them with undivided attention.
- Being a good role model in actions and speech. Realize that children often imitate their parents' behavior, regardless of all efforts to teach them good manners!

Parents have the awesome responsibility of raising their children to become all that they can be. Steps can be taken to aid parents as they endeavor to affirm their children's journey through childhood by empowering and encouraging them to make the best decisions. Henry Ward Beecher (1868) summed up admirable parenthood as follows: "Whoever makes a home seem to the young [to be] dearer and more happy, is a public benefactor" (p. 215). The greatest reward to parents and children comes when those who have been empowered go on to empower others.

Discussion Questions & Activities

1. Demonstrate knowledge to your child. Think about experiences when you were growing up. Share some choices you made—choices with both positive and negative outcomes—with your child.

2. Repetition promotes and advances learning. Make it a regular practice to encourage your child to make easy choices and thought-provoking choices. What are some ways you can include this in your daily lives with your children?

3. What are ways you can include your child in making decisions?

References

Balswick, J. O., & Balswick, J. K., Frederick, T. V. (2021). *The family: A Christian perspective on the contemporary home.* Baker Publishing Group.

Beecher, H. W. (1868). *Village life in New England.* Charles Scribner.

Cloud, H., & Townsend, J. (2017). *Boundaries.* Zonderevan.

Giving Children S.M.A.R.T. Choices

Hilary A. Rose, Ph.D., CFLE—Retired
Freelance Writer, Montreal, Canada

"Would you like to go inside and have lunch now?," I recently heard a well-meaning parent ask her 5-year-old child, effectively giving the child the choice of going inside to eat or not. Lunch (or any meal) is not really a choice, because eating (having a bath, brushing teeth, etc.) is not optional for growing children. Parents often ask questions such as "Do you want to …" or "Would you like to …" when the parent's goal is clearly for the child to do what is being asked (comply or cooperate). Offering a choice in such cases is illogical and confusing for children. After all, how should the parent respond if the child says, "No, I don't want to eat lunch"? Now the parent is in an awkward position because they gave the child a choice in a situation that really wasn't optional.

Sometimes we give young children confusing or too many choices—choices that can be overwhelming and inappropriate (Rimm, 1997). For example, recent research shows that children, like adults, find that choosing from among many options is cognitively demanding (Maimaran, 2017). Using an experimental design, this researcher presented children with large and small sets of items to choose from (e.g., books, games, snacks), and in each case, the children (average age 5 years) found that choosing from larger sets of options was more difficult than choosing from smaller sets of options. The researcher concluded that limiting choices to a few options is probably best for young children.

In addition, if children are offered choices, they should be minor choices that do not change the overall outcome. "Do you want your sandwich cut in halves or in quarters?" is a reasonable choice for a preschooler. For older children, of course, the choice should be more age-appropriate (Brazelton & Greenspan, 2000), such as the choice between a tuna or egg filling for a sandwich. It is important that parents retain control and responsibility for the outcome of the decision, while structuring or scaffolding (Shvarts & Bakker, 2019; Vygotsky, 1934) the child's choices so that the child ultimately learns to make good choices on her or his own.

Remember the 5-year-old who was asked about going inside to eat lunch; on this occasion, the 5-year-old didn't respond to his parents—and maybe not because he was being difficult. I think he didn't respond because the question itself is a difficult one. Here's what that 5-year-old may have been thinking: "I'm having lots of fun now, so why would I want to stop? But I'm hungry, too, and I want to eat. How can I stay outside and play, and go inside to eat at the same time? This is confusing. I can't answer this question." And so, as often happens, the 5-year-old says nothing, or whines, or says "No." Sometimes children don't comply with parents' expectations not because they are being uncooperative but because they are confused or feel unable to meet those expectations (Brazelton & Greenspan, 2000).

We sometimes think that we are doing our children a favor by giving them choices. But children, especially if they are young, tired, or hungry, can find choices overwhelming (Maimaran, 2017; Rimm, 1997). Young children are not cognitively or emotionally mature enough to make complex choices. We are not doing young children a favor by giving them such choices; we are doing them a disservice. Think about a choice as a decision that must be made. Good decisions require the ability to think logically, to consider alternatives, and to anticipate outcomes, and even adults defer making decisions that are too demanding (Maimaran, 2017). These cognitions, or thinking abilities, develop over time and with age (Inhelder & Piaget, 1958), and it is not realistic to expect that a young child like a preschooler is capable of complex thought processes.

Finally, we should think about the messages we are sending children when we give them choices: "You have the power to choose; I am deferring my authority to you" (Rimm, 1997). While these messages may be appropriate in some circumstances for older adolescents and young adults, they are often inappropriate for young children—unless the outcome of the choice is inconsequential, or it simply doesn't matter: "Which bedtime story do you want me to read to you tonight?" We should also remember that once the child is in a classroom with 30 other children, there will be fewer opportunities to make individual choices. Children who grow up with the expectation that they always get choices may be in for a shock when they hit the "real world" of public school.

Parents are legally and morally responsible for their children (Matthiesen, Wickert, & Lehrer, S.C., Attorneys at Law, 2022), and as such they need to maintain parental authority until children are developmentally ready to assume responsibility for themselves and their decisions. In each situation, parents need to ask themselves what their goal is. Is it important that children behave in a certain way (clean up their toys, go to sleep)? If so, without being harsh or coercive, make a *statement* to that effect: "It's time for you to do such-and-such now." If children's reactions are not that important (or even optional), then parents can ask a question: "Do you want to go to the park now?" Again, if the goal is children's compliance or cooperation, use a statement. Otherwise, parents can ask a question (make a request, offer a choice).

In conclusion, S.M.A.R.T. choices for children are as follows:

Simple, not complex. Especially with young children, we need to structure the choices we offer so that the actual choosing is made easy for the child. Otherwise, the child can become overwhelmed and frustrated. The choice should be between two equal or comparable alternatives. Three or four carrots? Green or blue pants? Jam or jelly?

Minor and inconsequential. Choices, by definition, are optional. At the same time, children need to learn that some things in life are not optional—like going to bed on time. If we ask, "Do you want to go to bed now?" we are implying that the child has a choice in the matter. Make sure that the choices you offer are truly optional, and that the outcomes of those choices are minor.

Age-appropriate. Regardless of how intelligent young children may be, they are still immature—cognitively and emotionally. Choices that are too complex are a burden, not a favor. Help your child learn how to make good choices by structuring or scaffolding them with the child's age in mind. As children get older, choices can and should get more complex or demanding.

Rare, not frequent. Having too many choices can be overwhelming and can lead to poor decision-making. Having choices all the time also sends the message that choices are an everyday right, not a once-in-a-while treat. Expecting to have choices about everything all the time is unrealistic, especially as children head off to school.

Thoughtful. Parents get tired and hungry, too. When we do, we often react automatically by giving children orders (telling them what to do) or choices (asking them what they want to do). Take the time to think about the implications of giving choices to children. Act thoughtfully instead of reacting automatically or emotionally.

As parents, we should think about the choices we give our children. Remember to consider what your goal is in each situation. Is your goal to get the child to comply? Use a statement. If it doesn't matter what the child chooses (ballet or art class; soccer or guitar lessons), ask a question, and give the child some input. Of course, if you give a child or adolescent a choice, you will have to respect their answer! Ultimately, as our children grow older, they will have to make many choices in life, often when we are not around to assist them. We can help them learn to make good choices by structuring the choices that we give them when they are young.

Discussion Questions
1. Discuss some potential problems that might occur when offering too many choices to children.
2. When offering choices to children, what are considered best practices?
3. Give an example of an age-appropriate choice for a 3-year-old.

References

Brazelton, T. B., & Greenspan, S. I. (2000). *The irreducible needs of children: What every child must have to grow, learn, and flourish.* Perseus.

Inhelder, B., & Piaget, J. (1958). *The growth of logical thinking from childhood to adolescence.* Basic Books.

Maimaran, M. (2017). To increase engagement, offer less: The effect of assortment size on children's engagement. *Judgment and Decision Making, 12*(3), 198–207.

Matthiesen, Wickert, & Lehrer, S.C., Attorneys at Law [Service Corporation]. (2022, January 13). *Parental responsibility laws in all 50 states* [chart]. https://www.mwl-law.com/wp-content/uploads/2018/02/PARENTAL-RESPONSIBILITY-LAWS-CHART.pdf

Rimm, S. B. (1997). *How to parent so children will learn: Clear strategies for raising happy, achieving children.* Three Rivers Press.

Shvarts, A., & Bakker, A. (2019). The early history of the scaffolding metaphor: Bernstein, Luria, Vygotsky, and before. *Mind, Culture, and Activity, 26*(1), 4–23.

Vygotsky, L. S. (1934). *Thought and language.* MIT Press.

Improving the T.E.N.O.R. of Interactions Using Logical Consequences

Hilary A. Rose, Ph.D., CFLE—Retired
Freelance Writer, Montreal, Canada

A new stepmother was telling me how frustrated she was trying to get her young stepdaughters (ages 5 and 7 years) ready to go to their summertime swimming lessons. As their new stepmother, she hated nagging them, and she hated yelling at them, but that's what she ended up doing to get the children ready on time. I suggested to her that she simply stop nagging and yelling. I encouraged her to state quietly, but firmly, that she was going to leave the house to go to the swimming pool at 8:30 a.m., and that they were coming with her, "ready or not." She asked me, "But what if they haven't gotten dressed yet?"

"Well, they go to the pool in their pajamas. They are changing into their bathing suits at the pool anyway." Then I added, "I bet they'll only show up at the pool in their pajamas once." A week later, my friend happily reported that her stepdaughters had indeed arrived at the pool in their pajamas just once. After that one occasion, they were always ready on time—and there was no need for any nagging or yelling. The girls learned that when they weren't ready on time (action), they would go to the pool in their pajamas (consequence). They also learned that by changing their action (getting ready on time), they could avoid the consequence of showing up in their pajamas. Best of all, they learned this lesson on their own—without any yelling or nagging.

An important life lesson for all of us is the cause-and-effect relationship between actions and consequences: in particular, when children behave in certain ways, certain things follow (Dreikurs & Soltz, 1964). In a national survey, 92% of parents agreed that it is important to teach children to take responsibility for their actions (Bibby, 2006). What is the best way to accomplish this goal? Many child psychologists and parent educators agree that the best way to teach children to take responsibility for their actions is by letting them experience the consequences of their actions (Dreikurs & Soltz, 1964; McKay & Dinkmeyer, 1996; Ryan & Deci, 2017). Learning the association between actions and consequences is the primary way we learn to take responsibility for our actions. As a bonus, allowing consequences to be the "bad guy" means parents can avoid the nagging, pleading, yelling, cajoling, or preaching that often comes with being the disciplinarian (Runkel, 2008).

Some parents, however, seem to want to "protect" their child from life's lessons (Dreikurs & Soltz, 1964; Runkel, 2008). Recently I heard about a teenage boy who was late catching the bus for a school field trip. His father, who had driven the boy to school, decided to follow the school bus for 1.5 hours on the freeway to get to the site of the field trip. Was the father angry at his son for the inconvenience of spending 3 hours (there and back) driving on the freeway? No—the father took his anger out on the teacher and the poor bus driver! According to the father, they should have waited for his son. By blaming others, and by not letting his son experience the consequences of being late (missing the field trip), the father robbed his son of an opportunity to learn to take responsibility for his actions.

Consequences are not a form of punishment (Dreikurs & Soltz, 1964; Ryan & Deci, 2017). Parents sometimes use random or arbitrary punishment to deter children's negative behavior. Consequences, on the other hand, are obvious outcomes or direct results of the child's behavior. If a child is late for dinner, the food may be cold—or all gone. In some cases (when safety or health is an issue), it may not be practical to let the child experience natural consequences. In such cases, parents can use a logical consequence—an outcome logically determined by the parent (or even by the child). If a child is late for dinner, the natural consequence would be that the child gets no dinner; a logical consequence might be that the child reheats his dinner in the microwave (and cleans up, too).

A recent book recommended that, to reduce resistance and promote cooperation, parents should discuss rule-breaking or misbehavior with their children in a supportive rather than a controlling way (Ryan & Deci, 2017). As an example of a supportive approach, logical consequences focus on problem-solving (often with the child's active participation) rather than punishment: "How can you get your homework done in time for you to watch some TV before bed?" As well, logical consequences are more effective in terms of fostering children's compliance or cooperation in the short term and helping children to internalize rules and expectations for behavior in the long term.

A Canadian study used an experimental design to explore children's reactions to logical consequences compared to mild (nonphysical) aversive punishments (Robichaud et al., 2020). In this study, children between the ages of 9 and 12 believed that logical consequences would elicit less anger ("If my mother acted this way, I would be angry …") and more empathy ("If my mother acted this way, I would understand why …") compared with mild aversive punishments. In another study involving adolescents, parents' use of logical consequences predicted compliance, whereas the use of mild aversive punishments did not (Robichaud et al., 2024). In other words, logical consequences work better.

In conclusion, think about the T.E.N.O.R. of your interactions with your children. Effective consequences are as follows:

Thoughtfully chosen. Avoid natural consequences if they are unsafe or unhealthy. In cases where safety or health is an issue, use logical consequences instead. What if a child misses the school bus? If it is unsafe to walk (natural consequence), the child could use allowance money for the gas for the car ride to school (logical consequence).

Experienced by the child. For learning to take place, children must experience personally the consequences of their actions. Sometimes parents want to protect their children from life's lessons, but parents can't protect children forever, and sooner or later children will be on their own in the world, expected to be responsible citizens.

Not about parental control over children. The goal of natural and logical consequences is to teach children about the relationship between their actions and the consequences, not about punishment. Parents' concerns about being in control and having authority undermine the effectiveness of natural and logical consequences.

Originating from the behaviors that lead directly to them. Parents should avoid arbitrary punishments, which have little to do with the child's behavior. For children to learn about actions and consequences, there must be an obvious link between them. If a child misses lunch, she can fix her own lunch (instead of having unrelated TV privileges revoked).

Rationally and clearly presented. In presenting consequences, parents should be warm and friendly, but firm. Parents should avoid presenting consequences as threats or in anger because this will feel like punishment. Even saying something like "You see? This is what happens when you …" will sound preachy and punishing to children.

Getting children to comply with parents' requests or rules can be challenging. Research shows that a supportive approach, like using logical consequences, is more effective than a controlling approach like mild (nonphysical) punishments. In addition, logical consequences lead to less anger and more empathy on the part of the child. In the long run, this approach also leads to greater internalization of the rules, meaning children take more responsibility for their actions—an important life lesson—and, as a bonus, parents end up nagging and yelling less.

Discussion Questions

1. How are natural consequences different from punishment?
2. What suggestion of effective consequences is most meaningful to you and why?

References

Bibby, R. W. (2006). *The boomer factor: What Canada's most famous generation is leaving behind.* Bastian.

Dreikurs, R., & Soltz, V. (1964). *Children: The challenge.* Hawthorn.

McKay, G. D., & Dinkmeyer, D. (1996). *Raising a responsible child: How to prepare your child for today's complex world.* Fireside.

Robichaud, J.-M., Lessard, J., Labelle, L., & Mageau, G. A. (2020). The role of logical consequences and autonomy support in children's anticipated reactions of anger and empathy. *Journal of Child & Family Studies, 29*(6), 1511–1524. https://doi.org/10.1007/s10826-019-01594-3

Robichaud, J.-M., Mageau, G. A., Soenens, B., Mabbe, E., Kil, H., Frenette, J., & Roy, M. (2024). Should parents combine reasoning with firm control to nurture adolescent socialization? Comparing logical consequences with mild punishments. *Canadian Journal of Behavioural Science.* Advance online publication. https://doi.org/10.1037/cbs0000409

Runkel, H. E. (2008). *Screamfree parenting: How to raise amazing adults by learning to pause more and react less* (rev. ed.). Harmony.

Ryan, R. M., & Deci, E. L. (2017). *Self-determination theory: Basic psychological needs in motivation, development, & wellness.* Guilford Press.

Actions Speak Louder Than Words: Being Role Models for Our Children

Kimberly Van Putten-Gardner, Ph.D., CFLE
Psychotherapist, Affinity: Counseling and Family Life Services, Columbia, MD;
and Family Science Instructor,
University of Maryland
College Park, MD

"Do as I say and not as I do." This is a common inference that I've heard from bewildered parents during family therapy sessions as they plead with their adolescent children to be respectful by not cursing, to be less angry, not to use drugs, to pursue a college education, not to engage in premarital sex, and so on. Unfortunately, such requests are hard for teenagers to follow.

As the social philosopher George Herbert Mead (1934), with his concept of "taking the role of the other" noted, children learn from observing their parents and others. All the interactions within the family atmosphere communicate to children what is valuable and become blueprints for future relationships and individual choices (Mead, 1934; Shulman & Mosak, 1988). During the adolescent years, teen children examine family interactions and values as they develop their peer relationships and begin to make their own life decisions.

Parents need to be vigilantly aware of the behaviors and attitudes that they model through parent–child and parent–parent interactions within the home (Dinkmeyer et al., 1997). Do you try to get your children's attention by cursing at them? Do your children see that the parent who acts out in anger by shouting and slamming doors is most effective in getting their own way in spousal arguments? If your child sees that such behaviors work for you, they will assume that those behaviors will work for them as well. Furthermore, teenagers are keenly attuned to the inconsistencies of their parents. For example, parents tell their children not to smoke marijuana, but parents will use and abuse other drugs, such as alcohol. Such behaviors send mix messages to teens.

I'm not suggesting that parents should be perfect examples (Terner & Pew, 1978). That would be impossible. Often, parents have made choices that have created challenges in their own lives and are attempting to instill values (e.g., values for education and marriage) in their children that would shield their children from the same difficult challenges that they have encountered.

Unfortunately, parents often attempt to instill values in their children by making demands. Rather than demanding that their adolescent child attend college or not engage in premarital sex, parents should clearly communicate their value beliefs to their adolescent children in a friendly, nondemanding way. By clearly communicating to your teenager what you believe, why, and the experiences in which your value beliefs are based, you are giving your child a message that may help him or her make future decisions (Shulman & Mosak, 1988).

In summary, rather than saying, "Do as I say and not as I do," parents should (a) strive to be good role models for their teens through the things they do, (b) say in a non-imposing manner what is expected of their teens, and (c) trust their teenagers to make responsible decisions.

> *What was silent in the father speaks in the son,*
> *and often I have found in the son the unveiled secret of the father.*
> —Friedrich Wilhelm Nietzsche

References

Dinkmeyer, D., Sr., McKay, G. D., & Dinkmeyer, D., Jr. (1997). *The parent's handbook: Systematic training for effective parenting.* American Guidance Service, Inc.

Mead, G. H. (1934). *Mind, soul, and society.* University of Chicago Press.

Shulman, B. H., & Mosak, H. H. (1988). *Manual for lifestyle assessment: Parental behavior and probable responses by child.* Accelerated Development.

Terner, J., & Pew, W. L. (1978). *The courage to be imperfect.* Hawthorn.

Four Messages Every Child Longs to Hear

Cynthia B. Wilson, CFLE, Ph.D.
Executive Director, The Florida Center for Prevention Research
Florida State University
Partnership Program Manager/Certified Parent Coach, Connected Families
Tallahassee, FL

Jim Jackson
President/Co-Founder

Lynne Jackson, OTR, CLC
Co-Founder/Content Director
Connected Families
Plymouth, MN

The great parenting myth is that if you get "it" just right, your kids will behave. As if somehow their behavior is your report card. This myth leaves many parents' confidence and well-being rising and falling based on the turbulent ups and downs of often unpredictable childhood behavior. When things "work," you feel good about your parenting. Likewise, when they don't work, you don't feel good about your parenting.

It does not have to be this way. **The stark truth is that sometimes, no matter how hard you try or how well you use a new technique, your kids will misbehave.** Getting free from the cloud of behavior-based discouragement begins by understanding what you control and what you do not control.

What you ultimately cannot control is your child's behavior. You may be able to control it in the short term, but if the methods used discourage your child, they will act out that discouragement later. However, you can control encouraging "messages" that you communicate to your child, especially when they misbehave.

Think about it: What messages do you want your kids to believe about themselves? *"I am loved! I matter! I am capable! I can make a difference!"* And perhaps many similar encouraging messages. This is not a typical way to think about discipline. It's common to treat children's misbehavior with hands on hips, a furrowed brow, and a loud, frustrated exhale. Before a word is spoken, children receive a message about themselves through such actions. The message is likely, *"You are a problem. You are a disappointment. You are a nuisance."* Add a parent's stern tone or yelling, and the messages deepen. Despite a parent's good intentions to guide their children well, **the messages children receive are often the opposite of what a parent wants to communicate.**

What if the most important goal of discipline was not to manage behavior but to communicate encouraging messages that shape children's sense of worth and identity? The Discipline That Connects With Your Child's Heart® approach (Jackson & Jackson, 2016) is designed to do just that. It teaches an approach aimed far more at encouraging identity messages than at "correct" behavior. What if, instead of evaluating your parenting by how your kids "did today," you evaluate based on what you did today to communicate the following messages?

You are SAFE with me.

   You are LOVED no matter what.

      You are CALLED and CAPABLE.

         You are RESPONSIBLE for your actions.

When parents and caregivers work intentionally to communicate these four messages, especially during discipline, their children will develop a strong sense of identity, purpose, and responsibility. Over time, children will act accordingly. Let's unpack these four messages:

"You are SAFE with me!" Kids learn best when they feel safe. Here's why. Our brains are designed to protect us from anything threatening, especially if it is large and comes at us fast and loudly. For our survival, we must quickly (a) aggressively defend ourselves or (b) run away when we are threatened (fight-or-flight response).

Although this self-protective mechanism works for us in the face of real danger (picture a large, roaring animal running at you), it works against us in disciplinary situations. Parents often try to regain control by rushing in (fast), towering over kids (large), with strong, loud commands to *"Stop it! Right now!"* This sends our kids into fight-or-flight responses and shuts down their frontal lobe. If we want our kids to learn anything helpful when they've misbehaved, we must approach them in a manner *opposite* of fast, large, and loud: We must approach *slow, low* (get out of intimidating postures and be calm), and *listen.*

Julie's 4-year-old daughter Brianna was intense—and so were their conflicts! Julie was learning to focus more on messages than proper behavior and started by rehearsing a new script to guide her thinking: *"I am going to respond with grace, love, and mercy."* She began narrating her own calming process: *"I'm pretty frustrated right now."* After slow, deep breaths, she'd respond with a gentle smile, *"Okay, now I'm ready to talk with you about this."*

Within a few weeks, Brianna's defiance decreased significantly, and she began following her mom's example. Her kindergarten teacher commented, *"She is an intense little girl, but I have never seen a child calm herself down so well! She just starts talking to herself."*

When we show up in tense conflict situations with "slow, low, and listen" at the forefront of our minds, we communicate to our children, "You are SAFE with me," and our kids do their best learning.

"You are LOVED no matter what!" If parents express love only when children behave well, they communicate to their children that love is conditional. Children may learn to perform to get love, which can be a very unhealthy life pattern. When children believe love is earned, their emotions and sense of value tend to rise and fall with their performance. They may even make compromising choices to gain approval or attention.

When parents express love even when their children misbehave, they effectively communicate that their kids are so valuable, they are loved despite what they do. Expressing love and kindness during these challenging times is the only way to convince our children they are loved no matter what. Unconditional love can be communicated in many ways: a gentle smile, a hug, or simply conveying love with heartfelt words.

Another powerful way to communicate love is by expressing sincere empathy. Empathy is about putting yourself in your children's shoes and feeling what it is like to be them. Once you identify your child's emotions, you can become a mirror and simply describe what you see: *"You're sad because ..."* or *"You're angry because ...."* Identifying your child's emotions helps them to do the same so that those emotions can be expressed more appropriately. Empathy also communicates powerful messages, such as *"You are understood,"* *"You are not alone,"* and *"I am for you."*

When children feel understood, they often want to make wiser choices. Even when consequences are still needed, kids are much more receptive to those consequences because they feel loved. The next time the situation occurs, they will be just a little closer to being able to express *"I'm really mad!"* instead of name-calling or hitting.

When your kids act out or throw a tantrum, try empathy. It will encourage you to react more calmly, help your kids build emotional maturity, and, most important, communicate to them that they are loved unconditionally—no matter what!

"You are CALLED and CAPABLE!" One powerful way to connect deeply with your child's heart is to identify their natural talents. It might seem counterintuitive, but it is even more important to identify those "talents" when kids use them to misbehave. When children get in trouble, they usually tap into their strengths and talents to accomplish what is important to them.

Your defiant child just might be tomorrow's leader. Or the one always yelling, *"It's not fair!"* might just grow to seek justice for all, not just themselves. This kind of encouragement opens even the most challenging of children to hearing about how they are built and what their life's purpose might be.

When parents step back and look beneath their child's immediate misbehaviors, they can envision how those talents might be used for good. If parents' primary goal is to "straighten them out" or fix the problems through punishment, these kids often grow discouraged, believing they are troublemakers, not talented people.

When kids believe the message "You are CALLED and CAPABLE," they hold onto the hope that they can positively use their gifts to impact the world around them.

"You are RESPONSIBLE for your actions!" Despite parents' most graceful efforts to stay calm, connect well, and guide kids toward wiser choices, kids still sometimes misbehave. They are still imperfect (just like us) and need corrective guidance (just like we do).

A first step in communicating this message is to help children understand the natural impact of their behavior. Natural consequences are the built-in "harvests" that come based on people's actions. For example, when a child lies, others may not trust her anymore. When an older sibling hits a younger sibling, the younger child might get scared. Both situations, as well as others, may be associated with various unpleasant feelings such as shame, guilt, and sadness, for example. Most importantly, relationships are broken. These are not imposed consequences; they are natural impacts.

Our instinct is to punish our children when they misbehave. Although that might temporarily modify behavior, it does little to build wisdom. The natural impacts of our children's behavior will be their best lifelong teacher if they are taught to understand and pay attention to how their heart feels when they hurt others.

This kind of wisdom is not taught through lectures. There is an art to helping children understand natural impacts through thoughtful questions, analogies, observations, and stories. As we gracefully guide our children to discover the natural impact of their behavior, they often want to make right what they have made wrong. This can look different depending on the situation, but the end goal is to restore relationships. It might mean giving a back rub to a brother after hitting him or truly apologizing and reconciling after a verbal argument.

When kids are too upset to reconcile misbehavior right away, privileges that are a distraction can be put on hold until they are calm and ready to reconcile. Guiding kids toward heartfelt reconciliation is a critical and often overlooked alternative to punitive discipline (punitive: *"Your Xbox is gone for a week!"* vs. restorative: *"Until you and your brother work things out, your screens and friends will be put on hold."*)

A final word: When parents embrace the Discipline That Connects® (Jackson & Jackson, 2016) principles, children grow in wisdom and true responsibility for their lives. Remember, **the most important thing is the messages that you send your child when you discipline.** Kids who grow up believing they are safe, loved no matter what, called and capable, and responsible for their actions are kids who grow up to change the world. Our kids need this. Our world needs them!

Discussion Questions

1. How is the Discipline That Connects® approach to parenting different from other typical parenting approaches that are more focused on behavior modification?

2. Why is it important to approach children in a "slow, low, and listen" posture rather than coming on "fast, large, and loud"?

3. What are some intentional ways parents can communicate these 4 messages to their children?

References and Suggested Resources

Jackson, J., & Jackson, L. (2016). *Discipline That Connects With Your Child's Heart*. Bethany House Publishers.

Jackson, J., & Jackson, L. (n.d.) *Discipline That Connects With Your Child's Heart* [Online course]. https://connectedfamilies.org/

Chapter IV
Health and Wellness

Raising Sexually Healthy Children

Sharon M. Ballard, Ph.D., CFLE
Professor and Department Chair,
Human Development & Family Science,
East Carolina University, Greenville, NC

Kevin H. Gross, Ph.D.

Many parents react with horror when the word sexuality is used in the same sentence with their child's name, particularly if their child is a preschooler. "We have a long time before we have to worry about that!" is the sentiment of many parents. The reality is that we are all sexual beings from the time we are born (actually, even before birth!) until the time that we die. Children are no exception. Children have difficulty achieving sexual health as an adult if sexuality is ignored throughout childhood. The Sexuality Information and Education Council of the United States (2004), in a comprehensive writing on sexuality education, identified several life behaviors of a sexually healthy adult, including the ability to "develop and maintain meaningful relationships," "appreciate one's own body," "interact with all genders in respectful and appropriate ways," "express love and intimacy in appropriate ways," and "express one's sexuality in ways that are congruent with one's values" (pp. 16–17). Using these criteria, most parents would agree that they want their children to be sexually healthy.

Both parents and children report wanting to talk about sexuality together, and the positive outcomes of effective parent–child sexual communication are well documented within the research literature (Pariera & Brody, 2017). Families are the primary socializers of their children. Not only are parents the preferred sources of sexuality information for many young people, but children do listen to their parents! Young people want their parents to engage in early, open, and ongoing discussions with them about a range of sexuality topics, such as dating, relationships, and sexual orientation, in addition to the basics, such as reproduction and birth control (Kuborn et al., 2023; Pariera & Brody, 2017). It is important for you, as a parent, to remember how influential you are in your child's life. However, knowing it is important and that your children want you to talk with them doesn't necessarily make it easy.

So, how do you overcome potential barriers and help your children achieve sexual health? First, ideas of sexuality need to be expanded. As the preceding description of sexual health states, sexuality includes more than just intercourse. It incorporates such things as body image, love, relationships, and gender issues and communication about these topics begins at birth. When you give your infant daughter a warning that you are going to wipe her nose rather than coming up behind her and taking her by surprise, you are conveying a respect for her body. When a preschooler sees his parents touch, hug, and kiss, this illustrates positive ways of showing affection. These examples illustrate the fact that sexuality education is already occurring in most families even when it is unintentional. It is helpful to think about additional actions that are intentional and can build on this foundation. What messages do you give regarding gender roles? Where appropriate, do you allow your child to make decisions, particularly decisions regarding their body? For example, if your son doesn't want to kiss Aunt Edna, don't force it. Are your children learning correct names for body parts as a way to instill respect for the body and provide a common language?

Second, there is a common idea that sexuality education occurring in the home consists of "the talk" that is often an awkward and ineffective conversation. Sexuality education should be an ongoing and intentional process. Rather than having one talk, parents can take advantage of teachable moments (e.g., potty training is a great teachable moment!) to discuss sexuality-related topics with their children. For example, when a little boy is learning to use the bathroom, he might ask, "Why does Mommy sit down when she goes potty, but Daddy stands up?" This provides a great opportunity to incorporate proper names for body parts into a discussion of the differences between girls and boys. Another example of a teachable moment might be when a 3-year-old asks about a pregnant woman. It is a good time to say, "She has a baby growing inside her—babies grow in a special place in the body called the uterus." This is generally all the 3-year-old wants to know. But by providing this information in an accurate manner, you have laid the foundation for future conversations about reproduction.

Answer questions as they arise and provide information that is developmentally appropriate. The result is a sense that sexuality is a natural part of one's life and not something about which to be embarrassed or ashamed. Additionally, if conversation is ongoing, parents can give children small bits of information that can continually build a foundation for sexual health. Preschoolers are curious about their bodies, and their questions should be answered in a truthful, thoughtful manner. Young children generally need only small bits of information. As they process each piece of information, they may then come back to you for more. Answers can be given in ways that children understand and that are consistent with your values. By treating their questions with respect and giving truthful answers (e.g., babies do not come from the stork!), children will learn that it is okay to ask Mom and Dad questions and that they can be trusted to give answers.

The parent who reacts with shock or embarrassment to the 4-year-old who asks where babies come from and avoids answering the question is less likely to be asked questions in the future. That child has learned several sexuality education lessons from such an awkward or negative interaction: It is bad to ask questions, it is wrong to be curious, the human body is something about which to be embarrassed, and, most important, don't ask Mom and Dad.

Finally, talking to your child about sexuality can be an important way to transmit your sexual values to your child. Clarify your own values and identify the goals and outcomes that you want for your children regarding sexuality. Convey these ideas in the messages that you send to your child. Are you setting the stage for continued honest communication about sexuality? Expanding your own definition of sexuality, engaging your child in ongoing, developmentally appropriate conversations about sexuality, and making communication an intentional process that reflects your own values can go a long way toward facilitating sexual health in your child.

As your child enters adolescence, she or he will encounter more and more sexuality information from a variety of sources and will be making difficult choices about sexual behavior. Remember that a positive and open dialogue about sexuality in your home when your child is young will increase the likelihood that, as a teenager, they are going to come to you rather than friends with questions and concerns.

Discussion Questions and Activities
1. How did you learn about sex? Was it from your parents? Friends? Media? Or maybe a combination of sources. Do you wish your own parents had talked to you more?

2. How can you learn from your own experiences to be effective in your sexual communication with your own children?

3. Check out *Tips for Talking to Your Kids About Sex & Relationships (plannedparenthood.org)* for tips and resources to help facilitate communication with your children about sex and relationships.

References
Kuborn, S., Markham, M., & Astle, S. (2023). "I wish they would have a class for parents about talking to their kids about sex": College women's parent–child sexual communication reflections and desires. *Sexuality Research & Social Policy, 20*(1), 230–241. https://doi.org/10.1007/s13178-022-00723-w

Pariera, K. L., & Brody, E. (2017). "Talk more about it": Emerging adults' attitudes about how and when parents should talk about sex. *Sexuality Research and Social Policy, 15*(2), 219–229. https://doi.org/10.1007/s13178-017-0314-9.

Sexuality Information and Education Council of the United States, National Guidelines Task Force. (2004). *Guidelines for comprehensive sexuality education* (3rd ed.). http://65.36.238.42/pubs/guidelines/guidelines.pdf

Breaking the Generational Curse: Integrating Family Science to Promote Self-Differentiation and Overcome Trauma-Driven Parenting

Felisha M. Burleson, M.A., CFLE
Doctoral Candidate
Founder of The Patchwork Society

A few years ago, during a therapy session, my therapist asked me why I think I am a better parent compared with my parents. I believe this is a multifaceted question with no simple answer.

I spent a short amount of time in the foster care system until I turned 18. As an adult and a parent, I can reflect on my experiences and the experiences of my parents. For instance, both of my parents lost their mothers at an early age. They did not have traditional maternal or paternal role models, only older siblings who were not necessarily maternal or paternal figures. Although capable, my parents did not have the typical parental guidance. Moreover, they grew up in the 1970s, when scientific understanding of family dynamics and best practices in parenting and early childhood development was less developed.

My journey has been about more than just breaking the generational curse or cycle of trauma. It has been about empowerment and, most importantly, self-differentiation. I have had access to tools and resources that my parents and many others might not have, which has been instrumental in this process. As adults, we have the power to take inventory of the skills we like and dislike from our parents, families, and other parenting people. We can decide which skills to keep and integrate and which to discard. This process, guided by mediators and moderators, can be formal, like therapy, life coaching, parent education, and case management; or it can be informal, through daily interactions.

I have worked to break that generational cycle, whether it was through case management, parenting classes, or education. My personal journey and professional experience highlight the critical role of self-differentiation in breaking the cycle of trauma-driven parenting. This leads us to consider the theoretical perspective of intergenerational trauma and self-differentiation, which provides a broader framework for understanding these dynamics.

The Science Behind It
While some call it generational curses, in social science, intergenerational trauma is often referred to as multigenerational trauma or transgenerational trauma (Chou & Buchanan, 2021). These terms are interchangeable in defining experiences that manifest trauma as well as traumatic responses over multiple generations (Chou & Buchanan, 2021). Kitamura et al. (2009) stated that parents often unconsciously replicate childhood parenting styles, perpetuating positive and negative patterns. Families with a history of trauma may continue to repeat or continue some of the

parenting practices associated with the traumatic experiences to their children and subsequent generations. Common forms of traumatic experiences stem from harsh parenting practices, including verbal, physical, and neglectful acts or omissions. Verbal acts include behaviors such as swearing, yelling, and name-calling. Physical acts include spanking (Erath et al., 2009). Neglectful acts include ignoring, isolating, scapegoating, and withholding food and necessities (Connell & Strambler, 2021).

Theory
Bowen's family systems theory, multigenerational, sometimes called intergenerational or transgenerational, explains how experiences, behaviors, and emotional patterns are passed across generations (Bowen, 1978). Bowen defined self-differentiation as maintaining one's identity and values while staying emotionally connected to others, enabling intentional decision-making (Józefczyk, 2023; Priest, 2019). Increasing self-differentiation allows parents to examine their upbringing objectively and make intentional choices based on their values rather than repeating familiar, potentially unhealthy patterns (Kerr & Bowen, 1988; Priest, 2019).

Role of Family Science Professionals
Family Science professionals offer critical support in breaking these cycles and promoting healthier family dynamics. Using a family systems approach, mediators and moderators, such as family therapists, Family Life Educators, family life coaches, and case managers, can facilitate this process of increasing self-differentiation (Priest, 2019).
- Family therapists allow parents to process their own traumatic experiences and reflect on them as they relate to their current parenting practices (Priest, 2019).
- Family Life Educators provide families with resources and teach them the life skills necessary for parenting (Ballard et al., 2020).
- Family life coaches help families develop goals and implement parenting practices (Allen & Huff, 2014).
- Case managers help families navigate various systems and provide guidance to position families for success (Speidel et al., 2020)

Mediators link family support services to desired outcomes, such as improved parent–child relationships through parenting education, implementing goals and skills through coaching, reduced family conflict via therapy, and increased stability and self-sufficiency through case management (Patel et al., 2017). Moderators identify factors such as family structure, socioeconomic status, and cultural background that influence the effectiveness of these services (Finders, 2016; Gardner, 2010). The family's readiness for change, commitment level, and approach also moderates the success of service delivery in achieving positive outcomes.

Applying These Concepts to Parenting
When people reach adulthood, they face the important task of determining how to parent their children. Often, they tend to adopt parenting styles similar to how they were parented because it is the only method they know. However, as they gain more life experience and knowledge, many adjust and modify their parenting approaches. This increased understanding and knowledge comes from various life experiences and interventions, whether intentional or not. Intentional interventions often involve working with Family Science professionals, such as counselors, life coaches, case managers, and Family Life Educators. These professionals play a critical role in

helping adults identify and understand their family and parenting values, challenge existing norms and expectations, and introduce new parenting skills relevant to their current circumstances. This process allows adults to make informed decisions about which practices to retain and which to change or adopt. Ultimately, this leads to more intentional and effective parenting tailored to their families' unique needs and values.

Conclusion

I began self-differentiation by leveraging the available tools, resources, and services, consciously and intentionally integrating behavioral changes into my parenting practices. When we know better, we do better, and this awareness has allowed me to break the generational curse of trauma-driven parenting. Bowen believed that increased self-awareness and differentiation of self could allow individuals to break free from unhealthy family patterns. The key is to develop a strong sense of self distinct from the family. Family Science professionals can work with parents to facilitate self-differentiation, allowing them to parent their children more thoughtfully and intentionally rather than just repeating the patterns of the past out of familiarity.

Discussion Questions

1. How has your own upbringing influenced your parenting style? Are there specific practices you have consciously chosen to continue or change?

2. Can you identify any patterns of behavior or emotional responses that may have been passed down through generations in your family? How have you addressed these in your parenting?

3. How do you measure the success of interventions aimed at increasing self-differentiation and breaking trauma cycles? What indicators or outcomes do you focus on in your work as a family professional?

4. What are the common challenges and barriers families face when trying to break generational cycles of trauma? How can professionals help mitigate these challenges?

References

Allen, K., & Huff, N. L. (2014). Family coaching: An emerging family science field. *Family Relations, 63*(5), 569–582. https://doi.org/10.1111/fare.12087

Ballard, S. M. (2020). The practice of family life education: Toward an implementation framework. *Family Relations, 69*(3), 461–478. https://doi.org/10.1111/fare.12443

Bowen, M. (1978). *Family therapy in clinical practice.* Rowman & Littlefield Publishers Inc.

Chou, F., & Buchanan, M. J. (2021). Intergenerational trauma: A scoping review of cross-cultural applications from 1999 to 2019. *Canadian Journal of Counselling and Psychotherapy, 55*(3), 363–395. https://doi.org/10.47634/cjcp.v55i3.71456

Connell, C. M., & Strambler, M. J. (2021). Experiences With COVID-19 Stressors and Parents' Use of Neglectful, Harsh, and Positive Parenting Practices in the Northeastern United States. *Child maltreatment, 26*(3), 255–266. https://doi.org/10.1177/10775595211006465

Erath, S. A., El-Sheikh, M., & Cummings, E. M. (2009). Harsh parenting and child externalizing behavior: Skin conductance level reactivity as a moderator. *Child Development, 80*(2), 578–592. https://doi.org/10.1111/j.1467-8624.2009.01280.x

Finders, J. K., Díaz, G., Geldhof, G. J., Sektnan, M., & Rennekamp, D. (2016). The impact of parenting education on parent and child behaviors: Moderators by income and ethnicity. *Children and Youth Services Review, 71*, 199–209. https://doi.org/10.1016/j.childyouth.2016.11.006

Gardner, F., Hutchings, J., Bywater, T., & Whitaker, C. (2010). Who benefits and how does it work? Moderators and mediators of outcome in an effectiveness trial of a parenting intervention. *Journal of Clinical Child & Adolescent Psychology, 39*(4), 568–580. https://doi.org/10.1080/15374416.2010.486315

Józefczyk A. (2023). Multigenerational transmission of differentiation of self— Toward a more in-depth understanding of Bowen's theory concept. *Journal of Marital and Family Therapy, 49*(3), 634–653. https://doi.org/10.1111/jmft.12645

Kerr, M. E., & Bowen, M. (1988). *Family evaluation: An approach based on Bowen theory*. W. W. Norton & Co.

Kitamura, T., Shikai, N., Uji, M., Hiramura, H., Tanaka, N., & Shono, M. (2007). Intergenerational transmission of parenting style and personality: Direct influence or mediation? *Journal of Child and Family Studies, 18*, 541–556. https://doi.org/10.1007/s10826-009-9256-z

Patel, C. C., Fairchild, A. J., & Prinz, R. J. (2017). Potential mediators in parenting and family intervention: Quality of mediation analyses. *Clinical Child and Family Psychology Review, 20*(2), 127–145. https://doi.org/10.1007/s10567-016-0221-2

Priest J. B. (2019). Examining differentiation of self as a mediator in the biobehavioral family model. *Journal of Marital and Family Therapy, 45*(1), 161–175. https://doi.org/10.1111/jmft.12301

Speidel, R., Wang, L., Cummings, E. M., & Valentino, K. (2020). Longitudinal pathways of family influence on child self-regulation: The roles of parenting, family expressiveness, and maternal sensitive guidance in the context of child maltreatment. *Developmental Psychology, 56*(3), 608–622. https://doi.org/10.1037/dev0000782

Weathering the Storm

Kristina Higgins, Ph.D., CFLE
Division Director and Associate Professor, Division of
Child Development and Family Studies
Tarleton State University

As we were leaving my grandmother's apartment one evening after a visit, my 10-year-old daughter piped up, "Do you remember when we lived with Mamaw for a month?" Memories of the early days of the COVID-19 pandemic came flooding back.

"Yes," I replied. "Do you remember why we had to live there?" "Because Dad was sick and we couldn't go home. It was so fun!"

Her enthusiasm took me by surprise. As a parent, the pandemic's early days was one of the most stressful times I could remember, but her perspective was clearly different. At the time, she was 6 years old, and her kindergarten year had abruptly ended at spring break. Her 20-month-old brother's childcare center shut down, and they did not leave the two-bedroom apartment for weeks. I would leave occasionally to grocery shop or pick up prescriptions, but only when necessary as I did not want to charge my octogenarian grandmother with the care of my children for too long. The isolation coupled with worrying about my husband's health, as he had contracted Covid before anyone knew what to expect from this illness, plus learning how to work from home with a kindergartener and a toddler, was overwhelming to say the least.

I asked her, "What do you remember?" Her perspective was enlightening. She remembered riding her bike and picking flowers outside of the apartment, teaching her brother to recognize letters and numbers, reading tons of books, and video calling family and friends. She also talked about how fun her first-grade class was because school was on the iPad. The entire year, she participated in a virtual learning class with nine other children and a phenomenal teacher, who kept the kids engaged and interested without compromising the foundational educational skills needed to succeed in future grades. While most are sighing in a collective relief that the world has returned to its new normal, my daughter reminisces about the fun times in the pandemic.

The world at large is keenly aware of the impact of the pandemic on all ages and generations, from the remote workforce who are now returning to the office, to the educational and social impacts on all ages of children and youth. Caregivers of young children were particularly vulnerable, suffering an increase in stressors related to their own employment needs (unemployment, low income) as well as their need to provide care while attempting to work or seek employment (Costa et al., 2022). Caregivers were simultaneously ensuring their children were engaged in age-appropriate activities, their care and routine was organized and monitored, and their behavior was corrected as needed. While some were able to manage these tasks, many were not, and preschool-age children showed increased misbehavior, aggression, and agitation.

My son's experience, on the other hand, was quite a bit different than my daughter's and more in line with typical research findings from the pandemic era. Although he does not remember the pandemic per se, the impact was felt and his social and emotional development has suffered. His childcare center closed for 6 months, and the only other children he interacted with was his older sister and occasionally a younger cousin. When he returned to childcare, teachers wore masks and face shields, ratios were low, and children were encouraged to play separately. This continued for 2 years, and in the peak years for social development and learning to play with others, he was unable to participate in this type of interaction. Although he began kindergarten this year, within 2 weeks he was moved to a pre-kindergarten classroom because, although he was 5, he was not socially or emotionally ready. He was fortunate that his teachers recognized this need and placed him in the correct class for his developmental level instead of insisting he stay with similarly aged peers.

I recently attended a roundtable session discussion with community leaders in early education focused on the differences between children who participated in a school readiness program and a comparison group. In this session, data were presented on pre-kindergarten- and kindergarten-age children and various domains of their development, including social emotional development, emotional management, and executive functioning (working memory, inhibition, and attention). Regardless of their participation in the school readiness program, children were behind the previous cohorts assessed in all these areas, which has the potential to affect their academic and social success for years to come without targeted intervention. I could not help but think about how this is my son's cohort, a group of children who missed the foundational years of social and emotional learning.

Interestingly, while the focus has been on the pandemic's negative impacts, Egan et al. (2021) noted positive impacts too. In a survey of 506 parents of children aged 1 through 10, they found that although negative impacts were noted by parents (such as an increase in tantrums, clinginess, anxiety, and under stimulation), some parents reported a positive experience. These parents felt the break in routine was helpful, and children had more time to play with their siblings than before the pandemic. These findings indicate that experiences were not universal but unique to each family.

As parent educators, and those who educate parent educators, we will always need to be mindful of the individual children and their experiences when the world shut down. Individual family experiences were unique, and we have cohorts of children at different ages who were impacted in different ways. Some children are more resilient than others, some were provided with more opportunities to interact than others, and some experienced more stress and trauma because of the stress on the adults in their lives. The importance of talking with families about their experiences during this time will help parent educators understand where the family is now and what is needed to support each individual family moving forward.

My family's experience is a prime example. Both of my children were in the same home environment; however, due to their different ages and educational experiences, the pandemic changed their lives in different ways. My daughter reminisces fondly about the pandemic, and due to a wonderful first-grade teacher and the support of a few close friends, the pandemic did not seem to have negative impacts on her development or education. Although my son does not remember lockdown in the way much of the rest of the world does, the negative impacts are clear in his social and emotional development. To quote Damian Barr's (2020) viral tweet in the early days of the pandemic, "We are not all in the same boat. We are in the same storm. Some are on super-yachts. Some have just one oar."

Discussion Questions

1. Consider your own family's experience with Covid. Would you consider it positive, negative, or neutral?

2. How does your experience during the pandemic align with or differ from the families you serve?

3. Which parts of your own experience with Covid could potentially bias you towards the families you serve? How will you resolve these biases to help strengthen families?

References

Barr, D. [@Damian_Barr]. (2020, April 20). *We are not all in the same boat. We are in the same storm. Some of us are on super-yachts. Some have just one oar.* [Tweet]. X. https://x.com/Damian_Barr

Costa, P., Cruz, A. C., Alves, A., Rodrigues, M. C., & Ferguson, R. (2022). The impact of the COVID-19 pandemic on young children and their caregivers. *Child: Care, Health and Development, 48*(6), 1001–1007. https://doi.org/10.1111/cch.12980

Egan, S. M., Pope, J., Moloney, M., Hoyne, C., & Meatty, C. (2021). Missing early education and care during the pandemic: The socio-emotional impact of the COVID-19 crisis on young children. *Early Childhood Education Journal, 49*(5), 925–934. https://doi.org/10.1007/s10643-021-01193-2

What's So Hard About Parenting Children With Mental Illness?

Elizabeth Mazur, Ph.D.
Professor of Psychology
Penn State, Greater Allegheny campus

"I don't get what's so hard about being a parent of a child with a disability," my aunt informed me the other day. "It's not like *you* have to deal with ADHD. Or anxiety. Or depression. It's not you who can't finish a paper for class, remember to do the laundry, or can't get out of bed in the morning. Now that's hard."

Oh, where should I start? Perhaps I should first check the opening sentence of the abstract of my 2018 research paper coauthored with Camille Mickle, "Child mental illness impacts the entire family, and previous research has consistently found that parenting children with mental health disorders is psychologically distressing" (p. 569).

I do suppose, however, if it was a contest between parent and child that, in this case, the child would "win." However, the results of our study of 146 online posts found that parents of children with mental illness have a range of parental concerns as expressed on four open U.S. Internet forums that support parents of children aged 5 to 18 diagnosed with ADHD, depression, anxiety, and bipolar disorder; parents' most frequent worry is the effect of their children's illness on themselves, specifically their feelings of helplessness, their need for advice on their own coping, and the stress of child discipline. Parents also frequently express worry about child symptoms, especially poor academic performance, and have questions about the efficacy and side effects of and their children's noncompliance with medication. We found, too, that most stressors were shared among parents of children with different diagnoses, genders, and ages, except parent–child verbal and physical conflict. Parents of children with bipolar disorders, co-occurring ADHD and oppositional defiant disorder or with co-occurring ADHD and bipolar disorder wrote more frequently about verbal and physical conflict than parents of children with only ADHD diagnoses.

This result is consistent with an earlier study (Theule et al., 2012) that found that co-occurring conduct problems in children with ADHD increased parenting stress compared with ADHD alone and that parents of children with bipolar disorder report that their children commonly experience intense and dramatic, seemingly uncontrollable, rage. Yet parents often say that although they know objectively that they have little control of the symptoms or severity of their children's conditions, their expectations for themselves is that they should.

Unfortunately, although most people realize that physical illnesses may be unremitting and erratic, few extend that understanding to parents of children with mental illness. Often relatives and other adults insist that all the child needs is firm discipline, a topic about which parents are already confused and concerned. In a classic 2004 text on developmental psychology, *Parenting Stress*, Dr. Kirby Deater-Deckard wrote that "compared to parents of healthy children, those of children who are disabled, impaired, or critically ill are far more likely to be acutely or chronically distressed" (p. 59). They feel little or no control over the symptoms or severity of their child's condition, no matter how "good" of a parent they are. However, in contrast to a disease such as cancer or cerebral palsy, parents of children with mental illness are frequently considered as potential originators of or contributors to their children's problems, either passively through genetic transmission or more actively and toxically through the home environment they provide. For example, has any article written for parents of children with physical disabilities begun similarly to the following?

> Most parents are good parents. But if your son or daughter has attention deficit disorder (ADHD or ADD) "good" may not be enough. To ensure that your child is happy and well-adjusted now and in the future—and to create a tranquil home environment—you've got to be a great parent (Carpenter, 2022).

So not only are parents expected, as most are, to do their best, mothers (mostly) and fathers of children with ADHD are told that they must parent better than best. Ironically, as Deater-Deckard pointed out, such expectations may lead to long-term problems in parents' own mental health, including higher levels of depression and anxiety.

If you are a parent of a child with mental illness or other disabilities—emotional or physical—you need to give yourself the benefit of the doubt. Has your adolescent child with mental illness ever told you that saying something such as "All you need to do is try harder/get out of bed/calm down" are unhelpful? Similarly, I give you permission to ignore the supposedly useful messages from family and other parents that "it can't be that bad," to "lighten up," "quit overreacting," and "look on the bright side." Find yourself friends who are sympathetic and adults who just listen, not judge. Check out discussion groups that provide online or in person support, such as those sponsored by the Children and Adults with Attention-Deficit/Hyperactivity Disorder (CHADD) and the National Alliance on Mental Illness (NAMI), the motto of the latter of which is pointedly, "You are not alone." Recognize that you are dealing with chronic emotionally distressing situations, which, as studies show, typically involve multiple stressors.

Parent educators, note how critical it is to address the diagnostic heterogeneity and complicated emotional development that characterizes many children with mental illness. As a parent, I can attest that it often feels like "two steps forward, one (or two) step(s) backward." It is important for practitioners to address not only the children's difficulties but also their families' challenges as well.

Discussion Questions

1. How might parenting a child with a mental disorder affect the parents' lives? How might siblings be affected? Can you think of any benefits of living with a child with a mental illness?

2. How might stigma play a role in the experience of parenting a child with a mental disorder?

3. What could you do as a Family Life Educator to decrease the stigma of mental illness?

References

Carpenter, D. (2022, September 26). 13 parenting strategies for kids with ADHD. *Attitude.* https://www.additudemag.com/download/raising-a-child-with-adhd/

Deater-Deckard, K. (2004). *Parenting stress.* Yale University Press.

Mazur, E., & Mickle, C. (2018). Online discourse of the stressors of parenting children with AD/HD, bipolar disorder and internalizing disorders. *Journal of Child and Family Studies, 27*(2), 569–579. https://doi.org/10.1007/s10826-017-0912-4

Theule, J., Wiener, J., Tannock, R., & Jenkins, J. M. (2012). Parenting stress in families of children with ADHD: A meta-analysis. *Journal of Emotional and Behavioral Disorders, 21*, 3–17. https://doi.org/10.1177/1063426610387433

Recommended Resources

Most affiliates of NAMI offer peer-led programs that provide free education, skills training, and support to both family members of and people with mental illness (https://www.nami.org/support-education/). Family Life Educators might be interested in staff development programs for health care providers, employees, and students working directly with people affected by mental illness that a smaller number of NAMI affiliates offer (https://www.nami.org/support-education/mental-health-education/nami-provider/).

CHADD provides resources for parents of children with ADHD. You can find a local affiliate at https://chadd.org/affiliate-locator/.

The Depression and Bipolar Support (DBS) Alliance offers a few types of free weekly, 90-minute online support groups for parents and caregivers of individuals living with a mood disorder. For more information, visit https://www.dbsalliance.org/support/for-friends-family/for-parents/#Support.

Fostering Parent and Infant Bonds in the Neonatal Intensive Care Unit

Hannah Mechler, Ph.D., CFLE
Early Childhood Education Faculty
Grays Harbor College
Aberdeen, WA

"Congratulations, you're expecting a baby!" This news tends to bring much joy and excitement to couples and families who prepare for the arrival of their newborn.

Eight years ago, my spouse and I received this same wonderful news. As the months passed, we eagerly prepared for our son's arrival until a routine check-up at my OB-GYN office resulted in my hospitalization at 30 weeks' gestation. Due to preeclampsia, I was put on bed rest in the hospital where my unborn son and I were routinely monitored. After a few weeks, it was decided that an emergency cesarean delivery was necessary due to my deteriorating health. At 32 weeks' gestation, my son was born and immediately taken to the neonatal intensive care unit (NICU) because he could not survive on his own. At that time, my son could not breathe, suck, or swallow independently. Thus, he was tube fed and connected to several types of oxygen machines.

He spent 1 month in the NICU, which included periods of time spent in an incubation chamber. My spouse and I were able to hold him 1 week after his birth for the first time, but forming skin-to-skin attachment only occurred at specific times due to the treatments he received.

For parents or people who know of a family whose infant has spent time in the NICU, concerns of how attachments and bonding may develop. To foster bonding between infants and parents while in the NICU, research has found that skin-to-skin contact reduces infants' cortisol and pain levels, while fostering attachment bonds (Haward et al., 2020). Participation in infant massage may also be positive for fostering closeness between infants and their parents, while synonymously fostering infants' brain development. In addition, parents' physical presence within the infant's NICU room may be important for building closeness between infants and their parents.

Reflecting on my own experiences, my spouse and I consistently asked NICU staff about what specified times were available for us to hold our son when he was not receiving treatments. Warm blankets were given, which fostered the development of bonding through skin-to-skin contact. We were also routinely present during scheduled feedings and bath times. Despite the oxygen cords sometimes impeding our movements, the experiences were heartwarming and joyous as we were able to engage in activities with our son that are routine when caring for infants. These interactions were profoundly significant, as they assisted my coping with depression. My experiences with maternal depression were spurred from my traumatic experiences while pregnant, in addition to my son's stay in the NICU, which posed heightened challenges due to lack of opportunities to care for my son without medical intervention and to engage in nurturing activities that are so common for many (e.g., holding, rocking) within the initial moments and days after birth. My development of maternal depression aligns with research conducted by Gerstein et al. (2019), whose research indicated that postpartum depression may be likely among mothers whose children are born prematurely and spend time in the NICU. Factors contributing to the development of depression include lack of engagement in nurturing behaviors between mothers and their infants due to time and conditions that may impede them within the NICU environment. Lack of certainty about the future of a child's stay in the NICU may also contribute to mothers' development of depression, anxiety, and posttraumatic stress disorder (Gerstein et al., 2019).

Today, my son has no memories of his stay in the NICU. However, those experiences and memories will forever remain with my spouse and me. As I have experienced and as research has found, fostering parent and infant bonds while in the NICU presents unique challenges for parents. This is coupled by ambiguity surrounding the length of stay that infants may have in the NICU, as well as the development of guilt, depression, and anxiety that may also be common for parents—especially mothers (Haward et al., 2020). However, having opportunities to engage in nurturing activities, such as feeding, holding the infant, participating in infant massage, and being present and speaking to the infant may be ways to develop essential bonds between parents and infants that affect the well-being of the parent–child dyad.

Discussion Questions

1. How can CFLEs or other professionals working with parents whose infant is in the NICU assist in fostering parent–child attachments? What theories may be used or referenced to support these attachment formations? How might these attachments affect maternal depression due to their experiences with their pregnancies, births, or complications that may lead to their infant staying in the NICU?

2. How might CFLEs or other professionals working with parents whose infant is in the NICU help with the stress levels or tension that may develop between family members due to stress they are experiencing?

3. What theories in the discipline of Family Science may be used to explain how stressors, such as experiences of a child's stay in the NICU, affect family functioning? How might these theories be applied to assisting parents cope with the stressors associated with their infants' stay in the NICU?

References

Gerstein, E. D., Njoroge, W. F., Paul, R. A., Smyser, C. D., & Rogers, C. E. (2019). Maternal depression and stress in the NICU: Associations with mother–child interactions at age 5 years. *Journal of American Academy Child Adolescent Psychiatry, 58*(3), 350–358. https://doi.org/10.1016/j.jaac.2018.08.016

Haward, M. F., Lantos, J., & Janvier, A. (2020). Helping parents cope in the NICU. *Pediatrics, 145*(6), 255–260. https://doi.org/10.1542/peds.2019-3567

Additional Resources

NICU Helping Hands. (n.d.). https://nicuhelpinghands.org/

Waddington C., van Veenendaal N. R., O'Brien K., & Patel, N. Family integrated care: Supporting parents as primary caregivers in the neonatal intensive care unit. *Pediatric Investigation, 5*(2), 148–154. https://doi.org/10.1002/ped4.12277. PMID

Breaking the Cycle: Understanding Adverse Childhood Experiences and Trauma

Angelina M. Mojica, CFLE
Director of West Texas Foster Care Homes Program
Saint Francis Ministries
Lubbock, TX

The year is 2018, my children are on break from school for the Thanksgiving holiday, and I am watching my 16-year-old daughter pack her bags and run into the arms of her boyfriend. As I watch her actions, it hits me like a brick to the head. I am witnessing the generational cycles coming full circle. I remember when I was 17 and wanting to escape my childhood trauma, breaking windows in my room because my parents were fighting hard against my rebellion but not realizing I needed help processing the many things I experienced as a young child. My parents had no understanding of the trauma I was trying to cope with. They did not know how to communicate their feelings; affirmations and encouragement were never spoken in my childhood home. My mom's response to my rebellion was to help me pack up my belongings and send me out of the house. I ran to my boyfriend's home as a refuge or what I thought would be a sanctuary for my pain. Now, I am the parent, and my daughter is running away from me, things had to change because the generational cycles were evident, and they needed to stop.

I'm no stranger to understanding trauma and educating others on adverse childhood experiences as I have worked in child welfare for many years. I have been educated and trained in how to help others parent their children with trauma to prevent generational cycles from reoccurring. So why am I struggling with my child? What did I miss in the scheme of it all? All the education and training I have obtained did not save me from seeing my child fall into cycles of abuse. "How an event affects an individual depends on many factors, including characteristics of the individual, the type and characteristics of the event(s), developmental processes, the meaning of the trauma, and sociocultural factors" (Substance Abuse and Mental Health Services Administration, 2014).

Here is what I have learned in my years working in the child welfare system, healing from my traumatic past, and raising three children into adulthood. What we experience in childhood and how we grow up have huge implications for how our adulthood unfolds. If we are to see changes in generational cycles of trauma, we must provide healing for both children and adults. One thing is for sure, there is no easy solution. Healing and breaking cycles involve an intricate web of understanding the issue, preventing, and treating the root issues.

Here are the roots of my daughter's childhood influenced by my actions as her parent. The exposure to domestic violence was my daughter's first understanding of a marital relationship. Yes, in total transparency, I was in a domestically violent relationship for 7 years. This was my second marriage, and it took me seven tries to escape. When I reflect on this situation, I see the repeated cycles that influenced my understanding of marital relationships. I too was once a young girl watching as my mother tolerated my father's abuse for the sake of keeping the family together and to avoid any further trauma at the hands of strangers. Hence, my tolerance for abuse for the sake of preserving the family, and my children witnessing arguments and verbal abuse. There was a night when my daughter witnessed me being dragged by my hair across the living room. This was the last straw for me, to hear my 2-year-old daughter screaming out of terror. When I broke free from the relationship, I was able to help rebuild my life. However, I did not take notice of the imprint made on my daughter's identity until she started to become an adolescent and interested in romantic relationships.

The experts say to break the cycle of childhood trauma, adverse childhood experiences (ACEs) must be identified and the trauma treated as soon as possible (Generational Trauma: Breaking the Cycle of Adverse Childhood Experiences, 2020). Growing up in my understanding of my parenting philosophy and being free of the relationship causing the pain and hurt, I was able to start working on the prevention of adverse effects. I started to limit the exposure to chaos and disruption in my children's lives. I kept school consistent; we had rules and expectations in our home. This helped my children feel safe and secure. They always knew what to expect and when to expect it. This is when I started to pursue my higher education; first my bachelor's degree in psychology followed by my master's degree in human services. My children became involved in music and sports activities, which helped them gain social skills, learn about healthy friendships, and connect with positive adults such as coaches and instructors. I tried my hardest to erase the past exposure of my mistakes, but it did not take long for things to resurface.

My daughter was a sophomore in high school with so many opportunities in front of her. My daughter's talent in sports gave her advantages and many opportunities to help build her future, and for a while, we were on the right path. At age 15, she began a relationship with a young man in a grade ahead of her, who slowly started to influence her choices. In the blink of an eye, my daughter was skipping all her sports games and practices. She began putting this person's needs above her own.

As a proactive parent, I saw the behaviors and would do the parent-to-child sit-downs and explain my expectations. Every time there was a situation, I tried to encourage my daughter, letting her know that she was loved and accepted but that the behaviors could not continue. My daughter would look me in the eye and say "Yes ma'am" or even take time to write me a letter expressing her remorse, but then not but a week later, we were doing it all over again. There was one morning when I was getting ready to go to work when my "mom radar" went off, and I checked her closet. I found the young man in her closet asleep. So I woke them up and asked the young man to give me his parents' numbers so he could leave under their supervision. He resisted giving me the information. With no choice, I called the police and had him escorted out of my house and told him he was no longer welcome in my home, hoping this was the lesson they took in to stop acting irresponsibly.

It was the Friday before Mother's Day weekend when my daughter came to me crying after her soccer banquet telling me she was pregnant. The abuse didn't stop; if anything, the young man became more possessive and threatening. My pregnant daughter was now being pushed and punched by this young man, and she didn't know what to do.

Here it is in black and white, the cycles of ACES: "Adverse childhood experiences often come from various sources of violence," said Mary Ciccarelli, M.D., an internist-pediatrician for Riley Children's Health. "This could be witnessing or experiencing violence, neglect or abuse in your home or community, being close to someone who dies by suicide or being sexually assaulted in childhood" (Indiana University Health, 2020). My daughter and I very much became the statistics that I now educate others about. Breaking the cycle requires so much more than just participation in classes or higher education. Yes, building the awareness that cycles are there and being honest with yourself about where you are helps. However, it also must come from within your spirit—the desire to change for the better. As much as I wanted for my daughter, she must also want it for herself. Although I implemented the appropriate discipline and expectations after my violent relationship, it was still required that I discuss healthy expression of feelings, love, and relationships with my children.

I began working with my daughter to help her build an awareness of choices and consequences. There were so many things we had to unpack, and it was not until she was ready to take that step and be truly honest with herself that the work started to bring about changes in her life. She also had to process all the things she was doing and allowing in her life. She began to take responsibility, stop lying to herself and others, and start implementing self-care. She started to believe in who she was created to be and the importance of her life—how much it mattered to herself and those who loved her. She started to build confidence and stopped being a "go with the flow" type of young woman. This is when she began to reframe her self-worth to resemble a person of worth, value, and love. Now, equipped with the knowledge of conscious thinking and choices, she understands the old programming is still rooted in her mind, but she is very proactive about reprogramming her unconscious mind so that when panic strikes, she no longer resorts to past behaviors. She is equipped with the understanding that she creates her life through the choices, habits, and actions she does or does not take.

Discussion Questions

1. How do generational patterns of trauma and ACEs impact the emotional and behavioral development of children, and what role can parents or caregivers play in breaking these cycles?

2. In what ways can unresolved trauma from previous generations shape family dynamics, and how might addressing this trauma create healthier relationships for future generations?

3. How can understanding the impact of ACEs inform strategies for breaking negative generational cycles and fostering resilience in both individuals and families?

References

Indiana University Health. (2020, December 10). *Generational trauma: Breaking the cycle of adverse childhood experiences*. https://iuhealth.org/thrive/generational-trauma-breaking-the-cycle-of-adverse-childhood-experiences

Substance Abuse and Mental Health Services Administration. (2014, March). *Understanding the Impact of Trauma*. Retrieved from National Library of Medicine: https://www.ncbi.nlm.nih.gov/books/NBK207191/

Additional Resource

Leonhardt, K. (2023, May 10). Breaking the cycle: Addressing generational patterns key to improving quality of life. *The Green Bay Press Gazette*. https://www.greenbaypressgazette.com/story/news/local/2023/05/10/breaking-the-cycle-addressing-generational-patterns-can-help-families/70194486007/

Neonatal Abstinence Syndrome: Experiences of Foster Care Parents

Elizabeth A. Ramsey, Ph.D., CFLE
Assistant Professor
Tennessee Technological University, Human Ecology
Cookeville, TN

The poetic creative representations in this piece came from a qualitative case study that I completed to understand the experiences of foster parents who cared for infants with *neonatal abstinence syndrome* (NAS). Newborn babies are diagnosed with NAS when a pregnant woman takes illicit drugs during her pregnancy, which may include prescriptions opioids, heroin, and other substances that cause the newborn baby to be born in an addicted state (March of Dimes, 2024). Infants with NAS experience a variety of symptoms, including tremors, seizures, excessive high-pitch inconsolable crying, low birth weight, feeding difficulties, diarrhea, vomiting, rapid breathing, breathing difficulties, trouble sleeping, stuffy nose, and fever (March of Dimes, 2024). The term *neonatal opioid withdrawal syndrome* (NOWS) is similar to NAS but is withdrawals caused specifically by prenatal opioid exposure.

To understand foster parents' experiences, I interviewed six participants who cared for an infant with NAS (Ramsey, 2017). Every story carried eerie similarities of little to no training on how to care for an infant with NAS and no prior knowledge of the baby's diagnosis. The parents would later discover that the baby in their care had a diagnosis of NAS. Each parent struggled consoling and soothing their infants who excessively cried and expressed looking for any information that could help them learn how to soothe and care for their babies.

The poems *Is This Normal?* and *The Sound of Crying* were created from the direct words and phrases taken from the lived experiences of the participants' interviews. Applying the method of poetic representation, I used the participants' words to write the poems (Richardson, 1993). Inspired by Gribch (2013), the poems were created to bring the reader as close as possible to the participants' experiences of caring for an infant with NAS.

Is This Normal?
(Taken from Rosie and Matthew, Interview 1)

Charles cried.
I mean a lot.
He would cry during the day.
But mainly at night
Really terrible
Family members would talk about how much he cried.
He cried a lot.
He was crying like crazy.
Rocking him in a chair – for two hours.
Just trying to get him to go back to sleep.

I don't know what to do for you baby.
Then, he would just pass out
I felt really uncomfortable because she would make comments about how much he cried.
Why is your baby crying?
Crying. Yeah.
Long periods of crying.
Really intense
Is this normal?
What's going on?
We're going to treat it like it's normal.
We don't know any different.
We still don't know.

The Sound of Crying
(Taken from Deborah, Interview 3)

The screaming is very, very high pitch
She hasn't stopped crying
Really high-pitched screaming
Pierced
Almost like breaking glass screaming
So, so high pitched
If you're really in tune with the baby, you can feel the pain.
A cry because something is broken
Crying because they're scared
They're frightened
You can tell
You can tell a difference
That high pitched crying
Until we were able to figure it out, to get her wrapped tight.
Everything starts over again.
Pierced.
So, so high pitched
I don't think I can do this another night.
I can't play mommy today.

I expanded on this qualitative research by conducting a correlational study to understand the training and support of foster parents and the relationships to their perceived abilities, motivations, and likelihood to continue fostering (Ramsey, 2018). I found that only 20% of foster parents were trained by their agency to care for infants with NAS and that 45% of participants expressed they were not trained to care for infants with NAS. Overall, foster parent training does not cover specialized topics such as caring for an infant with NAS. Recognizing this gap in parent education, Certified Family Life Educators (CFLEs) can fill a need by offering training for parents who care for infants with NAS. Recommended content areas include infant soothing strategies, withdrawal symptoms, daily infant care, parental self-care, and parental stress management (Ramsey, 2018).

Discussion Questions & Activities

1. Kangaroo Care has been identified as a helpful soothing strategy for infants with NAS. Search a reputable website, such as March of Dimes or Johns Hopkins Medicine, and read about Kangaroo Care. How would you describe this method of soothing to a parent?

2. Read Zero to Three's online article called "Colic and Crying" (https://www.zerotothree.org/resource/colic-and-crying/). Discuss ways to soothe a crying infant and self-care strategies for parents.

References

Grbich, C. (2013). *Qualitative data analysis: An introduction.* Sage Publications.

March of Dimes. (2024). *Neonatal abstinence syndrome* (NAS). https://www.marchofdimes.org/find-support/topics/planning-baby/neonatal-abstinence-syndrome-nas

Ramsey, E. A. (2017). *Experiences of foster parents who care for infants with neonatal abstinence syndrome: Preparation, readiness, and techniques* [Unpublished manuscript, Tennessee Tech University].

Ramsey, E. A. (2018). *The status of Tennessee foster parent training and support including fostering children with neonatal abstinence syndrome (NAS), and the relationships of foster parents' perceived abilities and motivations with the likelihood to continue fostering* [Doctoral dissertation, Tennessee Technological University].

Richardson, L. (1993). Poetics, dramas, and transgressive validity: The case of the skipped line, *The Sociological Quarterly, 34*(4), 695–710.

Attachment Theory and Its Cross-Cultural Applicability

Elizabeth Morgan, Ph.D., CFLE
Adjunct Faculty, School of Family and Consumer Sciences
Texas State University
San Marcos, TX

Attachment theorists and researchers across multiple fields (e.g., developmental psychology, social and personality psychology, developmental psychopathology, public policy, and intervention) are reflecting on the current state of attachment theory "to encourage greater understanding of different views within attachment theory" (Thompson et al., 2022). One area of difference centers around the universal applicability of attachment theory (Jin et al., 2012).

This article has three sections. First, origins of the universality perspective are reviewed. Second, arguments against the universality perspective are identified. Finally, suggestions for moving beyond the current impasse are summarized.

Origin of Universality Perspective

Attachment theory began as an explanation for infants' emotional ties to their primary caregiver(s) as well as for the link between these emotional ties and children's later emotional health and social competence (Bowlby, 1969). According to attachment theory, infants are biologically primed to form relationships with adults in their lives; maintaining proximity to preferred caregivers increases infants' likelihood of survival (Raina, 2023). The attachment relationship is unique from other adult–child relationships because the former "provides infants with a safe haven and a secure base, which is why attachment figures are sought in stressful situations such as when a person feels threatened or distressed" (Thompson et al., 2022, p. 545).

This unique relationship develops as a result of consistently sensitive and emotionally attuned responses by caregivers to infants' distress, smiles, or chortles. These dyadic experiences are marked by prosodic speech, mirrored facial expressions, and face-to-face communication. Bowlby identified these "nuanced and intimate" experiences as necessary for "promoting a sense of felt security and ultimately the development of secure attachment" (Ganz, 2108, p. 565).

While Bowlby developed attachment theory, Mary Salter Ainsworth developed an observational measure, the Strange Situation, for determining whether the findings would support or refute the primary tenet of attachment theory: Infants' early experiences with their primary caregivers would result in either secure or insecure attachment relationships. The Strange Situation, a series of brief separations and reunions between infants and their preferred caregivers, is primarily based on Ainsworth's observations of European American, home-based mother–infant interactions (Ainsworth, 1978). Ainsworth documented her observations of caregivers' and infants' reunion behavior, their interactions during periods together, infants' behavior during separations, and infants' behavior when joined by a stranger.

Ainsworth (1978) documented three distinctive patterns of infants' and primary caregivers' behaviors: one pattern was indicative of a secure relationship and two were indicative of insecure relationships (insecure-resistant and insecure-ambivalent). Mary Main (Main & Solomon, 1986) later identified a fourth pattern: insecure-disorganized/disoriented.

If, in the parlance of Bowlby, children have a secure attachment with their preferred caregiver(s), they develop a cognitive representation (internal working model) of the world as warm and friendly and explore their environment, confident that their primary caregiver will come to their aid if needed (Thompson at al., 2022; Weinfield et al., 2000). The internal working model is both a cognitive representation of past relationships and a template for future relationships. Thus, theoretically, children whose templates were derived from a secure attachment relationship would be more likely to experience the full range of emotions; express emotions in socially acceptable ways; form healthy and satisfying interpersonal relationships; view themselves as independent, capable, and loveable; and be competent members of the multiple environments in which they live, recreate, and work (Thompson et al., 2022). Conversely, infants who forge an insecure internal working model due to inattentive, rejecting, or nonresponsive caregiving are at risk for unhealthy social and emotional outcomes and are less likely to be competent members of their multiple environments (Weinfield et al., 2000).

In sum, proponents of the universality perspective contend the theory is applicable to all cultures and that "differences in particular cultural practices in early care do not necessarily violate broader generalities regarding the functions of attachment relationships: These functions "address the evolutionary adaptations by which infants can survive to maturity" (Thompson et al., 2022, pp. 550–551).

Arguments Against the Universality Perspective
Opponents of the universality perspective argue that attachment theory is "biased toward Western ways of thinking about young children and patterns of caregiving; these patterns are less applicable to many cultures emphasizing communal care" (Thompson et al., 2022, p. 551). For example, despite the majority of the world's children being cared for by multiple caregivers, the dyadic interaction patterns of European American caregivers and infants are considered the norms for sensitive and responsive caregiving (Keller, 2018). This despite anthropologists documenting links between agrarian communities' division of labor and their childrearing strategies (Keller, 2016). Distribution of the workload among adults includes "distribution of care and caretaking responsibilities" (Keller, 2016, p. 61). This division of labor necessitates infants being cared for by multiple adults; however, infants show attachment behaviors toward one or two of their caregivers (Keller, 2016). Further, communal cultures emphasize interdependence among their members in contrast to European American's support of their children's independence (Ganz, 2018).

Evaluating the interactions of caregivers and infants in communal cultures against the dyadic interaction patterns of European American caregivers has implications for social and public policy including whether to remove children from their homes on a temporary or permanent basis (Ganz, 2018; Keller, 2018; Raina, 2023; Ryan, 2011).

Suggestion for Resolving the Impasse
Thompson et al. (2022) suggested that proponents and opponents of universality identify areas of agreement and jointly address issues related to these areas. For example, gathering qualitative and quantitative data about the caregiving practices among communal and Indigenous cultures would allow for greater understanding of these cultures.

Discussion Questions and Activities
1. Review the literature and locate a journal article that addresses the impact of evaluating Indigenous childrearing practices with attachment measures based on Western societies. Discuss the impact of this practice on Indigenous, communal, and agrarian cultures.

2. Discuss the list of commonalities among members of the two perspectives on universality. Choose the commonality you believe should be addressed first, and explain your choice (see Thompson et al., 2022, pp. 551–552, for the list).

References
Ainsworth, M. D. S. (1978). *Patterns of attachment: A psychological study of the strange situation.* Lawrence Erlbaum Associates.

Bowlby, J. (1969). *Attachment and loss.* Basic Books.

Ganz, Z. (2018). Attachment theory's universality hypothesis: Clinical implications for culturally responsive assessment. *Smith College Studies in Social Work, 88*(4), 262–281. https://doi-org.libproxy.txstate.edu/10.1080/00377317.2018.1507369

Jin, M. K., Jacobvitz, D., Hazen, N., & Jung, S. J. (2012). Maternal sensitivity and infant attachment security in Korea: Cross-cultural validation of the Strange Situation. *Attachment & Human Development, 14*(1), 33–44. http://dx.doi.org/10.1080/14616734.2012.636656

Keller, H. (2016). Attachment. A pancultural need but a cultural construct. *Current Opinion in Psychology, 8*, 59–63. https://doi-org.libproxy.txstate.edu/10.1016/j.copsyc.2015.10.002

Keller, H. (2018). Universality claim of attachment theory: Children's socioemotional development across cultures. *Proceedings of the National Academy of Sciences of the United States, 115*(45), 11414. https://doi-org.libproxy.txstate.edu/10.1073/pnas.1720325115

Main, M., & Solomon, J. (1986). Discovery of an insecure-disorganized/disoriented attachment pattern. In T. B. Brazelton & M. W. Yogman (Eds.), *Affective development in infancy.* (pp. 95–124). Ablex Publishing.

Raina, S. (2023). Culturally diverse parenting: Deconstructing attachment theory. *Perspectives of the ASHA Special Interest Groups, 8*(6), 1500–1508. https://doi-org.libproxy.txstate.edu/10.1044/2023_PERSP-23-00050

Ryan, F. (2011). Kanyininpa (Holding): A way of nurturing children in Aboriginal Australia. *Australian Social Work, 64*(2), 183–197. https://doi-org.libproxy.txstate.edu/10.1080/0312407X.2011.581300

Thompson, R. A., Simpson, J. A., & Berlin, L. J. (2022). Taking perspective on attachment theory and research: Nine fundamental questions. *Attachment & Human Development, 24*(5), 543–560. https://doi-org.libproxy.txstate.edu/10.1080/14616734.2022.2030132

Weinfield, N. S., Sroufe, L. A., & Egeland, B. (2000). Attachment from infancy to early adulthood in a high-risk sample: Continuity, discontinuity, and their correlates. *Child Development, 71*(3), 695–702. https://search-ebscohost-com.libproxy.txstate.edu/login.aspx?direct=true&db=edsjsr&AN=edsjsr.1132388&site=eds-live&scope=site

Preventing Youth Substance Use: What Parents Can Do to Reduce Risk & Increase Protective Factors

Cynthia B. Wilson, CFLE, Ph.D.
Executive Director
The Florida Center for Prevention Research
Florida State University
Tallahassee, FL

Kaley G. Turner, CFLE, M.S.
Director of Program Evaluation
The Florida Center for Prevention Research
Florida State University
Tallahassee, FL

According to the 2022 National Survey of Drug Use and Health (Substance Abuse and Mental Health Services Administration [SAMHSA], 2022), 60% of youth aged 12 and older used some type of substance in the past month (i.e., tobacco products, vaped nicotine, alcohol, or an illicit drug). In the same year, 25% of youth aged 12 and older reported using an illicit drug in the past year, with marijuana being the most used illicit drug (SAMHSA, 2022). Of most concern is the fact that between 2019 and 2021, the number of overdose deaths among persons aged 10 to 19 increased 109%, with deaths involving illicitly manufactured fentanyl (IMF) increasing 192% (Tanz et al., 2022).

Many parents are rightly concerned about these statistics but don't know what they can do to prevent their tweens and teens from using alcohol and drugs. The good news is that there is a great deal that parents can do to build protective factors that serve as buffers against youth substance use and minimize the risk factors in their children's lives. While parents cannot control every influence in their child's life, the key is to minimize risk factors while maximizing protective factors, which stacks the odds in children's favor. The earlier parents begin, the better.

Understanding these risk and protective factors is the first step in helping children avoid alcohol and drug use once they become teenagers. However, parents must also be intentional about taking actions to help protect their children's well-being as early as possible. This article summarizes some of these risks and protective factors and provides specific actions parents can take to help protect their children from the potential harms of substance use.

Risk factors are "characteristics at the biological, psychological, family, community, or cultural level that precede and are associated with a higher likelihood of negative outcomes" (SAMHSA, 2019). Some risk factors are fixed and out of parents' control, while parents can actively influence others.

Protective factors are "characteristics associated with a lower likelihood of negative outcomes or that reduce a risk factor's impact. Protective factors may be seen as positive countering events" (SAMHSA, 2019).

The following summarizes risk and protective factors for youth substance use at the individual/self, family, and school/community levels, along with related actions that parents can do to prevent these issues or at least buffer against their effects.

Individual/Self.

Risk factors include attention-deficit/hyperactivity disorder (ADHD), anxiety, depression, posttraumatic stress disorder (PTSD), difficult personality, difficulty controlling behaviors and emotions, sensation seeking, impulsivity, and positive attitudes toward drug and alcohol use (Partnership to End Addiction, 2021a, 2021b; Prevention Network, n.d.).

Protective factors include the ability to control emotions/behaviors; attachments; communication, language, and academic skills mastery; ability to develop friendships; age-appropriate physical development; positive self-esteem; ability to use coping and problem-solving skills (Prevention Network, n.d.).

What parents can do: While parents cannot prevent all these issues, they can pay attention to their children's behavior, and if they have a concern, they can address it early. Untreated mental health issues can place children at higher risk of substance use and mental health problems in adolescence (National Institute on Drug Abuse, 2021), so early intervention is key. These concerns can be discussed with the child's pediatrician and/or a mental health specialist so that appropriate interventions can be explored, preferably before the child becomes an adolescent. Parents who notice that a child has difficulty controlling their emotions can help by modeling emotional regulation, especially during intense moments, and by actively teaching self-calming techniques such as taking 5 deep breaths or taking a break to calm down. Parents can also arrange play dates to help develop social skills, and role-play new social skills with the child before and after each play date when a deficit is noticed. For a child struggling with self-esteem, parents can foster opportunities to develop confidence in at least one area of life (e.g., a sport, instrument, or other hobby), as this has been demonstrated to increase self-esteem (Maidenberg, 2021). Children with higher self-esteem are better equipped to resist negative influences and peer pressure during their preteen and teen years. Parents can also teach coping skills by modeling appropriate coping, such as saying things to their child like "I am feeling really sad right now" or "I am feeling angry, so I need to take a 5-minute break to calm down before I talk with you." Actively teaching problem-solving skills also promotes the development of healthy coping mechanisms. Behavioral issues such as sensation-seeking and impulsivity can often be addressed by helping children find healthy, productive ways to channel their desire to take risks (e.g., playing games or learning a new sport) and practicing goal setting and short-term delayed gratification (Prevention Network, n.d.).

Family.

Risk factors include parents who use drugs or alcohol; parents who are hostile, overly permissive, or lacking warmth; poor attachment with primary caregivers; lack of consistent supervision; and sexual, physical, or emotional abuse (Prevention Network, n.d.).

Protective factors include parental involvement; supportive, reliable/consistent caregivers with structure, monitoring, and clear expectations expressed on behavior/substance use; and verbal rather than physical discipline (Prevention Network, n.d.).

What parents can do: At home, it is crucial that parents maintain open communication with their children and stay involved in their lives, even during the preteen and teen years. Parents should also clearly express behavioral expectations and model healthy habits, including responsible alcohol and drug use. This includes avoiding demonstrating reliance on nicotine, alcohol, or substances to cope with stress because it may influence children to adopt similar strategies. Additionally, parents should safeguard tobacco, alcohol, and prescription medications at home to prevent experimentation and ensure children's safety. Many parents may benefit from taking a parent education class to learn effective parenting practices, such as being kind and warm while still being firm and giving natural and logical consequences when children misbehave. Prioritizing family time and individual daily time with each child can build attachment and bonding. As children transition into the preteen and teen years and begin spending more time away from home, it is crucial that parents keep an eye on their activities. This includes being aware of their whereabouts after school, getting to know their friends, and establishing and enforcing basic rules (Prevention Network, n.d.). Research indicates that children and adolescents whose parents have a clear understanding of their activities and social circles are significantly less likely to engage in risky behaviors (Dickson et al., 2015).

School and Community.

Risk factors include community violence; school transitions or stress; poor school performance; lack of school connectedness; bullying or peer rejection; peers who use or have positive attitudes toward substance use; access to drugs or alcohol; and retailers selling alcohol to minors (Partnership to End Addiction, 2021a, 2021b; Prevention Network, n.d.).

Protective factors include relationships that allow genuineness; a sense of accomplishment and self-worth; opportunities that promote a sense of belonging, mastery, and value; antibullying policies and practices in school; participation in religious or spiritual activities; and the presence of a mentor (Prevention Network, n.d.).

What parents can do: Although parents may not have control over violence in their community, they can serve as a buffer against its effects by providing safe, secure, loving, and nurturing home environments that are free from violence (Suarez et al, 2024). It is important to maintain open communication with children so that they can talk about their feelings, fears, and experiences related to community violence and to demonstrate healthy coping mechanisms when faced with stress or adversity. Additionally, parents can build and strengthen their children's resilience, which can help them manage challenges they may experience with their peers and school and increase their ability to cope with academic or social stress. By modeling resilience, parents teach their children effective ways to manage difficult situations. For children or teens who lack school connectedness and are experiencing poor school performance or school-related stress, it is important that parents resist the urge to force their child to engage with school. Instead, explore and address what may be underneath their lack of desire to participate in school (e.g., bullying, lack of social skills; Prevention Network, n.d.). At the same time, encourage children to build positive relationships with their teachers and peers because these strong social connections can act as protective factors. Parents can also help cultivate positive peer relationships and additional trusted adult relationships and promote a sense of belonging for their children through involvement in religious and spiritual activities, community organizations, or recruiting a mentor for their child. Research has shown that families with the highest quality parent–child relations and high religiousness were at the lowest risk of adolescent substance use disorders (Hoffmann, 2023).

In conclusion, although parents cannot control every influence in their children's lives, they can still play a significant role in reducing risk factors and building protective factors that reduce the likelihood of them engaging in risky behaviors. By cultivating homes that are safe, nurturing, and full of unconditional love and connection; where the lines of communication are open; where resilience is modeled and built; and where children are free to build healthy relationships with other caring adults, parents can stack the odds in their children's favor. Although this is not a "silver bullet" of parenting that will 100% guarantee they will not engage in substance use, by building the protective factors discussed in this article, parents can significantly reduce the risk that their children will engage in underage drinking and drug use once they become teenagers.

Discussion Questions
1. Based on this information, how would you respond to a parent who feels like they cannot influence whether or not their teenager uses alcohol or other drugs?

2. What are some important things parents can model to their children to reduce the risk of substance use?

3. In what ways can parental involvement and open communication serve as protective factors against youth substance use?

References

Dickson, D. J., Laursen, B., Stattin, H., & Kerr, M. (2015). Parental supervision and alcohol abuse among adolescent girls. *Pediatrics, 136*(4), 617–624. https://doi.org/10.1542/peds.2015-1258

Hoffmann, J. P. (2023). Parent–child relations, religiousness, and adolescent substance use disorders. *Journal of Drug Issues, 53*(2), 335–356. https://doi.org/10.1177/00220426221121608

Maidenberg, M. P. (2021). 14 Strategies for building confidence in your children. *Psychology Today.* https://www.psychologytoday.com/us/blog/being-your-best-self/202103/14-strategies-building-confidence-in-your-children

National Institute on Drug Abuse. (2021, August 3). *Common comorbidities with substance use disorders research report.* https://nida.nih.gov/publications/research-reports/common-comorbidities-substance-use-disorders/introduction

Partnership to End Addiction. (2021a). *Playbook for parents of pre-teens.* https://cdn-01.drugfree.org/web/prod/wp-content/uploads/2022/01/19201051/Parents-for-Tweens-Playbook-062821.pdf

Partnership to End Addiction. (2021b). *Playbook for parents of teens.* https://cdn-01.drugfree.org/web/prod/wp-content/uploads/2022/01/19201051/Playbook-for-Parents-of-Teens-062821.pdf

Prevention Network. (n.d.) *Risk and protective factors for substance use and mental health disorders.* https://www.preventionnetwork.org/wp-content/uploads/Risk-and-Protective-Factors-for-Substance-Use-and-Mental-Health-Disorders-2.pdf

Suarez, G. L., Burt, S. A., Gard, A. M., Klump, K. L., & Hyde, L. W. (2024). Exposure to community violence as a mechanism linking neighborhood disadvantage to amygdala reactivity and the protective role of parental nurturance. *Development Psychology, 60*(4), 595–609. https://doi.org/10.1037/dev0001712

Substance Abuse and Mental Health Services Administration. (2019). *Risk and protective factors.* https://www.samhsa.gov/sites/default/files/20190718-samhsa-risk-protective-factors.pdf

Tanz, L. J., Dinwiddie, A. T., Mattson, C. L., O'Donnell, J. & Davis, N. L. (2022, December 16). *Drug overdose deaths among persons aged 10-19 years—United States, July 2019-December 2021.* Morbidity and Mortality Weekly Report, U.S. Department of Health and Human Services, Centers for Disease Control and Prevention. http://dx.doi.org/10.15585/mmwr.mm7150a2

Chapter V
Life Skills

The Practice Credit Card

Mary Bold, Ph.D., CFLE
Financial Planner
Abacus Financial Planning, LLC

The credit card has become a permanent fixture in U.S. family economics today. Besides providing a convenient means for paying for purchases, the credit card can serve as the first building block of a credit history. Researchers have found a positive relationship between credit card behavior and long-term financial planning (Cooper & Uzun, 2023). The downside is well documented: Credit cards can also stimulate high debt. Young adults are especially at risk of generating debt and find themselves deluged with credit card offers.

Credit card debt and credit card solicitations present a growing problem in the United States, especially for young people. In 2023, more than 42% of college students had credit card debt (Harzog, 2023). College campuses have long been a favorite marketplace for credit card companies. Today, laws offer some protection to consumers in that the companies cannot issue cards to anyone under age 21 who does not have steady income (or a co-signer). But companies have leeway in what qualifies as income and how that income is documented (Irby, 2021). Some parents agree to serve as co-signers, of course, because of the convenience a card can provide.

Parents can address some behaviors surrounding money management with their children before they finish high school. It is important to discuss several features of a credit card, such as the importance of paying the balance in full each month to avoid high interest charges on unpaid balances, as well as paying on time to avoid stiff late charges, which then have a negative effect on credit history, as information is publicly reported to nationally affiliated credit bureaus. In short, parents have a lot to communicate to emerging adults about credit card use. The following example shows how parents can learn from their children's own strategies to manage funds wisely.

To prepare my daughter for what could be a lifetime of credit card usage and make her credit-savvy before she left home, I intentionally sought a credit card for her at the tender age of 15. A local department store issued the card in my name and permitted my daughter to carry the card and use it for purchases on her own. We agreed that she would use the card for all her clothing purchases, which would require considerable planning to last the entire year. The allowance was $50 a month in the late 1990s. The rule was that a monthly bill of $50 or less would be paid by Mom. But if the monthly bill were even a penny over $50, the bill would belong to her—to be paid out of her own savings.

With your own children, you might want to vary this plan in terms of an amount according to your budget and the type of credit card. Some parents choose to work with more expenses throughout the months. Either way, children will learn how to save funds from one month to another, making accommodations for larger purchases. Another option might be to open a checking account for your child, along with being an authorized user on one of your credit cards to learn the fuller scope of financial management.

My credit card plan for my daughter was successful—but not in the way I imagined. She was worried about that one-penny-over-the-limit rule and so developed her own strategy for safety. On the first of every month, she went to the Customer Service desk and used the credit card to purchase a $50 gift certificate. Not only did she never go over the monthly limit, she also found her own way to plan for the year. She stockpiled several of those certificates to have more spending power at prime times, such as before the start of the school year. She also became aware of sales and seasonal markdowns; her stockpiled gift certificates provided a new benefit I had not even considered. I had a moment of feeling outsmarted, and then I realized that my daughter had learned the best lesson of all: that she was highly capable of protecting her own credit (by not overspending by even a penny) and budgeting for the long term.

The credit card can serve as a springboard for financial literacy whereby parents can share crucial information about credit and finances. Use of a card provides concrete evidence of how budgeting and planning can protect one's finances. Practical concerns such as payment due dates and safeguards against loss are obvious with the first use of a card.

Financial literacy is sometimes overlooked in family communication, but it is actually just part of a larger picture of financial socialization. The broader socialization reflects both home and school learning of values and behaviors (Sinnewe & Nicholson, 2023).

Nevertheless, there is a link between socialization and financial literacy and that may influence young adults' financial health. Sinnewe and Nicholson (2023) recommended that the larger social context be considered in the design of financial education.

Discussion Questions & Activities

1. Do adults expect too much from financial training for children and teens?

2. Considering human development, should we expect success from financial literacy or financial education?

3. A biosocial approach to finances would suggest that some of our money management is "baked in" with a genetic component. On the other hand, we may see how we were influenced by how our friends handled money or by hearing older relatives' tales of recessions. What are some examples of nature versus nurture in regard to finances?

References

Cooper, E. W., & Uzun, H. (2023). Credit card usage and long-term personal financial management. *Journal of Personal Finance, 22*(2), 84.

Harzog, B. (2023, August 30). *Survey: Over 42% of college students have credit card debt*. U.S. News & World Report. https://money.usnews.com/credit-cards/articles/survey-over-42-of-college-students-have-credit-card-debt

Irby, L. (2021, October 24). *Why credit card companies target college students*. The Balance. https://www.thebalancemoney.com/credit-card-companies-love-college-students-960090

Sinnewe, E., & Nicholson, G. (2023). Healthy financial habits in young adults: An exploratory study of the relationship between subjective financial literacy, engagement with finances, and financial decision-making. *The Journal of Consumer Affairs, 57*(1), 564–592. https://doi.org/10.1111/joca.12512

"Can You Afford It?"

Elizabeth B. Carroll, J.D., Associate Professor Emeritus,
Department of Human Development and Family Science,
East Carolina University, Greenville, NC

You are out shopping with your child when they spot a new toy they want very badly. Do you ever ask them, "Can you afford it?" One of the most important skills for the transition to adulthood is the acquisition of money management skills. Learning to manage money is something that comes with practice. An essential part of guiding the child into adulthood is providing opportunities for the child to practice making decisions about spending their own money. For the child to learn financial management skills, it is necessary for them to have money and the opportunity to make decisions about spending it. Consequently, asking a child, "Can you afford it?" is one of the wisest things a parent can do.

Children receive money in the form of allowances, spending money, gifts, incentives, and earnings. Many earn money by having paid tasks and others with part-time jobs (GoHenry, 2022). Adolescents, average age 15.7 years, self-reported annual spending was $2,316 (Piper Sandler Companies, 2023). In view of this, it is apparent that one of the major responsibilities of being a parent is to impart consumer education to children.

Overall, children report that they wish their parents would have actively taught them to manage money (LeBaron et al., 2018). Parents are role models and should be aware that children will learn through imitating their attitudes and behaviors about spending and saving money. It is easier for the child to learn to be a good money manager if they watch parents who use good money management techniques. In addition, the lessons about financial management should be developmentally appropriate for the child's age. Parents should begin teaching their children about money early (Smith et al., 2018). Preschoolers can sort coins; elementary-grade students can practice math skills by counting the change after they buy something; and teens can consider how peers and media influence their purchases. An understanding of what money is and how it is budgeted is an essential component of successful adulthood. The long-range negative impact of poor financial skills can be mounting debt and bankruptcy. The lifelong advantage of teaching children to be wise financial managers is worth the effort.

Teaching children about money management and spending choices begins from the time the child is old enough to go shopping and say, "I want that." Most parents cannot afford everything the child wants, and even if they can, indulging every whim can set up unrealistic expectations for the future. Planned shopping trips with a child, where the parent sets limits on how much they are willing to spend, can provide the child with the chance to learn to stay within a preset limit.

Many parents will choose to give their child an allowance as they mature. A Harris Poll conducted for the American Institute of Certified Accountants found that young people under 25 years old who were still residing at home received an average of approximately $120 per month (Dennis, 2019). Allowances offer opportunities for discussions about saving and making wise financial decisions. Children should be allowed to make some choices on their own and learn from the consequences if a choice they make turns out to be a mistake.

As children grow older, they may begin to earn money through special tasks that the parent or a neighbor may hire them to do and later through part-time and summer jobs. The older adolescent still needs parental guidance regarding savings as well as spending choices. This is an excellent time to discuss future financial goals such as college, buying a car, and creating long-term savings. It is important for emerging adults, those aged 18 and older, to realize that they are legally adults. They need to realize that poor financial decisions may have significant long-term effects, such as creating high levels of debt or negatively influencing their credit rating.

For the parent, lessons in money management are a constant balance between giving a child the freedom to make decisions while providing adequate instruction along the way. Just as children are not born knowing how to manage money, parents are not always automatically equipped with the knowledge to teach money management skills. This offers an opportunity for learning together.

"Can you afford it?" is one of the wisest things a parent can ask a child, adolescent, or young adult. It teaches them that there are limits to financial resources, and that they need to stay within them. When asked this question, children learn to budget and plan for purchases, while learning to be responsible for their own behavior. It prepares them for the transition to adulthood when they will be responsible for "affording it."

Discussion Questions

1. Assume you are shopping with a child. What are age-appropriate steps for teaching a child to pay for something with cash and make change?

2. How much allowance is appropriate for a child? Should all or part of the allowance be dependent upon the child performing household chores?

3. How do you encourage a child to save for future purchases?

References

Dennis, A. (2019, October 1). Children's average allowance in 2019: $120 a month. *The Journal of Accountancy.* https://www.journalofaccountancy.com/news/2019/oct/average-child-allowance-2019-201922088.html

GoHenry. (2022). *The youth economy report 2022, kids making money: The future of work.* https://cdn.gohenry.com/site-furniture/amp-us/pdfs/GoHenry_The_Youth_Economy_Report_2022.pdf

Piper Sandler Companies. (2023). *Piper Sandler completes 46th semi-annual generation Z survey of 9,193 U.S. teens.* "https://www.businesswire.com/news/home/20231010273091/en/"https://www.businesswire.com/news/home/20231010273091/en/

LeBaron, A. B., Hill, E. J., Rosa, C. M., Spenser, T. J., Marks, L. D., & Powell, J. T. (2018). I wish: Multi-generational reflections on parents teaching children about money. *Journal of Family and Economic Issues, 39*(2), 220–232. https://doi.org/10.1007/s10834-017-9556-1

Smith, C. E., Echelbarger, M., Gelman S. A., & Rick, S. I. (2018). Spendthrifts and tightwads in childhood: Feelings about spending predict children's financial decision making. *Journal of Behavioral Decision Making, 31*(3), 446–460. https://doi.org/10.1002/bdm.2071

Lessons Learned: When Transitioning From Being a Mother of a Teen to a Mother of a Teen Parent

Lisa Taylor Cook, Ph.D.
Assistant Professor, Division of Child Development and Family Studies
Tarleton State University
Stephenville, TX

Kristina Higgins, Ph.D., CFLE
Division Director and Associate Professor
Division of Child Development and Family Studies
Tarleton State University
Stephenville, TX

I clearly remember the day I received the phone call that my son's girlfriend was pregnant. He (Collin) was 15 and she was 17. I was wrong thinking the realization that their life trajectory was going to change would be the biggest challenge I would deal with as a mother of a teen father. These last 2 years of being a grandmother, and mother to a teen father, has demonstrated just some of the challenges that Collin will face as a single father. These challenges are ingrained into various systems and professional beliefs that make being a single father harder than it needs to be. I am a firm believer in Bronfenbrenner's ecological theory (Guy-Evans, 2024), so I found myself constantly reflecting on how Collin's support systems and interactions with various agencies and professionals were influencing his ability to care for himself and his daughter. My ever-changing role of supporting him maneuvering through the bureaucracy of the various social systems has created new stressors for me that I did not expect.

First within Collin's microsystem—his relationship with his father and I shifted. He was no longer our carefree youngest child; rather, he became someone who needed to mature to be able to provide care for another. I had to let go of the view of my 15-year-old boy still being little and needing me, and shift to the mindset of helping him prepare to care for his own child. Watching your son become a father is an emotional experience and even more emotional when your son is not fully a grown man during the process. I had to shift my guidance and desire to "fix" things for my teen son with the knowledge that he needed to struggle more as he would have to learn to figure things out in the moment with his own daughter. Babies do not come with instruction manuals, and I needed him to learn that everything was not going to be predictable and that neither he nor I could "fix" everything every time.

A noteworthy mesosystem interaction for Collin was between his responsibilities at home as a father and his expectations at school. In the school district where Collin attended, he tried to access student parent resources. However, I had to support him through accessing these resources because inclusion of fathers was limited. The enrollment paperwork was focused on expectant mothers, their pregnancy history, goals for completing high school, and so on. Only a few questions asked for the father's name and contact information (if the mother wanted to provide it). Collin found out that he would be a father in his sophomore year of high school; however, during that year and his two remaining years in high school, the parent resource personnel only contacted him when I requested information. My role as mother and grandmother expanded due to having to view my teen son not only as a high-schooler who needed guidance but also as a teen father who needed support. I frequently found myself advocating for him as he learned to advocate for himself. As a father he desired to be present at his daughter's appointments, assisted with her care around school hours, yet sometimes being an involved parent conflicted with school events. The case management services advertised on flyers for student parents included "instruction related to parenting skills, child development, family planning, and appropriate job readiness training," but these services were only available to student mothers due to the grant funding. Therefore, although my son had full custody of his daughter, he did not qualify for these student services offered through his school district.

Generic suggestions from the parent resource personnel included suggestions on services that were available within Collin's exosystem. These included (a) contact an outside agency for parenting courses that were only offered during the day when Collin would be in school, (b) contact the state childcare subsidy program to help cover childcare costs, and (c) contact the state work force department for assistance with future careers. No specific contact information such as specific departments within the state agencies, phone numbers, or email address were provided. Numerous times we were left with the daunting task of searching the Internet for agencies and calling various numbers hoping for assistance. Challenges with accessing state assistance included the operating hours of the programs, the fact that both parents were teens and often unable to sign up for services themselves, and a systematic bias that the mother requests the services for the child. When signing up for state services the parent must complete the paperwork or call to ask questions—this requirement is understandable due to privacy expectations—but challenging when the parents attend school during most of the state agency operating times. Thus, early pick-up from school and driving to office locations to get answers to questions, without the fear of being "disconnected" during a phone call, quickly became the norm. I was lucky to have flexibility in my job to be a chauffeur and a liaison between my son and various agency representatives. Multiple times, Collin was required to authorize care for his daughter for medical procedures; but, as a teen father, he could not be alone with her when these procedures occurred because he was not an adult at 17. When applying for Medicaid benefits, he was told that he could complete the paperwork because by the time it was processed, he would be 18 and an adult. If his birthday had been later in the year, he would not have been able to submit paperwork for medical coverage for his daughter because he was not a legal adult himself. At times, the look of confusion on the state agency personnel's face when they were unsure how a teen parent can sign paperwork for their child but are not able to sign paperwork for themselves was always interesting to witness. Honestly, times like this reminded me that not all answers are known and that some people truly do want to be helpful.

The assistance from my "village" of friends and family that helped me help Collin and his daughter was phenomenal. Even as a professional within the family science field, I did not realize how much emotional support I would need to be mentally and physically present to help Collin and through him my granddaughter. The texts of support, shoulders to cry on, hugs, and listening ears that allowed me to vent and talk through situations were immensely supportive and necessary. Being teen parents who are in school and working means they need support and thus, the roles of grandparents are increased to help when and where needed. I quickly learned that "us grandparents" in these situations need support too.

I continue to find myself reflecting on how to better prepare professionals who will work with families in similar situations to mine. In my education I learned that when working with families of young children the entire familial structure must be considered, but I truly did not understand what that meant until I became a mother of a teen parent. Even in the case of teen parents, the needs of each family can be different. Then, when considering challenges that fathers face in general (Shorey & Lanz-Brian Pereira, 2022), the challenges are increased for teen fathers exponentially. The support systems of teen parents, such as the grandparents, must be considered and provided for as well. I have always loved babies, and I knew I would love to be a grandmother, but I thought my children would be older when it happened. Being a mother of a teen parent and a grandmother to a teen's child is still rewarding, and I am ecstatic with my new title of Omah. I'm able to be the best Omah I can because of the support I have from others.

Discussion Questions
1. How has this article changed or reinforced your preconceptions on the challenges teen parents and especially teen fathers encounter when trying to access resources? What changes could be implemented to reduce the challenges faced by teens and teen fathers?

2. Thinking of your own community- what resources would be available to assist teen parents and their support systems? What would need to be done to ensure equitable access to the community resources?

3. After reading this article, develop a Bronfenbrenner's ecological map for the family and the resources that could benefit the family at various systems. What are other family system theories that could be applied to this family's needs?

References
Guy-Evans, O. (2024, January 17). Bronfenbrenner's ecological systems theory. *Simple Psychology.* https://www.simplypsychology.org/bronfenbrenner.html

Shorey, S., & Lanz-Brian Pereira, T. (2022). Parenting experiences of single fathers: A meta-synthesis. *Family Process, 62*(3), 1093–1113. https://doi.org/10.1111/famp.12830

Invest 5 to Save 10

Karen DeBord, Ph.D., CFLE
Professor Emeritus
North Carolina State University
Raleigh, NC

Parenting is hard work in a "hurry-up" world! And it seems as if life just keeps getting more and more rushed. Although we know that finding quality time with our children is critical, there are so many things usurping parents' time at work, at home, and in the community. These challenges can add stress to our lives and make us feel overwhelmed!

Whether it is the first thing in the morning or as soon as you walk in the door in the afternoon, children, toddlers, or middle schoolers want to share their stories, and they want the time and attention of their parents or primary caregivers. By devoting a few minutes focusing on the child as soon as you are together, it will help your relationship and keep the doors of communication open early in life. Later in life, you will be glad you devoted this short amount of time to connecting.

Invest 5 minutes to save 10 minutes
As opposed to turning on the television to fill the sound void, or each person retreating to their personal spaces with a device, make it a practice to try to spend at least 5 minutes with your children right after you get home. Your kids have been looking forward to seeing you, and they need your full attention for a few minutes just to help them feel more secure and loved. This also may help keep them from getting upset later in the evening when you pay attention to other things, like cooking, doing housework, or even working a little from home.

For young children, spend those first 5 minutes with your children on an activity that they choose, like reading, coloring, playing a game, working a puzzle, or telling you about their day. Get down on the floor with them or sit close to and give them your full attention. Kids won't be as satisfied if you are distracted or focused on something else (including your phone).

After you have spent a little time with them, help them start an activity that they can do themselves or with siblings. Television or devices should not be the preferred activity. They may be able to just continue what they were doing with you or help with a task in the home. This will give you some time to yourself to rest or ease into household tasks.

For older children, ask them to respond to specific questions or inquiries. "Tell me about your day" is not as effective as "Tell me about what you did in your science class today," "What was for lunch?" or "With whom did you sit?" Be sure to take the time to sit down with them to see what homework or school announcement may be in their backpack. Once you share their day, they may be ready to help you with some household chores you can work on together.

Create short morning and evening routines including a regular bedtime with some quiet time together before sleep. When possible, have your work time follow family time, or, better yet, after the children have gone to bed, separating work time from family time. Those "5 minutes" together can relieve family stress and save time you will need later for you.

Discussion Questions and Activities:
1. What causes stress in your home? What action can you take or plan can you make to relieve it?

2. Routines create a sense of safety, security, and knowing what to expect in children. Discuss a routine that you currently implement or would like to try that might provide your child(ren) with a sense of safety or security.

3. When you first return home from being out, set an alarm for 10 minutes and spend that time focused on your child(ren). Do you notice a change in their behavior later on?

Time as Money - Using Hour Concepts to Explain Family Finances

Jacki Fitzpatrick, Ph.D., CFLE
Human Development & Family Sciences, Texas Tech University, Lubbock, TX

It can be challenging for parents to teach children about money (LeBaron, Rosa-Holyoak, et al., 2018). Toddlers (2–5 years of age) have limited language and math skills, so they might only comprehend basic concepts (e.g., a quarter is bigger and worth more than a penny). Preschoolers mimic some adult behaviors without understanding the financial dynamics. For example, multiple stores offer mini-carts for child "customers" to fill with merchandise (Pinsker, 2020).

Elementary-age children (6–11 years) have more developed cognitive skills, and awareness of adults' financial activities. As parents engage in daily tasks, kids see them reach into purses or pockets and draw out cash, debit, credit, or SNAP cards. Children can be old enough to recognize that (a) cash and cards don't appear by magic, (b) parents have to spend money because items in stores aren't free, and (c) parents receive a salary (money for employment). However, children can lack financial literacy (Schug & Hagedorn, 2005) about what money is, how it works, and why parents can't always make more available to them. In this context, kids can have difficulty understanding parents' choices (e.g., how they earn money, how they make spending priorities) and motives (won't buy a new toy vs. can't afford a new toy). Children's confusion can be enhanced by digital (tap-and-pay) or buy now, pay later; no money down; NMD) transactions, which they assume allow for infinite purchases.

One approach to teaching financial literacy is drawing connections to moral or social beliefs. For example, parents can link money to values such as working hard, being responsible, and saving and planning for the future (LeBaron et al., 2018). Parallel to the American Dream, parents can convey that money will result from lifelong efforts to fulfill these values. This also aligns with the virtue ethics perspective on parent (Alden et al., 2009) and undergraduate education (Fitzpatrick, 2022).

This approach has some merits, such as promoting virtuous thoughts and actions. However, it has the limitations of explaining one abstract concept (money) by linking it to other abstractions (self-responsibility, motivation, delayed gratification). In addition, it might be difficult or impossible for some children to see their parents enacting such linkages. Kids are not typically present when parents do hard work as part of onsite employed tasks and receive a paycheck for such tasks. Even if they attend Take Your Child to Work Days, these events do not inherently provide a typical or realistic exposure to parents' employment conditions (Asher et al., 2012).

A somewhat more pragmatic approach can be trying to explain family finances via actual numbers. For example, parents can share information about their income/salary and monthly expenses. They can discuss budgets with their children and show line items (e.g., rent/mortgage, groceries, transportation, utilities, medical/insurance). Compared with the morality approach, this is more specific and concrete. However, it might still be beyond children's comprehension because they do not understand the ancillary expense concepts (e.g., What is a mortgage? How does insurance provide access to medicine?). It can be equally perplexing when parents summarize their financial dynamics by using analogies such as "money doesn't grow on trees."

There is a third approach available to parent educators and parents. It builds on children's own experiences of daily life (including limitations). This approach uses children's knowledge of time to explain family economics and resource management. More specifically, educators can guide parents in a money-to-hours conversion. Parents work through a list of income (how much they get paid per hour, how many hours they work per month) and expenses (based on the hourly rate, how many hours pay for rent/mortgage, transportation, utilities, groceries, school supplies/events, medical). If there is a deficit (more expenses than hours), then parents can use this to explain why the family cannot afford to engage in certain activities. If there is a surplus (more hours than expenses), then parents can use this to discuss how this surplus is used (e.g., put in emergency fund, savings for future years, family fun night).

If children are paid for some activities (e.g., chores, good grades), then parents can also help them to figure an hourly cost. For example, they can help their kids to calculate how many hours of chores they would need to complete to buy a particular item (toy, game, snack, sneakers). This can draw a pragmatic link between labor, payment for labor and expenditure of payment (e.g., LeBaron, Hill, et al., 2018). As children comprehend these linkages, they could realize that they will not be able to afford an item for months or years. In this situation, they can have the agency to adjust their expectations and choose more attainable options. This aligns with recommendations for providing both financial knowledge and financial communication skills during childhood (Duong et al., 2024; Tympa et al., 2024).

When some children learn that they cannot work enough hours to get a desired item, they will have strong emotions of anger, frustration, disappointment, and sadness. It can be difficult for some parents to endure expression of such emotions, but the endurance could provide teachable moments. After expression (when kids are calm enough to listen), parents can explain that they do not have control over the prices or required hours to earn enough money to meet the prices. This explanation can provide an alternative to kids' assumptions about parents' motives (e.g., they do not want me to be happy; they are just being mean). In addition, parents can self-disclose that they sometimes have the same experiences when they are unable to buy certain things (for themselves or others). This type of shared emotional experience could be an opportunity to build empathic communication and greater closeness (e.g., Herzog, 2016; Hoppe, 2018).

The prime advantage of this approach is that children directly experience time as finite. They get tired and know they cannot work 24 hours per day. Kids realize they need meal breaks to function (physically, mentally, emotionally). They can also understand that they cannot borrow time from the future (e.g., Fitzpatrick, 2023). For example, they cannot take a loan of extra hours from next week to stay awake longer today. It is possible their own physical constraints on time can help children comprehend why so many parents are navigating financial constraints.

A second advantage is it can allow parents to keep financial information private. For a variety of reasons, some parents are uncomfortable sharing economic details with their children. They do not want to reveal salaries, savings, or debts. In this hourly approach, these details can be withheld. Parents do not have to tell children how much money they make or how much they spend on specific items. They can simply explain their work hours (e.g., 40 hours per week, 250 hours per month) and link the hours to expense categories (groceries/food). The hours approach can also be used to explain extra jobs or side hustles (Clergé, 2023). Parents can show why they must work these extra hours and how they pay for aspects of family life. Finally, the hours formula can be used to explain the value of financial presents (cash, gift cards, bonds) from social network members such as grandparents, aunts/uncles, and friends. If these members work now or in prior years, then parents can explain how their work hours helped make this gift. It is possible that a comprehension of members' effort could contribute to children's gratitude. This aligns with parents' desire that children comprehend "the gift [effort] behind the gift" (Midgette et al., 2022, p. 1266).

Over several years, I have addressed this hours-to-money conversion in teaching about poverty and theories (e.g., Fitzpatrick, 1995, 2015, 2023). Students have comprehended the concepts and process quickly. I think it could be adapted easily for use with parent educators, parents and children.

Discussion Questions

1. Younger children (2-5 years) do not fully understand the abstract nature of time. However, some have an experiential sense of time. For example, they can comprehend the length of the car ride to school or an episode of their favorite tv show. How can parents use this experiential time to teach kids about money?

2. There can be a significant gap between parents and children's knowledge of time/money. Sometimes, the most effective instructor is the person who has most recently gained a specific skill or knowledge. They are effective because they have greater comprehension of the learning challenges and can offer insights for easier pathways to gains. This is a process of scaffolding knowledge within the zone of proximal development (e.g., Fitzpatrick, Kostina-Ritchey, & Hassanzadeh, 2016; Irshad, Maan, Batool, & Hanif, 2021; Vygotsky, 1978). How can older kids (6-11 years) be involved in money knowledge scaffolding for younger children?

References

Alden, A., Cassidy, D., Cooke, B., Gausman, B., Palm, G., Rice, M., Schultenover, J., Stokes, A., Stoner, S., & Zanner, K. (2009). *Ethical thinking and practice for parent and family life educators* (pp. 1–20). Minnesota Council on Family Relations. https://mn.ncfr.wp-content/uploads/sites/3/2014/02/ethical_thinking_and_practice.pdf

Asher, P., Adamec, B. H. & Panning, J. (2012). Second annual AGU Take Your Child to Work Day. *Eos: Transactions American Geophysical Union, 93*(19), 190–190. https://doi.org/10.1029/2012EO190011

Clergé, O. (2023). Intersectionality matters: Black women, labor, and households in Black suburbia. *RSF: The Russell Sage Foundation Journal of the Social Sciences, 9*(1), 86–103. https://www.rsfjournal.org/content/rsfjss/9/1/86.full.pdf

Duong, S., Elliott, L. E., Sidoti, O., Bachman, H. J., Libertus, M. E. & Votruba-Drzal, E. (2024). Money talks! The role of parents' discussion of money for preschoolers' math knowledge. *Journal of Numerical Cognition, 10*, 1–19. https://doi.org/10.5964/jnc.11351

Fitzpatrick, J. (1995, March). *The feminization of poverty.* Poster presented at the 11th Conference on the Advancement of Women in Higher Education, Lubbock, TX.

Fitzpatrick, J. (2015, October). *The great divide between poverty and privilege: The relevance of ecological theory.* Paper presented in the TTU Open Teaching Concept Program, Lubbock, TX.

Fitzpatrick, J. (2022). Microinclusive teaching in family science courses. *Family Relations, 71*(5), 2084–2103. https://doi.org/10.1111/fare.12794

Fitzpatrick, J. (2023). Demonstrating poverty constraints via an in person/online supermarket trip. In H. Scherschel & D. Rudmann (Eds.), *Teaching tips and techniques* (pp. 74–78). Society for the Teaching of Psychology.

Herzog, B. (2016). Establishing the therapeutic impact of empathy through "affect sharing." *International Journal of Psychoanalytic Self Psychology, 11*(2), 152–168. https://doi.org/10.1080/15551024.2016.1141609

Hoppe, S. (2018). A sorrow shared is a sorrow halved: The search for empathetic understanding of family members of a person with early-onset dementia. *Culture, Medicine, and Psychiatry, 42*(1), 180–201. https://doi.org/10.1007/s11013-017-9549-4

LeBaron, A. B., Hill, E. J., Rosa, C. M., Spencer, T. J., Marks, L. D. & Powell, J. T. (2018). I wish: Multigenerational regrets and reflections on teaching children about money. *Journal of Family and Economic Issues, 39*(2), 220–232. https://doi.org/10.1007/s10834-017-9556-1

LeBaron, A. B., Rosa-Holyoak, C. M., Bryce, L. A., Hill, E. J. & Marks, L. D. (2018). Teaching children about money: Prospective parenting ideas from undergraduate students. *Journal of Financial Counseling and Planning, 29*(2), 259–271. https://scholarsarchive.byu.edu/cgi/viewcontent.cgi?article=5017&context=facpub

Midgette, A. J., Coffman, J. L. & Hussong, A. M. (2022). What parents and children say when talking about children's gratitude: A thematic analysis. *Journal of Child and Family Studies, 31*(5), 1261–1275.

Pinsker, J. (2020, February 6). Why grocery stores have tiny kid-size carts. *The Atlantic.* https://www.theatlantic.com/family/archive/2020/02/kids-little-shopping-carts/606175/

Schug, M. C. & Hagedorn, E. A. (2005). The Money Savvy Pig™ goes to the big city: Testing the effectiveness of an economics curriculum for young children. *The Social Studies, 96*(2), 68–71. https://www.tandfonline.com/doi/pdf/10.3200/TSSS.96.2.68-71

Tympa, E., Nousia, A., Karavida, V. & Kanellopoulou, E. (2024). Parents' perspectives on teaching preschool children on financial saving and sharing need. *Journal of Social Studies Education Research, 15*(1), 38-56. file:///C:/Users/jafitzpa/Downloads/4593-16963-1-PB-1.pdf

Chapter VI
Perspectives

You - My Daughter

Marcia Pioppi Galazzi, M.Ed.
President & Founder
The Family Schools, Inc.
Brewster, MA

My hands
My eyes
My heart
All expanded
To create
The you,
The daughter
That created
Me,
The mother.
The teacher, who
Invited the student,
Created the learner,
Who shaped the teacher
Who learns,
At last,
To Love.

Growing Son to Man

Marcia Pioppi Galazzi, M.Ed.
President & Founder
The Family Schools, Inc.
Brewster, MA

What do I see in
This man in front of me.
Enveloping the boy I knew,
Who suffered, grew
So differently.
And better than I thought.

Assigned to become man,
With no blueprint, or plan.
From confusing messages
Searching paths to manhood
On divergent trails.

Carpenter, boatsman, marksman, cook,
Kind humorist, farmer, friend, philosopher, but
Never sure of what is supposed to be
The outcome of the love he gives to me.

A Stitch in Time: Knit One, Purl One

Clara Gerhardt, MBA, Ph.D., CFLE
Clinical Psychologist and Distinguished Professor
Department of Human Development and Family Science
Samford University, Birmingham, AL

The moments of our love string together like a pearl necklace, precious bead by bead, each representing a breath beheld, a second shared, a minute memorized.

Here is the soft pink angora thread, spun from many microfibers into a gentle filigree of flexibility.

Knit one, Purl one, Knit one, Purl one: the shorthand instructions for the knitter: K1, P1.

"In knitting, a purl stitch is the mirror image of the knit stitch but made in reverse. The yarn is in front of the stitch in a purl stitch, instead of behind it in a knit stitch. The purl stitch creates a little bump on the front of the stitch, while the knit stitch creates a bump on the back..."

The purl stitch is a basic building block – it happens when we pull the yarn from the front of the needles through a previous stitch and then it creates a little pearl like bump.

Purl, pearl, purl, pearl... each stitch is a wink in the tapestry of time.

A moment that connects to the previous moment and in so doing creates a pearl-like strand of memories. It represents all the instances we share. The mirrored front and back becomes the metaphor for parenthood—how children and parents complement each other, how we grow one another's resilience. I see my sister sitting in the sun backlit by the streaming morning light. In the distance the Outeniqua Mountains are crisply outlined. A patch of water glistens its turquoise reflection. My older sister Hanna, who in so many ways is a mother to me. My sister Hanna has incorporated some of the qualities I found in my mother Anna; the parent I lost too early in life. Similar names: Hanna, Anna, as if one name embraces the other.

We bought the wool together at a rustic farm store near Plettenberg Bay. Handspun from authentic angora goats. These animals roam peacefully on the farm looking at visitors with an inquisitive gaze. Their wool is processed and hand dyed. The exact shade of rose yarn was carefully chosen; a color aptly called "Love". A palette of warm harmonizing colors envelops my sister as she has become part of her setting – extending what she is wearing into what she is creating.

And so it is with life. Who we are merges with what we do. One is an expression of the other, fueling and feeding. Our creativity grows from who we are and gives us a warm sense of accomplishment as we turn dreams into stories, designs into expressions, ideas into products, moments into memories.

Knitting one stitch after the other while chatting, sometimes deep thoughts, sometimes light-hearted flippancies. Life contains the major dramatic moments, but its essence is captured in the countless times when we knit one stitch after the other, slowly, carefully, as they connect to form a row and then another. Minutes and days of our lives, some connected into the warm texture of a garment that will embrace us with its infused love.

Knit one, Purl one...

Knit, Pearl...

We knit the minutes into hours and hours into eternity.

The eternity where we are connected in love.

In memory of Anna and Hanna.

The Imperfect Perfection of Parenting

Clara Gerhardt, MBA, Ph.D., CFLE
Clinical Psychologist and Distinguished Professor
Department of Human Development and Family Science
Samford University, Birmingham, AL

In my parents' house, a finely woven Bokara rug covered the dining table. Antique carpets were so precious that they were put on tables rather than floors to protect their beauty. As a child I had ample time to look closely at the intricate patterns. Every carpet, however beautiful it was, had a purposeful mistake knotted into the design. This would show that the artistry of the carpet had indeed been created by human hands, as only the Divine could achieve perfection. Later in life it became a game to find these signs of humanness—where did the carpet makers place their mark into the landscape, where was that sign of authenticity, that imperfection that characterizes us in our vulnerability?

As parents we frequently recall our own memories of being parented. We look back at our childhoods with the eyes of a grown-up. When our parents made mistakes, they were the errors of authentic, fallible people. In my own world of childhood, I recall the distinct glow of belonging, being the apple of my parents' eyes. This made me resilient, able to overcome problems or bounce back from hardships.

The woven backing of the proverbial carpet, the core of which we are made, are the fibers of parental love. This intricate knotted pattern reveals the well-intentioned but at times imperfect parenting we experience in our parent–child relationships. As grownups and as parents, it is tempting to feel that the love of our children is our reward. For many of us, parenthood serves us our most demanding as well as most rewarding life lessons. Though we fail in numerous small ways, our children tend to trust and love us unconditionally—an immense gift we may hardly deserve but that we try to honor.

Our best parenting contains that error in the carpet, the expression of humanness. If we had to apply for the job as a parent, we could only have the courage to take on the challenge if the description read: "Perfection not a prerequisite, nor a requirement." As parents, we are reassured by the knowledge that we can be imperfectly perfect. We will give it our sincere effort and dedicate every fiber of our being toward best outcomes.

Parenthood: The Land of Vulnerability

Clara Gerhardt, MBA, Ph.D., CFLE
Clinical Psychologist and Distinguished Professor
Department of Human Development and Family Science
Samford University, Birmingham, AL

Through our children, we inhabit the land of vulnerability. From the time of their birth, invisible threads link us to our offspring, suspending us in uncertainty. The fibers of our being will change to accommodate a young life entrusted to our keeping.

Although different roads lead to parenthood, they all demand personal transitions, as we explore this new and wondrous landscape. Long before a child enters our homes, our minds create a mental space for this little being. We enlarge our world to welcome a possibility. Then the dream grows into a wish, gaining in urgency and culminating in the growth of our family. We have opened the door to parenthood and its accompanying frailty.

In an ideal scenario, we have given our consent to becoming parents, and in so doing, we will have imaginary cords linking our hearts to those of our children. A baby will reach into the corners of our soul and draw out our hidden resources. A youngster will guide us to find strengths within ourselves we did not know we possessed. She will give us hope and change our sense of the future. Through our children we might morph into better versions of ourselves. They are the best teachers of empathy, selflessness, and caring. For our children, we will walk through fire, climb mountains, cross oceans, willingly make sacrifices, and more.

Each parent walks a unique parenting path and finds their own way of fulfilling this role. Ultimately it is a child who will teach us our greatest parenting lessons. We know that parenting is an obstacle course like no other and that parenting stories have many endings. The outcome differs if we stir stressors into the mix. There can be wars within homes and between peoples. We acknowledge that there are unwilling and poorly equipped parents, socioeconomic hardships, incompatible partnerships. Strip the system of resources. Make the parents too young. Deprive them of an education. Take away sustaining values. Add addiction, mental illness, or the detour of crime. Desperation and depression are ingredients that can do endless damage. And still, we are optimistic. As a society we can pool resources, reach out, share, and sustain. In our own backyards, we can start small. An Andalusian proverb promises that every child is born with a loaf of bread under its arm—against reason, we hope that it will be fed, that life itself will create a place and an opportunity, as hope prevails.

Parent education makes a difference. We can identify family protective factors. Parenting represents reciprocities and possibilities, a lifelong dialogue. For some, parenthood is a conscious choice, a serious challenge. For others, parenthood takes them by surprise. We can instill values; we can care and love. Treat our children as we would like to be treated.

Within the stability of a dual parent or extended family system, the resources can be pooled to add to the richness of family life. Parenting can be sequential as one or the other parent plays a lead or secondary role during different life stages of the child. Total family strength can ensure a good outcome and families who celebrate and share life's joys together, can also build resilience. The cornerstones of parenting are nurture and structure. A tango between two essentials. It's about balanced parenting. Nurture is the fire in the hearth, the warmth that sustains. Structure is the predictability of routine, the benefits of a sense of place and belonging that carries rewards through self-regulation, reliability, task completion, and reserve.

Constructive parenting, if put in place in a consistent, appropriate, and loving manner, will allow our children to build their own lives around a web of possibilities. It's like a coral reef, a living, growing entity that shelters life. It is the platform from which parents can launch their children—safely, securely, and emotionally intact. It is the trellis on which the vine can climb to reach greater heights.

And it is the place where through our parental love, we gain the courage to explore the land of vulnerability.

The Seasons of Parenting

Clara Gerhardt, MBA, Ph.D., CFLE
Clinical Psychologist and Distinguished Professor
Department of Human Development and Family Science
Samford University, Birmingham, AL

Several seasons ago we splurged, and a horticultural team transformed our garden into a little Eden. Our intent was simple: "Low maintenance, minimal watering, no cutting, pruning, pampering … we are busy people." The gardener, with the greenest thumb, nodded. He planted the hardiest of hardy and made the wild forest the main feature. Diplomatically, he said that even Eden needs a little TLC and mentioned the benefits of an automated sprinkler system. In our mind, the zero-maintenance zone was a patch of white pebbles with a large Zen-like boulder. No further input required; we were putting nature on autopilot.

In my youth, my idea of parenting was as clear cut as my garden design: call in the professionals, find responsible and developmentally appropriate childcare, put on the automated systems and life could continue virtually unchanged. I was determined that nothing would upset my career and my self-centered pursuits. Raising children, I thought naively, is like completing a degree. Several years of intense input, the kids fly into the blue yonder and voilà: Task complete! Because I wasn't a parent, I missed the essence. I understood nothing. My heart had not yet been remodeled by a child. In time I would mortgage my soul for the well-being of my children, but at this point that truth was hidden from me.

Nothing could have truly prepared us for the arrival of our firstborn and the immensity of the emotions precipitated by this small person. Our parental hearts became suspended outside our bodies, held captive by a newborn. Should anything happen to this light of our lives, we would be destroyed. Surely siblings would reduce the emotional investment, halve it at least, or spread it evenly. Not so. With more children, the parental vulnerabilities increased exponentially.

Our parenting journey maintained a vulnerable component. Nothing could safeguard our hearts against the fear of the most catastrophic loss of all—the loss of a child, from which we were thankfully spared. As parents we could not truly control the future and well-being of our children. We could give it our all with good intent, but the task was intimidating. I would have to beseech a team of guardian angels to support us in this enormous responsibility. Supernatural powers were required to shelter, nurture, guide, love, and cherish these children to the "safety" of adulthood and beyond.

In my mind, the hands-on parenting role would end when they reached the safety of adulthood. But life brought young adults bouncing back into the parental home;

emerging adults challenged by life's demands. Our offspring may be living in mature bodies, but inside part of the child remains, asking for support, advice, acknowledgment, praise, security, and love paradoxically combined with desire for emotional space, independence, privacy, and autonomy. At times they still relied on the parental safety net. The perception of this magical backup, woven of parental love, gives them the acrobatic courage to leap, free fall, and trust that in the end they will land safely and unharmed.

As parents we never truly move out of the danger zone, we are invisibly linked to our children by our heartstrings. Our offspring run their own races, and we are spectators. They fight their personal battles; we agonize about the outcome. They experience the heartbreak of pain, and we cannot carry the burden for them. They drink from the well of joy, and our cup runs over. They are their own people, and we need to let them be, albeit with love.

Back to the garden: What a garden needs most is a shadow. This seemingly makes no sense, gardens need sunshine, and they need water. Then the insight that the shadow is the one cast by the gardener who tends the plants. As the gardener cuts, prunes, shelters, and nurtures, wondrous things happen. The flora can be coaxed; poppies and sunflowers bloom, berries grow, and, unless in their natural habitat, they respond to appropriate tending.

And so it is with our children. There is no maintenance-free parenting formula. No online distractions, no expensive gifts can replace the constructive shadow cast by parents tending their children; shadows that occur through parental availability and presence in the garden of life. It is our ongoing love as parents that supports the development of our children. If by Grace, we get it right, we find the optimal balance of structure and nurture that will sustain and promote growth. This ongoing attention will allow blooms and fruit to appear in wondrous ways.

Parenting continues seasonally: through long cold winters and into the gentle awakening of spring, unfolding into the warmth of summer and the maturity of fall. Little by little and day by day, good parenting is a lifelong task—not just for today or tomorrow, but through all the seasons of our lives.

Silver and Gold: The Family Photo Album

Clara Gerhardt, Ph.D., CFLE
Clinical Psychologist and Distinguished Professor
Department of Human Development and Family Science
Samford University, Birmingham, AL

In a sheltered corner of our bookcase, is a thick, leather-bound family photo album. Opening the pages, separated by thin rice paper, are the printed photos secured with transparent corner mounts. No online digital album—this one is a hard copy, a "feel-the-weight-of-its-importance" kind of book. Inside the sturdy front cover are some dried and pressed strawflowers, their yellow petals almost as bright as on the day they were first picked. Their other name is *Golden Everlasting*, and they seem to be fulfilling that promise between these pages. There are also a few silver leaves, from the silver tree plantation in Somerset West. Their botanical name is *Leucadendron Argenteum*, the second word referring to the typical silver sheen on the leaves. I did not pick nor dry them; that was my mother. It is like touching a remnant of what mattered to her; she is between these pages reminding me of her sunniness, her ability to see beauty in the ordinary. Silver and gold, leaves and flowers—she is reminding me of the longevity of memories dear to our hearts.

Slowly I turn the pages. We are eavesdropping on private moments captured by a camera. Here are the photographic reminders of days past, lives well lived. We smile with the innocence of youth, the joy of anticipation. Shiny hair, peachy faces; virtually unscarred by life's experiences and the accompanying lessons. That was several decades ago. There are other treasured photos. A double frame has been filled with images of previous generations: the families of origin. They stand rather formally and self-consciously, small groups of people. Great grandmother, my namesake, in a blurry haze of Victorian lace and a stern expression. Great grandfather in military uniform, a ceremonial sword by his side. Maternal grandfather: pointed beard, round glasses, and the same heart shaped lips as my mother.

The pictures move forward through the generations. An image of my parents, surrounded by at least two dozen bouquets of flowers, my mother wearing a formal dark suit. Childhood glimpses of my own generation, my brother as a cuddly toddler. My sister's children: my niece inquisitive and engaged at the tender age of four. Move forward in time. My children and then as the youngest representatives of this generational line up, my own granddaughters with the expectancy of youth in their faces.

The visual recordings span a good century and then some. Six generations, I counted them and wondered: Whose genes went where? Who was responsible for that creative genetic material that made some of us artistic? Who loved music, who had a fragile constitution? Who was the thrill seeker? Who was secretive? Virtues and vices, shaken up and surfacing again in new combinations. Ever changing like kaleidoscopic images. Who were these people really?

A few photos are missing. There is only one wedding photograph depicting my husband and I under a floral arch, a solitary memento marking the beginning of our marital journey. There were no other wedding photographs, no images of exchanging rings, nor cutting the cake. The person behind the lens, who had captured these moments, had not been able to give us the photos documenting that day. He prematurely lost his life in a cruel accident. He had given us a few proofs, but his recordings of family events had stopped midway. I wondered about the lost images. Had the negatives been destroyed in a major clean-up? Were they silently and patiently waiting in an attic somewhere as people moved houses, celebrated birthdays, and simply moved on?

Sometimes in life we cannot complete the cycles we had wanted or intended. We cannot record every event. We cannot reach across time. The quality of our wedding and ensuing marriage was not influenced by whether we did or did not have photos. Life swells and ebbs in its own way. Each generation lives within the boundaries and confines of their personal lives, firmly anchored in the here and now. With a little bonus, lives overlap and continue forward.

Recently I traveled across continents for a major family reunion. From the oldest to the youngest, they were all present. Four generations linked by name, tradition, and visible and invisible family connections. The metaphoric mantle of love was placed around my shoulders, and the family ties were knotted more firmly as we revisited and rediscovered places and relationships. We moved forward and backward in time. I rediscovered important family truths. But as one of the older members of the family, I was also quizzed about my memories of events and people. What was great grandma really like? Could she possibly be the genetic culprit for the idiosyncrasies of some of the offspring? Piecing it together like a complex mosaic, trying to see an intergenerational picture.

As I tried to unlock some of the family secrets for the younger members, someone in my circle reciprocated. In that big group of people collectively called "family," someone was giving me hope for the future while completing a segment of my past. Unknown to me, the missing puzzle pieces were being filled in, lovingly completing what needed completion.

After almost 30 years of wandering from one storage space to another, a forgotten box had found its way home. A daughter was reunited with all the negatives of photos taken by her late father. My niece, no longer the 4-year old youngster in the older family photographs, was now the mother of grown offspring. She had done what only the dearest and closest of kin could do: She had captured the soap bubbles of my youth, her youth, our family as she put together the many images her father had captured over the decades. Images of promise, love, childhoods lost and found once more, and threads of connection stretching across years and continents. In the process, she reunited me with my wedding photographs.

More than images capturing treasured moments, she had succeeded in filling in the blanks of personal stories. Importantly, she completed a cycle for her late father. Through his photos, he rejoined our circle; his presence was felt. Printed, cherished, and eternalized, the photos remind us not only of sacred rituals and transitions in our lives, but of the love of families, from one generation to the next. The way that families can step in for one another, can carry us when we need carrying, and can nurture us when we thought we were forsaken. We build on the foundations of our ancestors, and we reach forward to guide those who will succeed us.

Each individual life is woven into the tapestry of the family through oral and recorded history, through remembrances, keepsakes, and photographs. That is why reunions are so important. We pass on the baton of our collective memory; we piece together the patches of the family quilt.

Family ties bind us from one generation to the next. Over time they knit us together in desired and undesired moments, in awareness and ignorance. United as a family we are more, the sum being greater than the parts. Together we form an endless chain linking generations. Through our family ties, we find the courage and support for life's journey, knowing the threads that connect and support this family tapestry are tightly woven, in precious silver and gold.

—In honor of my namesake Clara W. with love and appreciation

The Daisy Chain of Parental Gifts

Clara Gerhardt, MBA, Ph.D., CFLE
Clinical Psychologist and Distinguished Professor
Department of Human Development and Family Science
Samford University, Birmingham, AL

My mother used to gather small bunches of flowers and dot them all over our home. Not the bold carnations or the confident roses. Her bouquets of wild gatherings consisted of a sprig of heather, a dash of marigold, a little branch that would only reveal its beauty on close inspection. My mom held onto life and happiness with a sense of wonder and gratitude. She lived her days fully; she focused on the moment, rather than being reminded of the passing of time. This was her gift: She could find and appreciate beauty in the most ordinary.

When my mother's last year on earth arrived, she changed slowly and almost imperceptibly. A brain tumor was robbing her true self from her. The last time she visited me, she again gathered miniature bouquets and sprinkled them in all our favorite places. I did not want to discard them. As they dried up, faded, and shriveled, I held onto them, as if I could hold onto my mother.

One sunny morning after her death, I replaced them with fresh flowers. I looked for the humble varieties. I searched out the small forgotten daisy, a curl of jasmine, a yellow bloom posing as a weed, a dark brown prunus leaf. I grouped this unlikely collection of God's flora in little vases and knew that it was right. My mom was no longer with us, but she had given me the skills to live my life fully and constructively. The ability to find and appreciate little flowers anywhere was now within my repertoire. I had internalized some of her gifts.

What my mother modelled in our one-to-one relationship I have translated into my formal teaching of parenting principles. There are many nuances in the quality of a parent–child relationship. We take it for granted that children are lovingly parented, and somehow all the goodness of the parent is poured into this receiving cup until it overflows. It's more complex than that. Parenting can challenge us like nothing else; it can bring immense joy, but disappointment and bitter tears are on the flipside of that coin. There can be the pain of loss when the relationship is severed, through family cutoffs, divorce, or through the final parting of death.

In teaching the formalities of parenting roles, we describe the many visible and invisible threads that set the loom. We acknowledge that for as much as our elders parent us, the children reciprocate by doing something in return—it is a bidirectional dance. We do this all against the backdrop of our own family histories. Parenting goes forward and backward in time, and it crosses generations.

By recognizing and understanding some of the patterns, learning techniques, approaching parenting as a skill set that can be expanded, parent–child relationships can become more rewarding. We can also train professionals who will guide other parents in finding the most constructive way through the forest of challenges. In formal parenting education, we make these collective experiences accessible to students and families. We try to keep the uplifting and rewarding aspects of parenting in mind.

Our relationships with the next generation have the potential to represent some of life's greatest joys and ongoing gifts. As Family Life Educators, we are particularly privileged to be close to the stage, where we can observe, encourage, and cheer on the actors partaking in one of life's true dramas and where we can become part of the audience to eavesdrop on the many dialogues that occur within the sacred space of the family.

And so, parents give to children, and children gift their parents in return. They exchange layers of experiences, which become memories, like a watercolor painting—not overworked but translucent. Layer upon layer, it builds to the depth of a meaningful and stable parent–child relationship.

At times it feels as if I lost my mother too early in my life. And then again, when I am reminded of how to be the best parent I can be for my own children, it comes into focus. All the small acts of kindness, the almost imperceptible moments, they string together like a daisy chain, and that becomes the floral crown of good parenting. Love is never lost. It is given from parent to child in a bouquet of gestures: the daily affirmation, the availability of shared time and experiences, the unconditional acceptance. Love grows and love links us like a daisy chain, generation-to-generation.

> *The greatest gift we can give to the world is creating a continuous, uninterrupted, loving family structure.*
> —Aldona Laita

Where I'm From

Mark Sfeir, Winchester, VA
Then, a 13-year-old grandson of CFLE Emeritus, Bob Keim

I'm from applesauce, Tonka, and toy trucks.
The bunk bed that was my tall fortress,
and hideout from my big brother Sami.

I am from the sycamore tree which I used to climb,
higher and higher as I grew older.
The maple syrup that my dad would get off a tree
and we would eat in front of a fire.

I am from the coconut that my family
had to drill open to get that sweet milk.
I am from funny uncles named Chuck, beach trips,
and waiting for that huge wave
that could sweep me off to shore.

I am from my cousins Gabe, Charlie,
and my little brother John.
From birthday songs and Easter eggs that we colored every year.

I'm from washing before you eat,
and look before you cross the street.
I am from my favorite Lebanese foods that mom made
when I grew up, jaj ou riz and fasoulia.
I'm from the berserk firework that almost hit my friend's dad.
I'm from Raffi tapes, Puff the magic dragon, and
being tucked in at night.
I'm from Christmas presents, family movie night,
and campouts in our backyard.

I'm from the Simpsons at 6:00 sharp every day,
dragon tales, and animal crackers.
I'm from starting small fires on my patio with
magnifying glasses and reading Harry Potter.
I am from playing tag to running cross country.
I am from Preschool to Middle School.
Toddler to young adult.

Courage

SaraKay Smullens, MSW, CFLE, LCSW, CGP, BCD
Clinical Social Worker, Writer, Consultant, and Family Life Educator
Philadelphia, PA

The need and desire for belonging begins early in children's lives and extends through adulthood. Difficult issues regarding "fitting in" and doing the right thing arise in every conceivable sphere, like stepping onto a playground with classmates and fearing you may not "measure up"; dealing with someone who demands help cheating on a test; having a close friend or romantic interest urge or insist on an unwise or unethical choice; experiencing the temptation to receive special favors and status others receive through manipulation, distortion, devious behavior, or lack of concern for others; or being urged to participate in the demeaning, shaming, or scapegoating of others. These are just a few examples, of situations that require a level of courage to achieve and maintain self-respect, show mutual respect to loved ones and friends, and act as an upstanding community member and citizen.

Through growing awareness, I began to realize that life is not fair; cruelty very often goes unchecked; and courage is a very difficult, often lonely state both to achieve in oneself and understand, appreciate, and welcome in others.

I saw how often people were punished or ostracized by those who did not wish to see, hear, or discuss their ideas. I saw parents punish children for voicing thoughts that did not meet their approval. I saw partners withhold love and humiliate in myriad ways when things did not go their way. I saw employers demand unethical conduct, punish those who did not acquiesce, and make life as difficult as possible for those whose competence threatened them. I saw political leaders use their power for manipulation and personal gain.

In developing this awareness, I saw that true courage has absolutely nothing whatsoever to do with the yearning of my youth: to feel accepted—to belong. Nor does it have anything to do with winning popularity contests or achieving power over the lives and choices of others.

Courage cannot develop unless an individual achieves the ability to stand alone. Those who develop in this way do not yearn for power and control over others. Theirs is a life art that brings clarity of thinking and vision. They achieve a reliable "emotional sense of direction" that promotes the courage to stand for and speak for what is worthy. But how does this quality develop?

To respond to this question, it is essential to look at the developmental attitudes and opportunities that lead to a child's confidence, direction, and resilience in our exceedingly fast-paced, complex world. And with this comes the ability to achieve courage and its accompanying insights and strengths.

It cannot be repeated enough that love and safety are crucial to children's physical and emotional survival. Children who experience this stability (at home and in their communities) feel worthy of success, can rise above hardship, and find fulfillment striving toward important goals (Smullens, 2021). With this sense of autonomy, they develop character, enabling them to stand alone and stand up for what they believe. The eminent Philadelphia psychiatrist Eli Marcovitz highlights the importance of dignity as "a prerequisite for mental health" that develops in children who are "nurtured, protected and valued." According to Marcovitz, dignity involves two essential components, pride and humility, which lead to "the development of standards, ideals, ethics, and responsibilities" (Marcovitz, 1982, quoted in Smullens, 2021, pp. 55–56).

Neglect, violence, poverty, and familial chaos affect children's neurodevelopment and subsequent ability to tolerate ambivalence, develop creative reasoning, and learn necessary coping skills when confronted with complex challenges (Perry, 2021, noted in Smullens, 2021, p. 55). Further, in all socioeconomic contexts, children who experience physical, sexual, and emotional abuse are robbed of early seeds that sprout courage. For theirs is an existence of perpetual fear, terror, violation.

Emotional abuse, always part of physical and sexual violence, is the most common pattern of abuse and merits its independent codification. Children who experience invisible cycles of emotional abuse are robbed of the early plantings of courage through rage, enmeshment (not given the opportunity to develop independent thoughts), rejection/abandonment, severe neglect, and extreme overprotection and overindulgence (Smullens, 2010, noted in Smullens, 2021). (I now regret that that in my 2010 study, I did not include the impact of parental *unscrupulous behavior*, in which children watch a parent select any means possible to reach their goals, regardless of the cost to others, and the children are encouraged to adopt this pattern of behavior.)

The capacity for self-reliance, empathy, and concern about others and the well-being of one's society—which I think of as "the art of mutual respect"—leads to the understanding that there are times when the common good is more important than personal aspiration.

On a macro level, we must promote this capacity by facing and addressing inequitable conditions that impair the lives of countless children who grow up amid hopeless poverty, and the constant presence of needless weaponry. Further, we must incorporate noted developmental guidance in our own families and communities, fostering feelings of being loved and of loving others in return. In this atmosphere, we can encourage children to make their own simple choices, which grow in complexity as time passes, and to become confident and feel pride in these choices. This growing security will help them become aware of the differences between attitudes that are beneficial to family life and societal stability and those that are not. This achievement promotes the ability to recognize the dangers in those who have no concern for the well-being of others, a truth those who are unscrupulous work endlessly to disguise and deny. It is also one that internalizes an understanding of the importance of saying no to some people and some activities and attitudes in order to say yes to safeguarding life—for us and others. Above all, those who achieve the capacity for courage will be able to "stand alone" and speak and act their truths, knowing that this choice is the only way to live in self and mutual respect.

Discussion Questions

1. Identify aspirational passages in our Declaration of Independence of July 4, 1776. What prevailing strengths can you identify in our country? What prevailing unfairness and injustice? How long have they existed? In what ways was this been addressed in the past? How is it being addressed in the present?

2. What acts have you studied or seen personally, professionally, or in our political world where one put identifying and speaking necessary truths above their own ambition?

3. Suggest examples you are familiar with in life or work where children are given the opportunity to develop self-reliance and character. How have you seen these opportunities violated?

4. What ways can children deprived of opportunity to develop courage be helped through Family Life Education?

References

Marcovitz, E. (1982–1983) *Bemoaning the lost dream: Collected papers of Eli Marcovitz, M.D.* Philadelphia Association of Psychoanalysis.

Perry, B. D. (2021, February 25). *A relational approach to working with maltreated children.* Conference opening plenary address at the American Group Psychotherapy Connect virtual conference.

Smullens, S. (2010). The codification and treatment of emotional abuse in structured group therapy. *International Journal of Group Psychotherapy, 60*(1), 111–130. https://doi.org/10.1521/ijgp.2010.60.1.111

Smullens, S. (2021). *Burnout and self-care in social work: A guidebook for students and those in mental health and related professions* (2nd. ed.). NASW Press.

Additional Resources

Applebaum, A. (2020). *Twilight of democracy: The seductive lore of authoritarianism.* Doubleday.

Eirik, S. (2001). The courage to love: Social interest and sexual-morphological meaning. *Journal of Individual Psychology, 57*(2), 158–172.

Frankl, V. (1965). *The doctor and the soul.* Alfred A. Knopf.

Kendi, I. X. (2019). *How to be an antiracist.* Random House.

Popkin, M. H., & Albert, L. (1987). *Quality parenting.* Random House.

Smullens, S. (2002). Developing an emotional sense of direction: A therapeutic model for the treatment of emotional abuse. *Annals of the American Psychotherapy Association, 6*(3), 17–21.

On Gender and Acceptance

Margaret Stridick, M.S., CFLE
Parenting Programs Coordinator,
Terrie Hess Child Advocacy Center
Salisbury, NC

My older sister was in the process of getting her Ph.D. when she told me she is a lesbian. I was in a committed relationship with my now husband when she shared this with me, and I had questions. I suggested that maybe she just hadn't found the right guy yet. She asked me how I felt when I was with mine, and when I told her, she said she had never felt that way with any guy—but she did with some women. And especially with the woman she was seeing at that time. That really resonated with me, and I remember saying, "Well, you can't argue with chemistry!" So, I accepted her news as a fact, not a choice, and I loved her even more because she entrusted me with this deep truth about herself.

We were raised Catholic. It was not easy for my sister to share this truth about herself with our mother. It took about 6 years before mom stopped praying for her conversion. I'm not going to lie; it was a bit awkward at family events with mom when we were first introduced to my sister's partner. There was a time when something made me and my husband cancel a planned visit and, because of institutionalized prejudice, they thought it was because my husband did not accept them, which was not at all the case. I did not find that out for a few years, and it hurt us all in the meantime. I was glad when she finally told me how they had interpreted it, so I had the chance to set things right. It just shows how important honest communication and acceptance are to family systems.

Discussion Questions

1. The author says she accepted her sister's news as "fact" versus a "choice." Why does this matter, and do you agree with this stance?

2. What role does, or should, religion play in either the acceptance or rejection of gender theory?

3. We often think of institutionalized prejudice in regard to race. What are some examples of how institutionalized prejudice might impact members of the LGBTQ+ community?

Chapter VII
Relationships

Couple Attachment Moments

Jerica Berge, Ph.D., MPH, LMFT, CFLE
Tenured Professor, Department of Family Medicine and Director, ACCORDS;
University of Colorado Medical School
Anschutz Medical Campus, Aurora, CO

Being emotionally accessible and responsive to each other, also known as *attachment*, are the basic building blocks of intimacy between two people (Cassidy & Shaver, 1999; Johnson, 2003). This term—attachment—is used in reference to the nature of the relationship between a parent and infant, as well as between couples (Johnson, 2003). The level of attachment may vary, from strong to weak, or almost nonexistent.

Isn't it ironic that one of the ultimate acts of attachment for couples, conceiving a child and becoming a parent, can decrease a couple's ability to be emotionally accessible and responsive to each other? Research indicates that couples' satisfaction with their relationship declines when they have children (Simpson & Rholes, 2017). At the very time that parents need emotional accessibility and responsiveness from each other most, they are both typically too tired and extended to relate to each other in this way. As their children age, increased stressors with developmental demands of parenting and adolescence can leave parents feeling at odds with each other (Simpson & Rholes, 2017).

On the other hand, research also shows that being intentionally responsive and accessible as a couple at important times, like the birth of a new baby, or working through challenging adolescent parenting issues, can lead to greater emotional adjustment, attachment, and growth for the individuals and the relationship (Bröning & Wartberg, 2024; Gordon, 2024; Simpson & Rholes, 2017). Thus, when couples exhibit attachment behaviors as parents, they can grow closer from the experience.

Being intentionally emotionally accessible and responsive to each other are essential for parents to strengthen their relationship, instead of unintentionally allowing their relationship to falter due to the stresses of parenting. Emotional responsiveness and accessibility do not need to be scheduled events for them to occur. In fact, continuous small gestures and efforts add up to create an overall atmosphere of emotional accessibility and responsiveness (Gordon, 2024). For example, when a partner gets home from work and it is clear that they have had a tough day, the other partner can simply check in to let him or her know that they are in tune with them. Likewise, when a parent clearly needs a break from interacting with the children, one partner can pull the other aside and recognize their feelings, then switch off for a while to allow the other partner to rejuvenate themselves.

Technology has also provided new and accessible ways to connect throughout the day such as sending a short text message of appreciation to your partner or a recorded message or picture sharing moments from your day to let them know you are thinking about them.

Along with the everyday spontaneous efforts to communicate emotional accessibility and responsiveness, partners need to find moments in which they can spend scheduled/planned time together without the children. Because couples have unique lives and schedules, parents will need to be creative in figuring out how they will make alone time happen.

Following are some examples of how to create planned couple attachment moments:
- Ordering in food for a date night after the children are in bed. Then "interview" each other about how their lives are going.
- Having a movie night or half-movie night in the middle of the week after the children are in bed.
- Swapping babysitting monthly with other couples (who have children) to have consistent date nights.
- Going to stores (malls, IKEA, etc.) that have in-house free babysitting and going shopping as a couple.
- Reading or listening to an audio book together nightly after the children are in bed.
- If both partners work, scheduling a Zoom meeting together for 30 minutes to check in with each other during the week.
- Getting up before the children every morning and exercising together. Or getting a membership at a gym that has in-house babysitting for free or a small fee.
- Going on semiannual or annual trips together while family members (especially grandparents) watch the children. For instance, one trip to celebrate the wedding anniversary and one 6 months later to celebrate parenting.
- Getting up before the children and having breakfast together.
- Having a nightly cup of hot chocolate, tea, or coffee after dinner to check in about the day while the children play or do homework.
- Meeting for lunch once a week while the children are in school or being watched by a neighbor (with whom you swap babysitting).

- Starting a new hobby together, such as woodworking, photography, cooking, or home improvement, to do on Saturdays when the children are at friends' houses, sports practice, school events, the babysitter, or other activity.
- Having quarterly weekend getaways as a couple to refresh (swap babysitting with another couple). These can be relatively cheap by exploring places within your own state.
- Joining a bowling league, or other team sport, together while the children are at home doing homework or with a babysitter.
- Send a short text message during the day letting your partner know something you appreciate about them.

By combining spontaneous daily efforts to be emotionally accessible and responsive with planned couple attachment moments, parents can feel closer to their partner and enjoy parenting more fully.

Discussion Questions

1. What is an example of a couple attachment moment?

2. Can you think of 1-2 couple attachment moments that you already have in your relationship, or that you would like to create?

References

Bröning, S., & Wartberg, L. (2024). Attachment orientations: Associations with romantic partners' self-regulation and dyadic coping. *Journal of Sex & Marital Therapy.* Advance online publication. https://doi.org/10.1080/0092623X.2024.2322566

Cassidy, J., & Shaver, P. R. (1999). *Handbook of attachment.* The Guilford Press.

Gordon, S. (2024). *The quality time love language and your relationship.* https://www.verywellmind.com/quality-time-love-language-4783540

Johnson, S. M. (2003). Introduction to attachment: A therapist's guide to primary relationships and their renewal. In S. M. Johnson & V. Whiffen (Eds.), *Attachment processes in couple and family therapy* (pp. 103–123). The Guilford Press.

Simpson, J. A., & Rholes, W. S. (2017). Adult attachment, stress, and romantic relationships. *Current Opinion in Psychology, 13,* 19–24. https://doi.org/10.1016/j.copsyc.2016.04.006

The Necessary Rules for Healthy Fighting

John H. Gagnon, Ph.D., CFLE, MFTL, ABMP
Private Practice, Stamford, CT

I have been a psychotherapist for 35 years. Throughout that time, I have seen individuals, couples, and families, including their children, in one configuration or another. Whenever I worked with issues of anger and fighting, I was taught to allow couples and families to express their anger without being "out of control." I had never seen a list by anyone that said, "Hey … wait a minute. There are ways that you can interact that will allow you to get through a fight without bashing each other to death or wounding one another beyond repair." And to the parents, we want to model better behavior than this for our children; they are apt to do as we do!

As the years went by, I began to insert rules in the way I conducted therapy. They first emerged in group therapy; before each session, I would lay out my rules of conduct for the group, and if anyone violated one, I called them on it, they apologized, and we moved on.

I can't remember what year I began to make a formal list of regulations for couples or families to follow, but I first called them "The Marquis de Gagnon Rules for Arguments," after the "Marquis of Queensbury" rules for boxing. I have worked on and refined the list a little bit, but in the main, it has remained pretty much the same for some 20 years or so. These days, I refer to them as "The Necessary Rules for Healthy Fighting."

When couples or families get to the issue of having unsatisfying or hurtful fights, I introduce the rules on a sheet of paper. I go through each one of the rules in the list while we are sitting in the therapy room. Next, I tell the clients to take their papers home and memorize them. I remind them that they are to use the rules at all times whenever they have a disagreement and to put the rules in a place, such as on the refrigerator door, where they can refer to them when necessary.

I require that each of the family members keep track of the rules for themselves, catching themselves whenever they might call someone a name, for example, then stop the fight, apologize for the mistake, and continue. At first one person may yell, "You aren't fighting by the rules" when they catch the "other" not using one of the dictums. I hear in the next session what happened, and I encourage them to stop any fight by saying simply, "Rules!" Then both parties are to go to their copy of the rules and continue the fight by them. No one may ever use the rules to show how "stupid" or "noncompliant" the other is.

Here they are:

- **All fights exist to "reach good ground"** at the end of a disagreement. Therefore, if one person "wins" a fight and the other "loses," the fight has not been conducted correctly and …
- Therefore, **trust, love, respect, caring, and kindness are key** elements in every fight.
- **Statements** of anger **may sound angry but must be simple:** "I resent that you left the dishes in the sink all day" is an example. It is also **useful for one to express one's feelings:** "It makes me feel like I am expected to be the slave here." However, the simpler the statement, the better.
- The **recipient** of resentment should **never defend themselves.** Accept resentments and **understand them for what they mean.** Listen to what your behavior "means" to your significant other(s). **Imagine yourself** being the recipient of what you did or didn't do.
- There **should be no name-calling**: "jerk," "numbskull," "asshole," etc. No one may be "wounded" in a fight.
- There is **no swearing at the other person** because swearing conveys a general lack of respect. Swearing as an adjective for an object may be OK as in "the damn dishes in the damn sink." Swearing at others, however, is forbidden.

- **No insinuated insults:** the intelligence, body image, opinions, ethics, spirituality, beliefs, or thinking of the other person are never "ridiculous," "stupid," and so on.
- **No threats**: arrest (unless warranted), hospitalization (unless warranted), physical harm, punishment where not due, threat to leave, separate or divorce, run away, and so on are not permitted.
- **No intimidation:** no coming closer in a menacing manner, picking up a weapon-like object, raising your hand as if to strike, grabbing the other person in any manner, and so on.
- **No raising the voice** beyond a common angry tone, **no dominating** the conversation, **no attempts to control** by out-shouting or making louder noises to "drive home a point." Anger is louder than regular speech, but it is not right to use loudness to shut the other person off. Therefore …
- **Allow room for each person to speak.** It is not allowed to talk nonstop, breathlessly, and not leave purposeful spaces for the other person to respond.

  In the simplest of fights, the entire thing might sound like this. First: "I resent your leaving the dishes in the sink all day." Second: "I don't blame you. I'd feel the same way." First: "Thank you for understanding. I don't want you to do that again." Second: "I will make every effort not to do that again."

  Here's another fight. First: "I resent that you told Billy he could stay up on a weekday night." Second: "I can understand how you'd feel like that. I figured that just this once wouldn't be a problem because this was a special TV show." First: "This was not a regular show that he could see again?" Second: "No." First: "This was not a series that he will want to stay up and see another time?" Second, "No." First: "Well … that makes lots of sense, then. Sorry." Second: "That's OK. I can see why you'd worry."

  Here's another fight. First: "I resent that you had Fluffy put down without discussing it with me! I loved Fluffy, too." Second: "God … I'm so sorry … I can see how that would make you feel left out at the end. I'm so sorry." First and Second hugging and crying together.

- **No leaving the present argument.** You may never bring up previous incidences of this event or talk about any previous fight, action, inaction, or behavior that has nothing to do with the topic of the current fight. You may not bring up any other topic to fight about. In fact, you may not project what will happen in the future if this ever happens again. Most wandering starts with, "OH YEAH, well how about the time when you …." This is forbidden. Each argument should be completely self-contained and limited to this instance of the problem right here and should not be allowed to go anywhere else.
- **Also, no leaving the argument by walking out of the room.** Each fight must be concluded. The adage "never go to bed angry" is a great idea, although it is sometimes impossible. When it is not possible to end a fight on a particular day, time should be agreed on for the next day during which to end the fight. Good fighters will find, however, that it takes about 10 minutes to end most fights when conducted by this set of rules.
- **Agree always with the other's basic feelings.** "I understand how you could feel like that." "I don't blame you for feeling that way." "I would feel like that myself."

- **Preserve another's sense of integrity and self-worth** throughout the fight. If you do not, you are "disqualified." Catch yourself, apologize, and continue when the apology is accepted.
- **The end** of a fight must **not be a "null sum (+1 and –1 = 0)."** Both parties should come away from the fight **feeling respected, and understood and also wanting to change some behavior that may be irritating or difficult for another to accept.** Compromise is always an excellent resolution to a fight, but the first person to see that they are wrong, to admit that, and to want to change is to be praised in the fighting process.
- **Love is the outcome of a good fight** within the context of a family, friend, or lover because with the reduction of anger, comes the return to positive feelings; one can't feel one's love for another when there is anger or resentment in front of it.
- Finally, **if anyone leaves a fight feeling "hurt," "injured," or "insulted,"** then the rules of fighting were not used properly or your fight was not conducted by these rules, and **you need to seek help for improving your ability to deal with conflict and anger in a healthier manner.**

So it is also the job of the family to take a "time-out," during which each member examines and discusses objectively what they did in the fight that caused it not to go well. No fighting may take place during this discussion. This is meant to be analytical and to permit people to "own" their respective problems. Anyone who starts a fight during this discussion is doing something wrong and must admit what they are doing wrong at that moment. This discussion is designed to help fine-tune the ability of the couple or family to problem solve the manner in which they fight that is not consistent with the rules given.

When couples or families use the "Necessary Rules for Healthy Fighting," they experience the value of this set of guidelines for all angry expressions or disagreements in their lives. Their ability to fight and share feelings improves, the acceptance of feelings increases, and defensiveness decreases.

Now ... go to your corners, come out for a healthy fight, and then end up in a different corner than either of you came from. In fact, you will more easily learn to wind up in the same corner!

Resources

One may find the following books to be helpful additional reading, but no one has made a list like mine before:

Stoop, D., & Arterburn, S. (1992). *The angry man: "Why does he act that way?"* W Publishing Group.

Ellis, A. (2017). *Anger: How to live with and without it.* Kensington Publishing Group.

Potter-Efron, R., & Potter-Efron, P. S. (2006). *Letting go of anger: The eleven most common anger styles and what to do about them* (2nd. ed.). New Harbinger Publications.

Potter-Efron, R. (2005). *Angry all the time: An emergency guide to anger control* (2nd ed.). New Harbinger Publications.

Commuter Marriages With Children: Benefits and Cautions

Richard S. Glotzer, Ph.D., CFLE Emeritus
Senior Lecturer, School of Social Work
The University of Akron, Akron, OH

There are between 150,000 and 1.5 million long-distance married commuters in the United States. Most commuters remain committed to their marriages and share childrearing and nurturance, including a common family residence. But by choice, they may work a sufficient distance from the family residence and must live away from home during the working week. Commuters travel to the family residence on weekends or at set intervals. Commuter families are challenged to develop unique ways of handling child rearing, family tasks, and other family routines. Commuting, most common among people in highly specialized fields, including college and university academics, construction work, and corporate business, has become an option for many types of workers, committed to career and spouse, in a fluid and unpredictable economy. It remains unclear the extent to which telecommuting (working remotely) will mediate the extent to which onsite employees will be required.

Research on commuter marriage remains underrepresented in academic literature. No one source tells the complete story. Two valuable accounts of commuter marriage are Bearce's *Super Commuter Couples: Staying Together When a Job Keeps You Apart* and Lindemann's *Commuter Spouses: New Families in a Changing World*. Both are available in many public libraries. The Worldwide Employee Relocation Council (WERC, talenteverywhere.org) and its national, regional, and state affiliates draw members from large corporations. WERC offers useful information on corporate moves to members but is oriented to the cost structure of moving. Several moving companies do the same. WERC tracks the issues families typically face in relocation, such as eldercare, intergenerational families, locating schools, spousal employment, and home sales. Home sales remain the highest relocation expense, and some companies are focusing more on "high impact" employee moves. Additional sources of information are Michigan State University's Sloan Center for Work and Family (http://sloanworkingfamilies.educ.msu.edu/welcome.html). Boston College's Carroll School of Management houses the Center for Work and Families and can be accessed online. It offers relevant papers that can be downloaded free or purchased at modest cost (http://www.bc.edu). Canadians may find Guelph University's Live Work Well Research Centre (liveworkwell.ca) and Vanier Institute of the Family (https://vanierinstitute.ca/) helpful.

Taking stock of one's own family circumstances, needs, and aspirations may lead the family to accept the myriad challenges of commuting. These include (a) the desire to maintain ties to their present community due to extended family, home ownership, a gainfully employed spouse in a secure and valued position, or not wanting to disrupt children's school and social progress; (b) local scarcity of professional employment for which one is trained and invested in psychologically; (c) financial need or crisis brought on by illness, debt, or family growth; and (d) opportunities for occupational or income mobility. Commuting is not as straightforward as it might seem. For example, physical and emotional wear and tear for all concerned are difficult to estimate. Working through the culturally laden assumptions of how married people with children should live can be surprisingly difficult. Dispelling notions of a family or marriage "in trouble" may be difficult to avoid, even with well-meaning friends and relatives. Family scientist Andrew Cherlin (2019) suggested that commuter families are investing in components of married life important to their specific family rather than the institutionalized standards influencing past family decisions.

In reaching a decision about commuting, family members should make a detailed inventory of the advantages and disadvantages involved, family strengths and weaknesses that may help or hinder handling it, and the pressures they believe they will face. Getting an informed and objective assessment of what the family is likely to encounter is an important second step. Working through various potential commuting scenarios with a family practice counselor or therapist offers an excellent way for identifying family strengths, potential stresses, and conflicts, as well hidden or unarticulated problems. For some families, consulting an accountant may also be helpful.

The effects of long-distance commuting on children, who are generally the most vulnerable family members, are hard to assess until commuting starts. Commuting with preschool-age children and those in the early elementary grades is most difficult and should be avoided if possible. Younger children lack the capacity to fully understand the long absences of a parent. If a decision to commute is made, there are helpful strategies for providing assurance to children and teens.

Predictability in scheduling trips home is important. Children should know parental arrival dates, be assured of individual time with the parent, and have information about the departure and the next visit. Activities should center on the family, and it is a good idea, especially for shorter visits, to bring as little work home as possible. When possible, involvement in the children's school (i.e., attending performances, assemblies, and parent–teacher conferences) is highly desirable. Resisting the Santa Claus Syndrome—bringing expensive gifts—is difficult but important because the anticipation of gifts shifts the visit's focus from the parent and child bonding relationship to a material level. Commuting might, however, allow time for the commuter to search out creative and thoughtful gifts related to school projects and children's interests.

Having children visit the commuting parent is helpful, replacing mystery with concrete experience and more readily understandable facts. Where commuting distances are substantial, the commuting parent can create a photo album of their distant residence, workplace, people they know, and the community. Photographs make the commuting parents' life away from home more tangible.

Cell phones (especially with video-call capabilities), emails, and traditional letter-writing are all important for commuters. Communication should be routine and predictable. Supplying children with self-addressed stamped envelopes facilitates writing notes or sending pictures. Writing can become an enjoyable activity for children and should not be forced. School websites provide a means for the commuting parent to stay informed about school activities and keep in touch with teachers, homework, and class projects. It may be possible to collaborate on school projects by contributing learning materials and ideas. The home-based parent can provide guidance or hands-on assistance.

Ideally, commuter families should have a time limit for the commuting experience. Be reasonably clear about when the experience will end and what will come next. The more flexible a commuter's schedule, translated into blocks of time for extended visits, the longer the family can accommodate the stress of commuting. The commuting parent should try to negotiate work-from-home days to extend family time. Open-ended commuting with no clear plan articulated or discussed creates ambiguity and anxiety for children. Permanent commuting, with few opportunities for visits or participation in family life, is corrosive to marital relations and children's welfare. Additional income cannot make up for prolonged absence from the home and the lives of the people we love. Not surprisingly, commuting works best for adults with grown children. However, carefully considered, with limits, goals and strategies set, commuting can be a positive chapter in a family's development.

Discussion Questions and Activities

1. What are some suggestions for parents to give assurance to children when one parent is commuting?

2. Review one of the online resources that the author included about commuter marriages. Identify some helpful strategies you found for commuting couples.

References

Bearce, M. (2014). *Super commuter couples: Staying together when a job keeps you apart.* Equanimity Press.

Cherlin, A. J. (2004). The deinstitutionalization of American marriage. *Journal of Marriage and Family, 66*(4), 848–861.

Lindemann, D. (2019). *Commuter spouses: New families in a changing world.* Cornell University Press.

Embracing Fathers' Opportunities to Prepare Daughters for The World of Boys

Scott S. Hall, Ph.D., CFLE
Professor, Early Childhood, Youth, and Family Studies
Ball State University, Muncie, IN

While raising my three daughters, I shuddered at the thought of boys taunting, flirting with, and perhaps even groping them. I often pondered how I could help prepare my daughters for the world of boys. Having been an adolescent boy myself, I can attest that they are not completely lacking merit and virtue—but as a father, I found myself somewhat prejudiced against the male counterparts to my unsuspecting daughters.

Yet turning my daughters against boys might only create suspicion toward me and against other males that would likely be important to them some day. Promoting a positive but cautious perception of boys can be a challenging balance to find.

Research indicates that involved fathers play a critical role in contributing to daughters' healthy psychological and social development, including the promotion of confidence, social competence, psychological maturity, and sexual restraint (Blickman & Campbell, 2023). Applying Erikson's theory of psychosocial development (Erikson, 1968), scholars have suggested that fathers play an especially important role in bridging a daughter's family identity and bond to a social identity and connection outside of the family (Snarey, 1993). Part of that identity will be manifested in and shaped by interaction with male peers. Because a father is typically the first male figure a daughter loves and admires, he serves as a template for future male–female interactions and relationships (Katz & van der Kloet, 2010; Lee, 2018). For example, daughters exposed to more paternal deviance (e.g., drug use, violence) have reported lower expectations for the relationship investments and behaviors that they are likely to encounter from potential male romantic partners (DelPriore et al., 2019). In short, fathers have a unique and valuable opportunity to influence a daughter's self-image and how she interacts with the world of boys.

Of course, fathers should also be cautious about assuming their young daughters will ever be romantically interested in boys. Pushing such assumptions too strongly could hamper his relationship with daughters who experience non heterosexual attraction. These daughters might find it difficult to be open and honest about their feelings, could fear his rejection, and may close off any meaningful communication and connection with him. Regardless of their attractions and intentions, however, girls still engage with the world of boys, and that world can include the presumption of mutual, heterosexual attraction.

As a young father, I tried to spend one-on-one time with each of my daughters in a variety of formal and informal ways. I sometimes made it a point to mention how my daughters will gradually attract more and more attention from boys and that such attention is not always what it seems. Sometimes the boys just want to be around a cute girl, sometimes they want a kiss or a hug, and sometimes they want to be a real friend. We talked about knowing and identifying the differences among these motivations. For example, a friend would respect their physical and emotional boundaries. I tried to instill in them the expectations that girls be treated as people, not objects; that girls should not kiss (or be otherwise physical with) a boy just to keep his attention; and that being smart and a role model for positive behavior are just as, if not more, important than being pretty and fun. Involved fathers can be very effective in encouraging a daughter's autonomy by helping her be more open and vocal about her opinions and values (Corwyn & Bradley, 2016).

After such a discussion with my then 7-year-old daughter, she told me she understood, and then added, "… but I'm still just a kid." She was right, and fathers should be careful not to say too much too early about this topic in ways that can scare their daughters or vilify the entire male population. Boys can be a big part of girls' lives—in one way or another—and creating a deep-seated suspicion toward them may inhibit healthy cross-sex relationships. However, waiting until puberty to teach these lessons is undoubtedly too late. They need to hear them many times in many ways so that they internalize the messages. How tragic it is when a naive young (or older) girl puts up with demeaning treatment and abuse from a boy whom she believes likes or loves her just because of the attention he gives her? How tragic it is when girls starve or sexualize themselves to attract empty affection from boys who have only selfish interests at heart?

Fathers, embrace the teaching moments that help your daughter seek appropriate and healthy attention from boys and to feel confident to stand on her own when she is not the focus of every boy around. These moments might come when you watch television, movies, or online videos that includes messages about girls and about relationships; when they tell you about what they have learned or observed at school; or when they ask you about your relationships with women. Also, be sure to mention your daughter's personal attributes that go beyond her pretty eyes and her sweet smile. Well-meaning fathers might say too much about their daughters' looks and not enough about more significant reasons they value them as people.

In summary, fathers of daughters should
- realize that a warm, accepting father helps a daughter feel confident, important, and worthy of positive male attention.
- explain why boys give attention to girls and how to identify selfish and exploitative motives.
- emphasize that a boy who genuinely cares about a girl will not expect her simply to abandon her personal or family values and comfort.
- encourage their daughters to value positive characteristics that have nothing to do with their looks.
- convey these messages early and often through words and treatment of their daughters.

Important lessons about boys might come across differently from a father than a mother in that he has more direct experience and insight related to the world of boys. However, if a mother is in the picture, she can help encourage and support the father to be active in these important relational and socializing processes, especially if he experiences discomfort with broaching these subjects. She likely has important experiences and insight that are also worth sharing. Nevertheless, daughters typically yearn for a father's attention and can learn much from him about how to feel valued (Hall & Tift, 2007). Fathers, give your daughter the attention she craves; she's likely to seek it elsewhere if she doesn't get it from her dad.

Discussion Questions

1. As fathers' and mothers' roles seem to become more similar, do the social contributions fathers make to their daughters become less unique?

2. What signs can fathers teach daughters to look out for that indicate that boys just want to use the daughters as objects?

3. How can fathers instill a healthy level of caution regarding boys without creating paranoia and anxiety in their daughters?

References

Blickman, R. S., & Campbell, C. G. (2023). Moving toward an integrated model of the father–daughter relationship during adolescence. *Family Relations, 72*(5), 2664–2678. https://doi.org/10.1111/fare.12787

Corwyn, R. F., & Bradley, R. H. (2016). Fathers' autonomy support and social competence of sons and daughters. *Merrill-Palmer Quarterly, 62*(4), 359–387. https://doi.org/10.13110/merrpalmquar1982.62.4.0359

DelPriore, D. J., Shakiba, N., Schlomer, G. L., Hill, S. E., & Ellis, B. J. (2019). The effects of fathers on daughters' expectations for men. *Developmental Psychology, 55*(7), 1523–1536. https://doi.org/10.1037/dev0000741

Erikson, E. H. (1968). *Identity: Youth and crisis.* Norton & Co.

Hall, S. S., & Tift, J. N. (2007). The daddy–daughter dance: Insights for father–daughter relationships. In S. E. Brotherson & J. M. White (Eds.), *Why fathers count* (pp. 77–90). Men's Studies Press.

Katz, J., & van der Kloet, E. (2010). The first man in her life: Father emotional responsiveness during adolescence and college women's sexual refusal behaviors. *The American Journal of Family Therapy, 38*(4), 344–356. https://doi.org/10.1080/01926187.2010.493474

Lee, S.-A. (2018). Parental divorce, relationships with fathers and mothers, and children's romantic relationships in young adulthood. *Journal of Adult Development, 25*(2), 121–134. https://doi.org/10.1007/s10804-017-9279-4

Snarey, J. (1993). *How fathers care for the next generation: A four-decade study.* Harvard University Press.

Nurturing Traditions: Nurturing Family

Arminta Lee Jacobson, Ph.D., CFLE Emeritus
Professor Emerita, University of North Texas
Denton, TX

Holidays remind me of the importance of nurturing and maintaining traditions and rituals in the lives of our children, our families, and our communities. Several years ago, our oldest son, Trey, arrived home for Christmas after his first semester in college. My husband, his younger brother, and I were waiting for Trey to carry out our family "traditions" of decorating and cooking as a family. Trey let us know dramatically and in no uncertain terms how disappointed he was. He said "I have been cooped up in my dorm studying for finals and couldn't wait to come home and have Christmas. I thought you would have Christmas music playing when I drove up, the tree decorated, and cookies baking." For him what was important for a slightly homesick college freshman was Christmas as he remembered it. After that year, we made sure the Christmas tree was decorated and music was ready to play when we spotted him arriving home from college for winter break. And to carry out another family tradition, joking and having fun, Trey heard his favorite Christmas music record from early childhood when he walked in the door, *Christmas on the Farm.*

Our family holiday traditions can include the kinds of rituals important to families, as studied extensively by James Bossard and Eleanor Boll and reported in their book,

Ritual and family living (1940). In his book, *The intentional family: How to build family ties in our modern world* (1997), William Doherty says we have rituals for connections or bonding, love rituals, & rituals that bind us to the larger community (1997). According to Doherty, *connection rituals* help families feel closer together and build trust and loyalty. *Connection rituals* can be as simple as our routines at family meals to ways we celebrate holidays. *Love rituals* are how we express intimacy and make other members of the family feel special. How we celebrate birthdays and tell each other goodbye are examples of love rituals. *Community rituals* include family events such as weddings and funerals that involve the larger community. Early in the history of this country, most ritual celebrations were carried out in the larger community.

Holidays for most faiths include all three of these rituals. *Connection rituals* include the special traditions and routines we have at home, like drinking hot chocolate while we decorate the Christmas tree. *Love rituals*, making each family member feel special, include traditions such as hanging our children's tattered hand-made Christmas ornaments on the tree year after year, hand-making a gift, and calling distant family members on Christmas afternoon. *Community rituals* and traditions include worship services and yearly observances such as Christmas Lighting celebrations and the Fourth of July parade. Families are part of the larger whole – the community, where we live our traditions and rituals.

Why do family rituals have so much importance for us? Why do we repeat them over and over again? Think of families as a whole – not just a group of individuals. Routines and rituals are how we stay organized as families and how we maintain equilibrium and stability (Kabanova, 2022). We have *rules* about how we do things, the structure for our rituals and traditions. It is clear how we are supposed to act and celebrate. Our rules may be related to culture, our religious beliefs, or may be passed down by families through generations.

Doherty (1997) says family rituals and routines are important to us in four ways: for *predictability*, for *connection*, for *identity*, and for *enacting values*. Rituals and routines are important for children of all ages, especially infants and young children. We know that young children like to read the same books over and over and the same way each time; that grandchildren like to play the same games every time they visit. Through *predictability*, infants and young children learn to trust their caregivers and their world. This is the basis of secure attachment and emotional and social development. Children also learn basic principles of life, particularly cause and effect. They learn concepts about people, objects, time, and social relationships and strengthen their memories through the repetition of ritual.

Traditions and rituals also build individual and family *connections*. The shared experiences of traditions and rituals are a way of strengthening ties and bonds and building a sense of family and community. Through shared family and community experiences, children develop a sense of family, cultural, and community *identity*. *Identity* helps provide an organizing principle for family life (Anderson & Sabatelli, 2011). The child knows "This is who I am. This is where I belong." Families enact *values* that are dearly held and reinforce them through family traditions. This is especially true when cultural and religious beliefs are expressed through ritual and celebration.

What is the message for parents? Be intentional and develop rituals and routines to which you can commit and maintain and reflect your most important values and beliefs. When parents include ritual and traditions in family life, they model and teach children that the world and others can be trusted. Children learn the most important people in their lives care and take time for them. They also develop a sense of who they are as a member of their family and community, what is important, and what is valuable.

As rituals and traditions involve routines and organization, they also provide children important structure for their lives. They help regulate their behavior, provide clear expectations about what is expected, and facilitate building ties and bonds and a sense of community and loyalty.

As you celebrate holidays, family celebrations and religious traditions, look beyond the work of getting ready and reflect on how traditions and the rituals express who you are, what you believe, and how we care about others and our families and communities.

Discussion Questions

1. What is a ritual or tradition in your family? How has the ritual or tradition helped your family members build connections, express love or identify with your culture or community?

2. What is a new ritual or tradition you would like to develop in your family? If there are children in the family, how would it nurture their well-being and development?

References

Anderson, S. A., & Sabatelli, R. M. (2011). *Family interaction: A multigenerational developmental perspective* (5th ed.). Pearson.

Bossard, James H. S., & Boll, Eleanor S. (1950). *Ritual and family living A contemporary study.* Philadelphia: University of Pennsylvania.

Doherty, W. J. (1997). *The Intentional Family: How to Build Family Ties in Our Modern World.* United States: Hachette Books.

Kabanova, K. V. (2022). Traditions and their role in the development of family and society. *Psychologist, 1.* 72-80. https://doi.org/10.25136/2409-8701.2022.1.35918

My Father's Wisdom From Under the Clock Tower: Teaching Forgiveness

Gregory Roger Janson, Ph.D., LPCC-S †
Associate Professor Emeritus,
Child and Family Studies, Department of Social & Public Health,
Ohio University, Athens, OH

From the return of the prodigal son to Gandhi's final act of forgiveness toward his assassin as he lay dying, the nature of forgiveness has been the subject of religion, philosophy, and psychology. Forgiveness can arise from ethical discrimination: What is right? Or from an affective dimension: Our empathy and our ability to experience the pain of others leads us to forgive. Teaching forgiveness can rely on faith or reason, but it is a challenging process to move beyond a few expected words. Somehow we must help our children to experience forgiving—not just forgiveness—if they are to understand its nature and to make it a living part of themselves. As an observer of my father's life, I witnessed an unusual act of forgiveness, an event that spanned a large portion of his life.

My father died a raw March morning after a 15-year battle with prostate cancer, a battle he fought with patience, grace, and humor; a battle he fought without complaint, as he had lived his life. He was 88 when he died. I was always sure of his love, although he never spoke of it. I was less sure about his thoughts and feelings; those were his own.

There should have been time to understand each other better. We both lived long enough to know each other as men, not just as father and son. But life has a way of intruding. I often wished he were more demonstrative, more emotive, more open. I wished I were more present with him. I often reflected on our relationship with thoughts like these.

I knew my father had been abandoned by his own father at birth. I knew he had left high school during the Great Depression to support his mother, whom he adored. During the Second World War, I knew he served in the Medical Corps, in the First Army field hospital. He was among the first into the concentration camps. His decorations, including a Bronze Star, sat in a bureau drawer for the duration of his life. He never spoke of any of these experiences.

His beloved mother died when he was in Europe. At the end of the war, he returned home, spending 6 months sitting on a beach in Maryland, staring at the sea. He met my mother at that time. They married and he worked his way through college and law school at St. John's University in Brooklyn, where my brother and I were born. Six months before he died, he shared with my mother that he had lived in a Catholic orphanage from age 2 to 5. During the first part of the 20th century, that is where devout mothers who were unable to support their children took them until things improved. His mother returned for him.

I know of these things from my mother; my father never spoke of them to me. Knowing them helped to explain to me his reticence, his stoicism, his emotional reserve. As a counselor and a traumatologist, it became easier for me to understand his emotional reserve as generational, as formed by abandonment and loss, and by the horrors of war. He shared none of this with me.

The one story I remember my father sharing with me was about meeting his own father for the first time. His story had a profound impact on me.

My mother, the product of a large and boisterous Greek family, was the emotional antithesis of my father. It was she who called my father's father and asked him to come to New York—without telling my father. She knew that he would have quietly refused. My father was 34 years old and had never seen his father or wanted to see him. Apparently, my mother felt otherwise. My father believed that his father was responsible for his mother's hard life and early death. Yet I never knew my father to be anything but patient and kind; he never held a grudge, and I never saw him angry. I never knew my father to utter a harsh word to my mother, my brother, or me.

Out of respect for my mother, he reluctantly agreed to go to Union Station that afternoon. He did not agree to bring my grandfather back.

He told me that during the subway ride to Union Station he stared out the grimy windows, uncertain of what he would do. He had seen pictures of his father, but his father had no way to recognize him, so they were to meet under the clock tower. My father said he could easily walk away if he chose to.

"I stood on the mezzanine, leaning against the railing. I looked down and saw him standing under that enormous clock. Everyone was moving except him. He was just standing there, all alone. I knew I didn't owe him anything. I just stared for a while, not thinking, and then I realized, it just wouldn't be right to walk away. It wouldn't be right. So, I walked down and brought him home to meet you."

This was the heart of his wisdom. The work of Robert Enright describes various qualities of forgiveness: "restraint from pursuing resentment or revenge," "forgoing of resentment or revenge when the wrongdoer's actions deserve it and giving the gifts of mercy, generosity, and love when the wrong-doer does not deserve them," and "the overcoming of wrongdoing with good" (International Forgiveness Institute, n.d.). My father demonstrated these to me.

Looking back as part of an effort to distill the essence of his life and wisdom into a few words that could be of use to others, I realize that he shared far more than I imagined. Beyond sharing this story with me, he never spoke about forgiveness. There were no explanations, no qualifications, no telling me how I should think or feel. He simply lived forgiveness by example. He quietly showed me and let me judge for myself. He did it so respectfully that I never felt as though he was teaching me.

This was his gift as a "living" teacher: to embody the wisdom he sought to share in a way that enabled me to experience it, to feel it, and to make it my own. I am a different kind of teacher than he was, but I have come to realize that the ultimate foundation of his wisdom was not just his love for me, but his faith in me. That realization enabled me to pass on that love and faith to my own children and to share with them the wisdom necessary to a good life, well lived. Perhaps that was his greatest gift to me … and to them.

Discussion Questions

1. What does forgiveness mean to you?

2. Do you believe the act of forgiveness is rooted in faith or reason, or something else entirely? Why?

3. Is forgiveness unique to man? Or do you also see forgiveness in the animal world?

4. Are there times when you *shouldn't* forgive?

5. People often say we should forgive others, we should "let it go" to find peace within ourselves. Does this make forgiveness a selfish act?

†Gregory R. Janson passed away in June 2024. His daughter, Dr. Jennifer Tobin, provided the discussion questions as well as the following tribute:
I am very lucky, as his daughter, that I got to know him as a father, but also as a kind, compassionate, and forgiving man.

Reference
International Forgiveness Institute. *What is forgiveness.*
https://internationalforgiveness.com/what-is-forgiveness-2/
https://internationalforgiveness.com/product-category/Forgiveness-Research-Tools/

Three Pillars of Strength Among Latin American Families

Brian Jory, Ph.D.
Professor of Family Science, Berry College

Rachel Bascope-Vidal
MSW Candidate, Georgia State University

In the past quarter century, Latinos have become the largest minority group living in the United States, encompassing more than 62 million people or roughly 20% of the U.S. population. The densest populations live in California, Texas, Arizona, New York, and Florida, but there are large numbers in Colorado, Georgia, Illinois, New Jersey, and New Mexico. Despite the political rhetoric about immigration, the increase of the Latino population is mostly from births in the United States, not from immigration. More than 90% of Latin American children living in the United States were born in the United States (Kohornen, 2023).

Latin Americans are a diverse group. Sixty percent trace their heritage to Mexico, and the remainder to Central America, South America, Cuba, Puerto Rico, Haiti, and the Dominican Republic. Most Latin Americans are fluent in both Spanish and English; only 22% state that they are not fluent in English. In fact, there are more Spanish speakers in the United States than in the entire country of Spain. However, Portuguese, French, Dutch, and some indigenous languages are also prevalent, depending on their country of origin (Office of Minority Health, U.S. Department of Health and Human Services, n.d.).

Our goal in this chapter is to shed light on three pillars of strength among Latin American families, keeping in mind that many Latino families struggle with the challenges of intergenerational acculturation, family separation, underemployment, racial discrimination, and a broken immigration system. Our list of Latin American family strengths is far from exhaustive, and we recognize that there are questionable aspects of Latino families such as strongly gendered male and female roles, machismo among some Latino men, and authoritarian parenting practices. Just the same, we hope that our focus on the strengths of Latino families will help all parents, and those who work with families, appreciate the values and skills necessary to raise happy, resilient, and competent children.

Pillar One: The Culture of Familismo
One characteristic that Latino families share is a common cultural view of families, sometimes called familismo (Olayo Méndez, 2006). We describe *familismo* as the shared values of family loyalty, emotional closeness, parental warmth and nurturance, sacrifice for family, respect for elders, and mutual support among extended family members. *Familismo* can be contrasted with the Anglo American values of individuality, self-assertion, self-promotion, egalitarian parent–child relationships, and the primary focus on the nuclear family over the extended family. Nobody needs to say to a Latino that it *takes a village;* this idea is a foundation of their cultural view of families.

A study by Yvita Bustos and Catherine DeCarlo Santiago (2022) presents evidence that familism among Mexican immigrant families is a preventative factor in shielding immigrant children from depression and anxiety. The researchers focus on the specific factors of family cohesion, parental support, and parental warmth toward their children, primarily the warmth of mothers, as the primary forces of prevention and resilience.

Latin American families value sharing memories, laughter, and energy. They raise their children to share with their family and spend time with them. For example, it is common for Latino families to get together on weekends to share a meal or hang out with the whole family, including extended family. Similarly, if there is an event for one of the children, whether as small as a soccer game or as big as celebrating a birthday, the whole family is expected to be there to show their support and love. This teaches Latino children the value of family loyalty and shows them that they have a family to support them during the good and bad. This creates tight bonds, and, with the help of open communication, children are more willing to ask for and accept advice from their family. Children raised in this environment learn to work through problems as a group and know that they are not alone. Through these experiences, parents keep the tradition of being close to immediate and extended family members, as well as family friends.

Pillar Two: High Expectations for Problem-Solving Skills and Education
A study by Cecilia Ayón and her colleagues (2015) identified four parenting styles among Latin American parents, and overlapping all four styles, was a tendency for Latino parents to be authoritatively strict and hold their children to high expectations at home, in the community, and in school. They instill problem-solving skills from a young age such as being able to figure things out on their own without asking for help. Children are typically assigned responsibilities from a young age, with the goal of developing problem-solving skills. Children are taught to think of alternate ways to

complete a certain task without asking for help. For example, a child may be tasked with helping the parents cook. With this, the child learns how to be safe in the kitchen, how to use kitchen utensils properly, and make simple meals for themselves or their siblings. If a day comes when the child is hungry and the parents are busy, the mom will say, "You know how to make at least one meal, you can do it, go and make it, or wait until I am done." The parent not only encourages the child to do the task on their own but also has faith that the child will do a good job.

The Latino expectation for success spills into school. A study by Renee Ryberg and Lina Guzman (2023) found that Latin American parents have the same, often higher, expectations for their children's success in school as Anglo families. Their study found that more than half of Latino children have at least one parent who has completed some college, and nearly one in four have at least one parent with a bachelor's degree or higher. Despite the expectation that their children will succeed in school, not all Latino parents are equally equipped to provide the support their children need. The same study found that the parents of roughly one in five Latino children have less than a high school diploma. There is considerable discrepancy among Latinos depending on the country of heritage: Parents from Cuba, South America, and Spain tend to have higher educational attainments than parents from Mexico and Central America, where higher education is less available. Latino children who have at least one parent born in the United States are more likely to succeed in school compared with children with neither parent born in the United States.

If neither parent has been raised in the United States (i.e., exposed to the U.S. education system), there is plenty of room for struggle. For example, a first-generation Latino child may not be able to ask their parents for help because of a language barrier or confusion over the different ways topics are taught in this country. So when a child comes home with challenging homework, the parents will probably help them as much as they can, but as the child gets older, the parents may insist that the child take responsibility and be able to do their homework alone. The child will need to pay attention in class, ask questions, and take notes. Whatever level of support parents can offer, Latino parents will expect the child to do well in school and encourage them to finish strong.

Pillar Three: A Strong Sense of Belonging and Responsibility to Others
Latin American families value being a well-mannered person as a representative of the family in the community, an expression called *bien educados* (Fontes, 2002). It is common for Latino families to be well connected and involved in their communities, and there is a strong expectation of being selfless and willing to help others. For instance, if a parent and child are walking on the street and see a neighbor struggling to take their bags home, there is an expectation that the parent and child will stop and offer to help their neighbor—even if they are in a hurry, even if they are going in the other direction, even if the neighbor lives up a steep hill. Taking time to be kind and help others is not an option in Latino culture—it is a firm expectation that parents teach their children from a young age.

While Anglo parents may question this kind of generosity and selflessness, citing the demands of time and obligations, there is a payoff for Latino children: A study by Alan Dettlaff, Ilze Earner, and Susan Phillips (2009) found that Latin American children were 8 times less likely to be victims of physical neglect than Anglo American children. These same researchers found this to be a double-edged sword in that Latin American families are twice as likely as Anglo American families to be referred for emotional abuse of their children. Although it is true that imposing devotion to the needs of others on a child, especially by an authoritarian parent, may cross the line into emotional abuse, it is just as likely that this statistic is partially a result of cultural confusion. The point is that the security of belonging and inclusion that Latino children experience is encased within the responsibility to come to the aid of others even when it is inconvenient and requires self-sacrifice.

We hope that our discussion of the three pillars has shed light on the strengths of Latin American families, their parenting styles and practices, and we encourage readers to learn more about their cultural beliefs and customs.

Discussion Questions

1. Familismo fosters the idea of being present and pouring oneself into one's family. How does familismo compare with individualistic culture in the United States in terms of family support, especially in times of need?

2. Latin American families tend to have reasonably high expectations for their children's success while offering encouragement in the development of problem-solving skills and self-discipline. What are some positive ways that problem-solving skills aid in the development of children, especially as they attend school and transition into young adults?

3. Latin American families emphasize raising well-mannered and humanitarian children who are familiar with the needs of others and who respect authority. How do you think this practice impacts the community they are a part of?

References

Ayón, C., Williams, L. R., Marsiglia, F. F., Ayers, S., & Kiehne, E. (2015). A latent profile analysis of Latino parenting: The infusion of cultural values on family conflict. *Families in Society: The Journal of Contemporary Social Services, 96*(3), 203–210. https://doi.org/10.1606/1044-3894.2015.96.25

Bustos, Y., & DeCarlo Santiago, C. (2022). Effects of familism, parenting, and family cohesion on child internalizing symptoms among Mexican immigrant families. *Journal of Child and Family Studies, 32*(1), 243–256. https://doi.org/10.1007/s10826-022-02423-w

Dettlaff, A. J., Earner, I., & Phillips, S. D. (2009). Latino children of immigrants in the child welfare system: Prevalence, characteristics, and risk. *Children and Youth Services Review, 31*(7), 775–783. https://doi.org/https://doi.org/10.1016/j.childyouth.2009.02.004

Fontes, L. (2002). Child discipline and physical abuse in immigrant Latino families: Reducing violence and misunderstandings. *Journal of Counseling and Development, 80*(1), 31–40. https://doi.org/10.1002/j.1556-6678.2002.tb00163.x

Korhonen, V. (2023, October 11). U.S. Hispanic population by sex and age 2022. *Statista.* https://www.statista.com/statistics/259812/hispanic-population-of-the-us-by-sex-and-age/

Office of Minority Health, U.S. Department of Health and Human Services. (n.d.). *Hispanic/Latino Health.* https://minorityhealth.hhs.gov/hispaniclatino-health

Olayo Méndez, J. A. (2006). Latino parenting expectations and styles: A literature review. *Migration: A Critical Issue for Child Welfare, 21*(2), 53–61.

Ryberg, R., & Guzman, L. (2023). *National profile of Latino parents' educational attainment underscores the diverse educational needs of a fast-growing population.* National Research Center on Hispanic Children and Families. https://doi.org/10.59377/665j6906g

Parenting Through Turbulent Times

Ainsworth E. Joseph, Ph.D., D. Min., PD MFT., CFLE
Assistant Professor, Department of Discipleship and Lifespan Education
Seventh-day Adventist Theological Seminary, Andrews University,
Berrien Springs, MI

Parenting is the most important vocation because it exerts the first influence upon the life of a child. However, no one goes to school to become certified in parenting before becoming a parent, and there is no manual given to guide in the parenting profession and role. The reality is, we embark on parenting the way our parents parented us. We bring the dysfunctions of parenting from our own parents who acquired less knowledge or had less access to knowledge than we do, and the vicious cycle of dysfunctional practices continues. Knowledge is powerful, and it enables us to break dysfunctional cycles. This article sets out to address an area of parenting that is crucial to children's emotional well-being.

According to Balswick et al. (2021), some parenting styles encourage growth and empowerment, whereas others hinder or block growth either by fostering dependency or expecting premature self-reliance (p. 114). Our contemporary culture fosters "premature self-reliance" of children, which may be due to technological advancement and work demands on parents, leaving them with little time. However, as Balswick et al. posited, an important aspect of socioemotional parenting focuses on the attachment quality of the relationship between parents and children (p. 120).

Attachment
This is where it all begins! Attachment is the process through which infants and their parents relate in patterns governed by signals and responses that lead to the development of a caring, protecting, and trusting relationship. Humans are born and wired with needs, and when these are being satisfied, an attachment develops. Therefore, we can begin to see the landmarks for emotional injury from early childhood development. Although attachment behavior is especially prominent during childhood, it stays active throughout adult life.

Attachment behavior is a normal, essential, and healthy part of the human instinctive makeup. So, "separation anxiety and the activation of intense attachment behaviors is seen as a natural and inevitable response to the loss of the attachment figure" (Atwood, 1992, p. 300). Therefore, one of the best things parents can do for their children is to help them develop healthy attachment.

Types of Attachment

John Bowlby and Mary Ainsworth are the founders of attachment theory, and through their work, we can now understand the diverse types of attachment and the ways in which it takes place and develops. Let us quickly examine the types of attachments.

Secure attachment: The child has developed a balanced view of parents from a wide range of feelings and memories of both positive and negative experiences from their interactions.

Anxious attachment: The child's fear of abandonment becomes driven by anger and hurt at parents. The child places a high value on intimacy, which makes them overdependent on attachment parental figures in the past and present.

Avoidant attachment: The child dismisses love and emotional connection and shows low tolerance for any heightened emotions displayed by parents and others. Although they may idealize their parent(s), their actual memories do not support the ideals.

Fearful attachment: The child has difficulty trusting others because of past disappointments and may be uncomfortable with gestures of emotional closeness. Trauma and loss usually inundate the child's life.

Parental Behavioral Responses

The parental behavioral responses to their child can either enhance or ruin the parent–child attachment bond, which the child needs for emotionally healthy development. According to Linda Wark (2006), there are different terms used to explain the transactional behaviors that exist between parent and child that build secure attachment. I believe that Wark's seven key behavior traits that contribute to secure attachment are timeless and relevant for parenting today.

1. *Empathy, Sensitivity, Attunement.* In brief these really have to do with parental ability to gauge the child's emotional state and corresponding emotional need and give the proper response. This requires being emotionally sensitive to the manifested signals the child is sending. Sometimes parents can become too busy with their own lives and responsibilities, or they are simply nonchalant about the child's developmental needs. Practice and learn to tune in and focus on what your child needs in the moment.

2. *Availability.* This is a crucial factor in a child's development and maintenance of secure attachment. There needs to be consistency as opposed to sporadic availability. The child needs to be able to predict parental availability. However, parents must be careful to avoid *ambiguous presence*, which means, as a parent, being physically present but emotionally absent from one's child. As Linda Wark (2006) shared, "Parents who are emotionally available have internal access to giving, loving, and nurturing, and they easily communicate these to their children" (p. 14).

3. *Responsiveness.* To put it simply, this occurs when the child takes the initiative to reach out to the parent, and the parent responds engagingly with an answer or takes the right action if needed. As a counselor, I saw a young man who was in his late teens and had trouble completing high school. In doing an assessment of his

developmental history, I discovered he was suffering from abandonment resulting from parental separation. However, where he found himself stuck was on a promise his father had made one Sunday to visit and bring him pizza. On the Sunday in question, he refused to eat his mother's delicious homecooked meal because his dad was bringing pizza. Sadly, the hours went on, night came, and his father never showed up. Through the father's lack of responsiveness, the boy was emotionally damaged.

4. *Consistency.* As discovered by Bowlby (1973, cited by Wark, 2006), predictable discipline, structured routines, and reliable interactions help create the child's internal working model (p. 14). As time elapses, children develop knowledge, understanding, and concepts of their parents based on their consistent or inconsistent interactions. Either way, the parents are framing the child's thoughts and feelings about who they are as parents. In our busy culture, we grapple with the commodity of time. However, what the child needs and will remember is the consistency of the time you carve out to give them your undivided attention. Be consistent with your child.

5. *Touch.* There is enough evidence to substantiate the value of touch in a child's development, and even in our adulthood. Children thrive when they receive hugs, kisses, cuddles, and pats; enjoy rubs on the shoulder, head, and back; and are allowed to sit in a parent's lap. Other forms of physical contact through fun activities and even household chores are also beneficial. Science shows that, among other benefits, endorphins improve mood and well-being, and they are released through welcomed, pleasurable touch.

6. *Eye Contact.* Ours is a digital world that allows for virtual contact. However, there is nothing like face-to-face eye contact and interaction. Although in certain cultures, eye contact between a child and an adult may be discouraged, as it is between genders, it is proper and acceptable to make eye contact in Western culture. We communicate a great deal through our eyes. My mother used to say, "Eyes communicate the soul," and you can tell a whole lot about a person by looking into their eyes. For the same reason, a child can discern much about their parents through eye contact, just as the parent can through eye contact with their child. Moreover, the eyes provide direction and discipline. As a child, my parents only had to look at me in church, and I got the message they were conveying.

7. *Frequent Playful and Joyful Contact.* Although we mature into adulthood, we never lose the child in us. Parents can still jump around, crawl, and play hide-and-seek, ball games, tabletop games, jump rope, skip, and even digital games with their children. Plan such activities into your schedule and engage your children in fun parent–child activities. Your children will never forget it, and they will always appreciate you for it.

Conclusion

In summary, the findings of Dan Siegl and Tina Payne Bryson (2020) provide an easy to remember and follow framework for healthy attachment development, which they termed the Four S's. *Safe* means providing a safe harbor; *seen* requires paying attention to children's positive and negative emotions; *soothed* is the act of being attentive to the hard things children experience and teaching coping skills; and finally, *secure* is providing a faithful, ongoing, trustworthy presence. The attachment goal of Sigel and Bryson is that the children experience what they termed "felt" and "known" through a parent tuning into their experiences. What parents end up with at the end of their life's journey is their children. The healthy attachment parents develop with their children not only enables them to navigate through life; they in turn take care of aging parents in the family lifespan development. We owe it to our children to help them develop healthy emotional attachment, which will serve them well throughout their lives.

Discussion Questions

1. As you reflect on your childhood upbringing which of the seven parenting attachment behaviors attachment were adequately practiced by your parent(s)?

2. Which of the seven parenting behavior attachments were lacking in your childhood upbringing?

3. On a scale of 1-10, how would you rate your parenting behavior practices for each of the seven attachment behaviors?

4. Which parenting attachment behavior do you believe is most critical?

References

Atwood, J. D. (1992). *Family therapy. A systemic behavioral approach.* Wadsworth Publishing.

Balswick, J. O., Balswick, J. K., & Fredrick, T. V. (2021). *The Family: A Christian perspective on the contemporary home.* Baker Academic.

Sigel, D. J., and T. Payne Bryson (2020). *The power of showing up: How parental presence shapes who our kids become and how their brains get wired.* Ballantine.

Wark, L. (September/October 2006). Attachment. What to tell parents about their young child's attachment. *Family Therapy Magazine.* The American Association for Marriage and Family Therapy.

Nurturing the Couple

Dorothea M. Rogers, D.Min., LMFT, CFLE

No doubt—the husband and wife roles change when children come into the picture. The nonstop rigors of childrearing can cause parents to become fatigued and disheartened. Couples can realize that although their marital relationship is different, the situation will undergo continual change, and, overall, the dependent stage with children is temporary. Even though parenting is for a lifetime, most children will eventually grow up and leave home. Having the support of one's spouse to rely on and bounce ideas and frustrations off of while raising children is healing for couples. Staying close and connected as couples is necessary relationship maintenance. The husband and wife set the tone for the family, and the quality of that relationship governs the quality of the family. Moreover, spending alone time with a spouse each day is rewarding and offers a safety net from the world as couples reconnect during this quality time.

Finding one-on-one time in marriage after children come is difficult but essential. Couples who spend time alone, even for a few minutes a day, can reconnect as they are away from phones, other people, and whatever else could be a distraction. "Acts of love are usually expressed naturally when people spend quality time together" (Balswick, et al., p. 242). Quality time together can include rituals. For example, rituals of connection, such as getting together at the end of the day for a few minutes and how to say goodnight, are helpful ways to stay connected with one another (Gottman & Gottman, 2018).

During one-on-one time, couples can share what is going on in each other's lives. Concerns can be discussed and solutions sought during a few private minutes. Even a few minutes together alone builds a rich communication—a bonding that has created a sense of unity that holds firm when tough times come (Covey, 1997). Balswick et al. (2021), asserted, "It is through expressing our feeling that we learn how others respond to important experiences in their lives. Emotional expressions allow us to gain insight into the character of the other (p. 243).

Additionally, one-on-one time can help the whole family. The strength of the marital bond creates a sense of security for the entire family. "The greatest thing you can do for your children is to love your spouse" (Covey, 1997, p. 154). Children see how their mother and father treat each other, and children have a sense of security from what they see. "Love is an act of will—namely an intention and an action. ...We do not have to love. We choose to love" (Covey, 2022, p. 169). The marital relationship has a powerful effect on the entire family, and when couples spend time together nurturing their relationship, the family unit is strengthened. Further, parental boundaries are important in one-on-one time and need to be clearly understood by the children.

All parents need time together as a couple. Time for couples requires boundaries, set by parents, and must be respected by children. Because children emulate their parents, parents need to be aware that their children are observing them. As Cloud and Townsend (2017) affirmed, "Parents have a sober responsibility: Teaching their children to have an internal sense of boundaries and to respect the boundaries of others. ...Children have the responsibility to learn and listen" (p. 193). Further, parents can use the "No one interrupts" rule. Parents need to be able to have conversations without children interrupting.

Following are a few suggestions for how parents can spend some time alone together:
- Date your spouse. Go to a movie or a play, walk along a beach, or just go for coffee, and do not talk about the kids. A date two or three times a month is a great rejuvenator of couple hood.
- Spend time doing an enjoyable activity, such as working on a puzzle.
- Set aside a time each night after the kids are in bed. Couples can share about their day, plan for the future, or even spend time in prayer.
- Take a weekend away once or twice a year. This away time will create couple renewal in marriage intimacy, and it can be fun!

Spending time alone with a spouse is not only necessary but also rewarding as the bond that unites them also carries them through tough times, allowing them to have the energy to parent their children. Couples must be cognizant that the quality of their relationship sets the tone for the rest of the family.

Discussion Questions & Activities

1. Determine your priorities. All people have responsibilities. Discuss with each other where and when you will spend time together, daily, nightly, weekly, once a month, and/or a weekend getaway.

2. How can you show empathy and respect during alone time with your spouse? For example, ensure that you are truly listening to each other, and if you are not clear on something, genuinely ask for clarification.

References

Balswick, J. O., Balswick, J. K., & Frederick, T. V. (2021). *The family: A Christian perspective on the contemporary home.* Baker Academic.

Cloud, H., & Townsend, J. (2017). *Boundaries.* Zondervan.

Covey, S. R. (1997). *The 7 habits of highly effective families.* St. Martin's Griffin.

Covey, S.R. (2022). *The 7 habits of highly effective families: Creating a nurturing family in a turbulent world.* St. Martin's Essentials.

Gottman, J., & Gottman, J. S. (2018). *The 10 principles of effective couples therapy what science tells us and beyond* [Class handout]. PESI.

[No] Surprise: Our Children Still Need and Want Us

Sterling Kendall Wall, Ph.D., CFLE
Full Professor, Family & Consumer Sciences
University of Wisconsin – Stevens Point
Stevens Point, WI

Years ago, my small young family took a Saturday off from the routine of graduate study and work and went down to the Garden of the Gods, in Colorado Springs, to eat lunch amidst the amazing natural architecture of the famous red rock outcroppings. We selected a camp site that was off the beaten path with a picnic table and shade. After we set up the food and had fixed lunch for our 3-and-a-half-year-old son, Sterling, he announced that he was going to go eat by himself, up in the rocks. We helped him pack up his plate and watched as he wandered off. I struggled slightly with feelings that it had already started, "he doesn't want to be with us," I thought.

The rest of us continued to eat our lunch, converse, and, after a few minutes, noticed that atop the rocky mound into which our son had headed, we could just barely see his head and face as he ate his lunch. He had situated himself in a precise location where, in his own lunch spot and mostly hidden from our view, he still had a line of sight directly to our table.

I realized then that he needed us after all, just perhaps in a different way. It may be surprising for some parents to hear that even as teens our children still want and need us. This is contrary to how the media all too often portrays parenting during the teen years as a constant battle between parents and independent young adults. Indeed, a first version of this story was written just a few years after a survey of 200 teens found that 21% rated "not having enough time together with parents" as one of their top concerns (Global Strategy Group Inc, 2000). Similar messages still ring true worldwide even today, almost 20 years later, with teens still needing and wanting a relationship with their parents, just in different updated ways (Kids Health N.Z., n.d.). It's not that teens need to replace their parents with friends; indeed, the strength of the teen's friend network is positively correlated with the strength of the relationship with their parents, and for teens with smaller friendship networks, that parental relationship is even more important (Schacter & Margolin, 2019).

That children and teens still want and need direct connection with their parents seems to run counter to our fast-paced consumer culture within which we live. The good parent is no longer seen as a close confidant or mentor, or even the parent who plays catch in the back yard. Rather, we sometimes feel that the good parent is the parent that can provide the goods and services to their child, driving them to baseball practice where they can play catch with someone else. Direct time with parents seems to be squeezed out by a plethora of activities for our children, in spite of findings that young teens who have warm relationships with their parents report greater closeness and warmth towards them later in their early 20's (Brennen, 2022). An old adage states "things are to have, people are to love; as long as you don't get that mixed up, you'll do okay." Sometimes we do get it mixed up as we start to believe that possessions, success, and achievement are the main conduits to happiness. This even starts to play out in our activities with our children.

For example, several years after eating lunch in the Garden of the Gods, I found myself pursuing the final leg of my academic career in Auburn, Alabama. We lived near a small fishing pond. At this time, I was working three jobs, going to school, and our family had grown to four children. Sterling, about six years old, was set on going fishing. Day after day it seemed that he would ask me to take him fishing. Day after day, I would give some excuse about how I was too busy, or that it was raining, and that fish don't bite in the rain. Finally, he asked, "Can't we just try, Dad?" I had 30 minutes, so I packed him and his 5-year-old brother Taylor, the fishing pole, tackle box, and their 2-year-old sister, Mariah, into the pickup. It was sprinkling just a bit, but we were going to "try" anyway.

We got down to the fishing hole and I baited his hook with a hunk of bread (the bluegill love it) and he and Taylor went over to the bank to try their luck while I helped Mariah throw bread to the ducks from the pickup bed (it was safer, the ducks couldn't jump up on her from there). I watched as the boys took turns casting and reeling, with the other holding the umbrella over the person fishing. It was so cute, but I didn't even see a glimpse of the usual school of bluegill, and they did not receive a single bite on their line, "due to the rain" I said, just as I had warned.

When time was up, we piled into the cab of the pickup, slightly damp. As I was trying to formulate some wise "I told you so" to my son, thinking we had failed since we had not caught a single fish, he piped up first saying, "This was the best day of my life!" I was surprised! I reminded him that we had not actually caught any fish, to which he replied, "Yes, but we went fishing!" It was an eye opener for me; I thought the goal was to catch a fish, to obtain a prize, to achieve. He had only said he wanted to "go fishing"; he'd never actually said he needed to "catch a fish."

I have been reminded of the priority of spending time with my children, even in seemingly simple activities on numerous occasions. Once, lying under our van while making some repairs, I saw two little legs appear by the side of the car. Our 4-year-old, Meaghan, wanted to know if she could help. "Not this time, Meg; this is important and I have to get it done. Why don't you see if you can help mom with dinner?" She received the same response from mom, "Not tonight, Meg, I'm in a hurry, why don't you go play?" Fortunately, children are persistent, and forgiving. Before long I saw two little legs again and she picked up a wrench and started pounding on the car door (mimicking my sounds from under the car). I quickly slid out and showed her how she could help me by hitting on the tire and rim instead. Her smile was priceless that night as she told everyone around the dinner table how she had helped dad fix the car. She smiled just as big when she got to make special desserts or dinners with mom.

Spending time with parents in seemingly simple activities is not only important for young children. When asked to think back to their childhood and picture the best time they had as a family, many adults mention such activities as singing songs together in the living room, camping out two hours from home, playing games on Friday nights, or even scrubbing the kitchen floor with mom (Olsen & Defrain, 2000). Trips to Disneyland and other expensive vacations are not mentioned as often as these seemingly simple times together.

In summary, contrary to the popular notion that children and adolescents want nothing to do with parents, they still need and want to be directly involved with their parents, perhaps in ways that are different from what we expect as parents. Furthermore, most children and parents report having strong relationships and sharing similar values–and are not characterized by the high level of conflict that seems to be so popularized in the media (Demo & Cox, 2001). Indeed, as long as parents can maintain connection, guidance, and love, even when the going may get a little tough in the teen years, things tend to turn out just fine more often than not (Walsh, 2014).

When he was 15, I went to Sterling's track meet making my way into the stands as he hung out on the field with his teammates. Once the call was made for the "boys 200-meter dash," he went across the field and started warming up and getting ready to race. I was distracted by our 3-year-old, Hannah, and when I looked up, I saw that Sterling had broken away from the group and was slowly walking towards us across the field, waving his arm until I saw and responded with an answering wave. He then went back, got set, and ran the race. Whether they are sitting just barely out of sight on that rocky ledge, or out on the field getting ready to run the race of their lives, our children still want us to be there, to see them, to be a part of their life.

Fast forward 15 or so years. I am so grateful that a relational foundation was laid early on with our children because those things we thought were a big deal back then pale in comparison to what we all grapple with now as adults. For example, we are so glad that we can be there and listen as our child, much older now, explains about their challenges of coming out, but that they are not "that kind of gay," that if they can tell someone else is gay, they are usually not interested in them, that they went to the national "conservative" gay convention where there were only 30 people! Our hearts are able to pain with them over the challenges of finding meaningful personal and intimate connections with others with such a limited pool available to them.

We are so grateful we can be there and listen as another now adult child confides in us about challenges with a partner's pornography usage. So glad they reach out to us regularly to connect, not necessarily about just that, but about life, to maintain the bond, to help them feel tethered in an uncertain world and life.

So grateful for conversations about faith, and agreement or thinking the same has little to do with it. I asked another of our now adult children "Do you think mom and I are happy that you are getting married?" and they teared up a little saying, "well, it's not how you raised me...." Natalie and I were so happy to inform them, "Honey, your life is your life, mom and I have not even once sat up at night thinking oh gee, if only you would do this, if only you would get married in the church. We are so happy for you." On a separate occasion they asked, "so, do you and mom worry about your kids salvation since so many have gone different paths than you?" We replied, "sweetheart, we are so busy trying to work out our own salvation in our own way, your life is yours to live, and I wouldn't trade any of you. I can't think of anyone with more Christlike love and charity than you and your sibling, you are such kind people. Maybe while we work on certain areas commonly discussed in church, you are working on other areas of your life, probably things I should be working on too. As Wally Goddard once said, "we are all reaching for the same light." But, more importantly Natalie asked our child, "how do YOU feel about it?" To which they replied, "After hearing you guys say that, I actually feel a LOT better now!"

Discussion Questions & Activities

1. What are some of your most meaningful and memorable experiences you remember sharing with your parents growing up?

2. After identifying some of your own powerful memories, think about your family now and the children in your own care. What meaningful memories have you made that stand out for you?

3. Next, identify at least 3 specific ways you could create more new memories with your children.

References

Brennen, S. P. "Parenting Practices in Teen Years Set the Stage for Closeness, Warmth Later On." *Penn State University,* Penn State News, www.psu.edu/news/research/story/parenting-practices-teen-years-set-stage-closeness-warmth-later/. Accessed 12 Aug. 2024.

Demo, D. H., and M. J. Cox. (2000). Families with young children: A review of research in the 1990s. *Journal of Marriage and Family, 62*(4), pp. 876–895. https://doi.org/10.1111/j.1741-3737.2000.00876.x

Global Strategy Group, Inc. (April 2000). *Talking With Teens: The YMCA Parent and Teen Survey: Final Report.*

Kids Health NZ. (n.d.). *Parenting teens – Spending quality time together.* Retrieved March 26, 2024, from www.kidshealth.org.nz/parenting-teens-spending-quality-time-together.

Olson, D. H., & Defrain, J. (2000). *Marriage and the family: Diversity and strengths.* Mountain View, California: Mountain View Publishing.

Schacter, H. L., and G. Margolin. (2019). "The interplay of friends and parents in adolescents' daily lives: Towards a dynamic view of social support." https://doi.org/10.1111/sode.12363

Walsh, D. A., and E. Walsh. *Why Do They Act That Way?: A Survival Guide to the Adolescent Brain for You and Your Teen.* Atria Paperback, 2014.

Appendices

Appendix A

Discussion Ground Rules

- The discussion stays in the room. You may speak for yourself outside the room, but you will not presume to speak for others or about others.
- Listen respectfully. This is a dialogue, not a debate.
- Speak from your own perspective. Use lots of "I" statements: "I think," "I feel," "I believe," etc.
- Use textual evidence when possible. Statements such as "In the text, it states," According to the text," "The author said," "On page xx, the author says."
- Agree to disagree.

Discussion Guiding Principles

- Read the material selected for discussion.
- Try not to interrupt classmates.
- Practice active listening. When needed—clarify, paraphrase, agree, disagree, elaborate, or summarize.
- Be aware of your nonverbal behavior. Body language sends subtle messages.
- Be sensitive to others—they have experiences that you may never know about or begin to understand.
- Stay on topic.
- You may pass if desired. No one will be forced to answer or talk.

Source: Developed by Elizabeth A. Ramsey, Ph.D., CFLE.

Appendix B

Discussion Ideas

- Discuss the implications of the article.
- If you have a group facilitator, members of the group should be encouraged to share their ideas before the facilitator shares.
- Discuss similar examples related to the topic you have seen illustrated in other families.
- Apply the article to your current life situation or your family of origin.
- Discuss the importance of the topic as it affects parents and children.
- Share how you might consider following the article's suggestions.
- Identify and discuss issues that may arise when you seek to carry out suggestions made.

Source: Developed by Robert E. Keim, Ph.D., CFLE Emeritus, and modified by Elizabeth A. Ramsey, Ph.D., CFLE.

Appendix C

Various Reasons Children Misbehave: Look for the "Why" Behind the Behavior
- Accidents
- Anger
- Anxiety (tensions in family, etc.)
- Attention seeking
- Boredom
- Conflicting preferences or values—or priority of what is important (not always a right or wrong way to do something)
- Confusion or misunderstanding
- Curiosity
- Experimenting, perhaps unaware of possible consequences
- Fatigue
- Fears
- Frustration
- Inadequate feelings
- Low regard for self, low self-esteem
- Jealousy
- Mixed messages of parents or inconsistent parenting
- Modeling influences of others: parent, sibling, friend, TV, video games, or social media
- Moodiness, bad moods, emotional problems
- Peer pressure
- Personality related, temperament
- Physical/emotional problems, including sickness, allergies, etc.
- Power
- Reinforcements from the past, possibly unintended
- Role identification
- Revenge
- Testing limits
- Past trauma
- Adverse childhood experiences (ACEs)

Source: Developed by Robert E. Keim, Ph.D., CFLE Emeritus, and modified by Elizabeth A. Ramsey, Ph.D., CFLE.

Appendix D

Responsive Parenting Suggestions

Send "I" Messages rather than saying "you did this" or accusing someone of something. Express your feelings about an issue. Example:

"When you look at your phone when I am talking to you, I feel like you aren't listening to me and that I'm not important to you."

Say something good about the other person related to the issue you are concerned about. For example, if your child has not been taking out the garbage without being asked, focus on when they are doing things the way you want. Rather than saying, "You never take out the garbage without being asked," say, "I know you are busy, but it is very helpful if you can remember to take the garbage out without being asked. That makes my life easier, so thank you."

Talk about the matter differently: Focus on the issue at hand. Do not attack the person with name-calling or by degrading them. Talk about what is happening by using metacommunication. For example, "We sound like two kids arguing! Let's start over."

Take a time out: Suggest talking about it later—"when we are both calmer."

Recognize that people have different thresholds or tolerance levels impacting how long they can carry on an argument. Then:
- reflect on alternative solutions to satisfy both people involved and remain open to new ideas or
- try venting your feelings by jogging, cleaning, or talking with a friend.

Write a letter, and then tear it up or throw it away. If you need to send it, consider delivering it in person to explain what you meant if there is any danger of it being misunderstood.

Listen to yourself. Identify negative self-talk and negative thinking.

Do something unexpected or different by forcing a different response:
- Stop and hug the other person or hold hands while talking.
- Listen to understand them and acknowledge that understanding.
- Say I'm sorry when it fits, expressing genuine feelings. Be willing to forgive the other person without putting them down.
- Try sitting down to talk or change the atmosphere in some way.
- Reverse roles: Try taking the other person's position, discovering his or her feelings by taking the other side of the argument.
- Use humor and try to see how silly things are by laughing with each other, not at each other.

Listen to what the other person is saying.
- Think before speaking. Be more caring with your words. Really listen to what the other person is saying.
- Ask yourself, "Am I letting them know I hear what they are saying and feeling?"

Key Ideas from Parent Educators

- "Do I convey in a friendly or caring manner that I understand?"
- "Am I reflecting on key ideas or words that have been said?"
- Keep silent until the other person finishes, then respond reflectively on what you heard. Check to see that you understand what was said. Ask: "I'd really like to know how you think so I can improve things between us. Please tell me."
- Listen, acknowledge what has been said, and then thank them. Tell them you will consider what has been shared. Consider them in a way that maybe you haven't before.

Suggestions by Robert E. Keim, Ph.D., CFLE Emeritus, modified by Elizabeth A. Ramsey, Ph.D., CFLE

Index

A
Acceptance of body image, 12
Acceptance of diverse body shapes, 12
Active listening, 72
   o in parent-child communication, 17, 18
Active parenting, 32-33
Actualizing tendency (Carl Rogers), 71
Adams, Rebecca A., 41-42
Adolescent self-esteem, 12
Adverse Childhood Experiences and Trauma, 133-134
Affirmation, 33-36
Allowances, 148-150
Attachment, 194-195
Attachment theory and cross-cultural applicability, 138-140
Attention-Deficit Hyperactivity Disorder (ADHD), 128-129
Authoritarian parenting, 83-85
Authoritative parenting, 82-85

B
Ballard, Sharon M., 23-25, 82-85, 119-121
Bascope-Vidal, Rachel, 190-193
Basic care, (stimulation, guidance, love, and affirmation), 33-36
Bedtime, 41-42, 61-63, 66-67
Berge, Jerica, 43-44, 174-176
Body image
   o and media, 12, 36
   o and self-esteem, 11, 12
Bold, Mary, 11-12, 45-46, 47-49, 49-51, 146-148
Bonding, 131
Breaking generational parenting cycles, 122-124
Burleson, Felisha M., 122-125

C
Carroll, Elizabeth B., 148-150
Cassidy, Dawn, 7, 51-52, 52-53
Chandler, Kristie, 53-55
Child development, 23, 37-41, 38
Choices for children, 107
   o (S.M.A.R.T. method), 108-110
   o progressive choosing, 78-79
Clarke, Jean Illsley, 25-27, 55-58, 58-60
Cobb, Rebecca A., 61-63
Cole, Charles L., 13-15
Cognitive development, 36-37,
Communication
   o about sexuality, 119-121
   o with children, 115-119
   o in relationships, 13-15
Commuter marriages, 180
Compassionate parenting, 74-77
Conflict resolution, 13-15, 18-20
Consequences, 74-76, 80
   o logical and natural, 42, 69-70, 74-76, 110-113
Control, 77-82, 106-107

Cook, Lisa Taylor, 151-153
Couple attachment, 174-176
Courage, 170
Credit cards and financial literacy, 146-148
Crying, 24, 136-138,
Cultural influences on parenting, 60, 138-140, 185-187, 190-194

D
DeBord, Karen, 63-66, 153-154
Decision-making in children, 108-110
Differentiation of self, 122-124
Digital safety, 47-49
Digital media and children, 47, 63
Digital tools for family engagement, 21
Discipline, 51-52, 68-71, 92
Discussion
   o ground rules
   o guiding principles
   o ideas

E
Ecological theory (Bronfenbrenner), 151-153
Education and parental involvement, 21-23
Elmore-Staton, Lori, 66-68, 68-71, 86
Emotional intelligence, 23, 88, 90, 96,
Empowerment, 106,
Encouragement, 58-60,

F
Failure, 86-88
Fathering, 151-153, 182-185
Family
   o Communication, 11-12, 16-17, 18-20,
   o dynamics, 86, 122-123, 135
   o engagement in schools, 21
   o influences on self-image, 11
   o meal discussions, 30-32
Family Science professionals, role of, 123
Family Systems Theory (Bowen), 123
Financial literacy, 146-148, 155
Fitzpatrick, Jacki, 155-158
Forgiveness, 188-190
Fostering parenting and infant bonds, 131-132
Four horsemen of the apocalypse, 13

G
Gagnon, John H., 176-179
Galazzi, Marcia Pioppi, 159, 160
Garrison, Cynthia R., 71-73
Gender
   o constancy, 36
   o development in preschool, 36
   o schema-theory, 37
   o identity, 36,
   o typing, 36
Gerhardt, Clara 10, 160-161, 162, 162-164, 164-165, 165-167, 168-169
Glotzer, Richard S., 180-182

Goals
- child-centered vs. parent centered, 88
- short-term vs. long term

Goddard, H. Wallace, 74-77, 77-82
Guidance and discipline in parenting, 41, 51-52, 68-71, 77-80
Goddard, Wallace H., 74, 77
Gross, Kevin H. 82, 119-121

H
Hall, Scott S., 182-185
Handling differences in relationships, 13-16
Hardman, Alisha M., 68, 86-88
Health and wellness, 119-142
Higgins, Kristina, 125-128, 151-153
Home-school communication strategies, 21-23

I
"I" messages, 16-17, 18-20, 206,
Identity formation in youth, 36-37
Impact of parental behavior on children, 13-16
Imperfection, 93-94, 162
Importance of play in child development, 25-27
Influences of mass media on self-image, 11
Intentional parenting, 88-91
Intergenerational trauma, 122-124

J
Jackson, Jim, 115-119
Jackson, Lynne, 115-119
Jacobson, Arminta L., 6, 185-187
Janson, Gregory R., 188-190
Johnston Pawel, Jody, 98-101
Jory, Brian, 190-194
Joseph, Ainsworth E., 194-197

K
Keim, Robert E., 6, 8, 16-17
Kohlberg's theory of gender development, 36-37
Krause, Lisa, 27, 58, 60

L
Latin American Families, 190-194
Learning from mistakes, 29
Lee, Cameron, 88-91, 91-93
Life lessons from the pandemic, 104-106, 127
Life skills, 146-155
Logical consequences, 42, 43, 69-70, 110-113
Listening, skills in parenting, 17-18, 73
Lying, 98-101
- reasons for lying, 100

M
Machara, Margaret E., 93-95
Maslow's hierarchy of needs, 34
Mazur, Elizabeth, 128-130
Mechler, Hannah, 131-132
Media influence on children, 11, 63-66

Mental health challenges in children, 128-130, 143
Misbehavior, reasons for, 205
Modeling behavior, 114-115
Mojica, Angelina, M., 133-135
Morante, Ana, 17-18
Morgan, Elizabeth, 138-141
Motivation, 45-46, 59-60
- External and internal, 43-46

N
Nelson, Julie K., 18-20, 27-30, 95-98
Neonatal abstinence syndrome, 136-138
North-Jones, Peggy, 30-32
Nurturing
- couple relationship, 197-199
- traditions in families, 185-187

O
Overindulgence, 26, 58-60
Over nurture, 59

P
Parent, as teacher, 38
Parental influence on peer pressure, 49, 143
Parental monitoring, 35
Parent-centered goals, 88
Parent-child communication, 11-12, 16-18, 21
Parenting
- Approaches and styles, 41, 82-83, 88
  Authoritarian, 83-85, 191, 193,
  Authoritative, 82
  Cultural relevance of, 84
  Demandingness, 82-85
  Intentional, 88-91
  Neglectful, 84
  Permissive, 83-85
- Children with mental illness, 128
- Compassionate, 74-77
- Intentional, 88-91
- seasons of, 164
- styles of, 83
- as a teen, 151
- trauma-driven, 122-124
- through turbulent times, 194
- vulnerability, 162, 164
Play, importance of, 25-27
- free vs. guided, 26
Peer pressure and parental guidance, 49
Perfection, 93-95
Positive discipline strategies, 68
Positive reinforcement, 69-70
Potter, Brenda L., 32-32
Powell, Lane H., 33-36
Psychosocial theory of development (Erickson), 102, 183
Ramsey, Elizabeth A., 7, 36-37, 102-103, 103-104, 136
Praise, encouragement, and motivation 59-60
Preventing youth substance use, 142-145

R
Raising daughters, 182-184
Raising sexually healthy children, 119

Ramsey, Elizabeth A., 7, 36, 102, 103, 136-138
Recognizing and managing emotions in children, 24
Respect, 170-172
   o in marriage and relationships, 13-15
Responsiveness
   o as couples, 174-175
   o in parenting, 82-85
Responsive parenting suggestions, 206
Rewards and reading, 45-46
Rituals, 98, 185-187
Risk and protective factors, 142-144
Rogers, Dorothea M., 106-107, 197-199
Rogers, Jim R., 104-106
Role of "I" statements in conflict resolution, 18-20
Role modeling, 114
Rose, Amelia L., 37-41
Rose, Hilary A., 108-110, 110-113
Roughhousing, 95-97
Rules for healthy fighting, 176-179

S

Saying "I'm sorry" in relationships, 16-17
School and community impact on risk factors, 144
Screen time and children, 63-65
Self-actualization, 34-35
Self-differentiation, 122
Self-esteem development, 11-12, 27
Self-efficacy, 52
Sexuality education, 119-121
Sfeir, Mark, 169-170,
Sibling rivalry, 102-103
Small, Cynthia J., 21-23
Smullens, SaraKay, 170-173
Social Learning Theory, 105
Social media influence on self-image, 11
Social Network Theory, 53
Socioeconomic status and parenting, 123

Strategies for handling peer pressure, 49-50
Stress management for parents, 194
Stridick, Margaret, 173-174
Structure and nurture in parenting, 163-165
Substance use prevention, 142-145
Supporting children's mental health, 128

T

Tactful communication between parents and children, 12
Teaching, 77
   o children decision-making, 108-110
   o financial responsibility to children, 146-148,
      148-150, 155-157
   o forgiveness, 188,
   o vs. discipline, 51-52
   o with compassion, 74-77
Technology's impact on families, 63
Time as money, 155-159
Time management with children, 154-155
Traditions, 185-187
Trauma, 122-125, 125-128
Turner, Kaley G., 142-146

U

Uninvolved or neglectful parenting, 84
Universality Perspective, 138-141

V

Values and sexuality education, 119-120
Van Putten-Gardner, Kimberly, 114-115

W

Wall, Sterling, 199-203
Weathering family challenges, 125
While Activities", 43-44
Wilson, Cynthia B., 115-119, 142-146
Work-life balance in parenting, 199

www.ingramcontent.com/pod-product-compliance
Lightning Source LLC
Chambersburg PA
CBHW052309300426
44110CB00035B/2322